Hermeneutics of Mission in Matthew

Israel and the Nations in the Interpretative Framework of Matthew's Gospel

Bitrus A. Sarma

MONOGRAPHS

© 2015 by Bitrus A. Sarma

Published 2015 by Langham Monographs
an imprint of Langham Creative Projects

Langham Partnership
PO Box 296, Carlisle, Cumbria CA3 9WZ, UK
www.langham.org

ISBNs:
978-1-78368-909-5 Print
978-1-78368-907-1 Mobi
978-1-78368-908-8 ePub
978-1-78368-874-6 PDF

Bitrus A. Sarma has asserted his right under the Copyright, Designs and Patents Act, 1988 to be identified as the Author of this work.

All rights reserved. No part of this publication may be reproduced, stored in a retrieval system or transmitted, in any form or by any means, electronic, mechanical, photocopying, recording or otherwise, without the prior written permission of the publisher or the Copyright Licensing Agency.

Except where indicated, the Scripture quotations in the work are from the *New International Version* 1979, 1984 by International Bible Society.

British Library Cataloguing in Publication Data

Sarma, Bitrus A., author.
   Hermeneutics of mission in Matthew : Israel and the nations
in the interpretative framework of Matthew's Gospel.
   1. Bible. Matthew--Hermeneutics. 2. Missions--Biblical
teaching.
   I. Title
   226.2'06'01-dc23

ISBN-13: 9781783689095

Cover & Book Design: projectluz.com

Langham Partnership actively supports theological dialogue and a scholar's right to publish but does not necessarily endorse the views and opinions set forth, and works referenced within this publication or guarantee its technical and grammatical correctness. Langham Partnership does not accept any responsibility or liability to persons or property as a consequence of the reading, use or interpretation of its published content.

To my wife Sanatu and our children Esther, Grace, Rejoice, David, and Yambale with thanks for your unfailing encouragement and support.

Contents

Abstract xi
Acknowledgements xiii
Abbreviations xvii

Chapter 1 1
Introduction
   1.1 Purpose and Direction of the Study 1
   1.2 Contribution of the Study 12
   1.3 Methodology and Procedure of the Study 13

Chapter 2 23
Mission in Matthew: The Role of the Triune God
   2.1 Introduction 23
   2.2 The Father's Redemptive Role in Mission 25
      2.2.1 He Sends the Angels 27
      2.2.2 He Sends the Prophets 29
      2.2.3 He Sends out Workers into His Harvest Field ... 30
      2.2.4 He Sends the Son 31
   2.3 The Son's Redemptive Role in Mission 35
      2.3.1 He Saves from Sins 36
      2.3.2 He Heals Sicknesses 38
      2.3.3 He Restores and Leads Israel as Shepherd-King ... 39
      2.3.4 He Fulfills the Torah 40
      2.3.5 He Mediates the Knowledge of the Father 41
      2.3.6 He sows the seed of the Kingdom 43
      2.3.7 He Sends for Mission 44
      2.3.8 He Forgives Sins 47
      2.3.9 He Cleanses the Temple 49
      2.3.10 He Judges the Nations at the end of the Age ... 50
   2.4 The Holy Spirit's Redemptive Role in Mission 51
      2.4.1 He is the Agent in Jesus' Miraculous Conception ... 53
      2.4.2 He is the Agent at Jesus' Baptism 54
      2.4.3 He Anoints and Empowers Jesus for Mission 55
      2.4.4 He Speaks through the Disciples 56
      2.4.5 He is the Spirit of Prophetic Inspiration 57
   2.5 Summary and Conclusion 58

Chapter 3 61
   Mission to Israel: Foundations and Framework
      3.1 Introduction 61
      3.2 Redemptive Events, Institutions, and Mission.........................64
         3.2.1 The Exodus...68
         3.2.2 The **Torah** **77**
         3.2.3 The Davidic Shepherd-King 82
         3.2.4 The Temple...89
         3.2.5 The Exile and Restoration...93
      3.3 Prophetic Ministry and Mission..96
         3.3.1 Prophetic Ministry before John the Baptist.....................98
            3.3.1.1 A Panoramic View of Promise-Fulfillment in Matthew...... 98
            3.3.1.2 The Use of the OT in the NT: Direct Prediction,
                    Typology or Christological Readings 100
         3.3.2 Prophetic Ministry of John the Baptist 108
      3.4 Geography and Mission 113
         3.4.1 Bethlehem and Ramah 114
         3.4.2 Egypt...116
         3.4.3 Nazareth..116
         3.4.4 Galilee..119
         3.4.5 Mount Zion/Jerusalem 124
      3.5 Intertextual Typology and Mission 127
         3.5.1 The Wilderness..130
         3.5.2 The Mountain 132
         3.5.3 The Sign of Jonah 134
         3.5.4 The Stone 137
      3.6 Summary and Conclusion..141

Chapter 4 145
   Mission to the Nations: Foundations and Framework
      4.1 Introduction 145
      4.2 Redemptive Events, Institutions and Mission..........................148
         4.2.1 Abrahamic Promise and the Nations.................................149
         4.2.2 Gentile Women in Jewish Genealogy................................155
         4.2.3 "A Single Universal Righteousness" of the Torah..............159
         4.2.4 The Temple: a House of Prayer (for all Nations) 162
         4.2.5 Jesus and the Elect in the Blood of the Covenant 166
      4.3 Prophetic Ministry and Mission...168
         4.3.1 Prophetic Ministry Prior to John the Baptist....................169
            4.3.1.1 Yahweh's Servant Heals both Jews and Gentiles..........169
            4.3.1.2 The Nations Put their Hope in His Name.................173
         4.3.2 Prophetic Ministry of John the Baptist 181

  4.4 Geography and Mission 183
    4.4.1 Magi from the East 183
    4.4.2 Galilee of the Gentiles 186
    4.4.3 Mount Zion and Eschatological Pilgrimage 190
  4.5 Intertextual Typology and Mission 193
    4.5.1 The Mountain 193
    4.5.2 The Sign of Jonah 195
    4.5.3 The Stone 197
  4.6 Summary and Conclusion 200

Chapter 5 203
 Conclusions and Recommendations
  5.1 Conclusions 203
  5.2 Recommendations 208

Bibliography 213

Abstract

This work is an investigation of the hermeneutics of mission in the Gospel of Matthew. The work seeks to respond to the question: What is the framework of Matthew's mission theology? The writer puts forward the argument that Matthew utilizes the Old Testament as the foundation of God's own initiative in mission to Israel and the nations. Matthew sees God working through the history of Israel, the nations, and geographical locations as an ongoing series of divinely orchestrated actions toward the realization of salvation in Jesus. By his citations, allusions, and echoes, Matthew suggests that the Old Testament is a book of promise of God's salvific purposes and that Jesus is the fulfillment of those promises. God's scheme of salvation is understood as an umbrella under which people, events, and places are divinely coordinated for the salvation of humankind through Christ the Messiah. For Matthew, the purpose of God to save fallen humanity is the grand narrative of the Bible. He therefore uses promise-fulfillment as the interpretative framework of his mission theology and explores this single framework from four dimensions. These dimensions include redemptive events and institutions, geography, prophetic ministry, and intertextual typology.

Acknowledgements

The journey in the PhD has been an exciting and challenging one. I thank our Father in heaven for his grace upon my life. He carried me through the demanding experience. But in the course of this dissertation I have become highly indebted to many, some of whom I may not be able to mention for lack of space. If the following list looks like the Pauline greetings in Romans 16, it is intentional as a mark of gratitude to faithful servants of the Lord who have been kind and supportive along the way.

There is no way any recompense can be adequate in appreciation of the role of my primary reader, Rev Dr Randee I-Morphe, through whose hard stretch and push this work came to good conclusion. His broad and deep knowledge of available resources on the subject and the New Testament and Old Testament helped me immensely in giving direction to the study. And like a good coach he endured with me to the finishing line. My indebtedness also goes to my external reader, Distinguished Professor Craig L. Blomberg at Denver Seminary (Colorado, USA). His thorough and critical examination of the work and generous comments cannot be quantified in words. That a world-class professor could stoop down to lift me up, I am touched. My second reader, Dr Jim Crouch, deserves appreciation for his contribution. I am thankful for his comments and encouragement.

Professor George Janvier was Barnabas, the son of encouragement, in the course of the adventure. He knows that PhD work can be discouraging and was always available to give the necessary encouragement. He also ensured that resources and finances needed for the study were available. The same goes for Associate Professor Bulus Galadima, the Provost of JETS. He was always available to encourage and could go the extra mile to ensure that my needs were met. Professor Samuel W. Kunhiyop believes that others can make it. As the Provost of the Seminary at the commencement of the program, he gave me all the encouragement and assistance I needed.

Similarly, in our 2009 research trip to University of Stellenbosch, South Africa, Professor Hendrik L. Bosman and Professor Jeremy Punt provided the needed moral support and encouragement and went the extra mile to give good shape to my proposal. I thank God for their humility and large hearts. I also thank the library staff at the University of Stellenbosch, Faculty of Theology, for their faithful services. They made our research a lot easier.

Although the 2009 trip to the United Kingdom for research at Tyndale House was aborted due to the British Embassy's refusal to grant us visas, Tyndale House kept us posted and updated through their newsletters. Similarly, there were families in the UK that had already made preparations to host and take care of us at their own expenses. We owe them gratitude for their kind and generous hearts.

Each of my course mates, Rev Joel K. T. Biwul, Dr Matthew Michael, Rev Stephen Baba, and Pastor Ishaku B. Kubgak, contributed significantly in shaping my life and thinking. We also laughed and cried together in the humbling adventure.

Many others who are also special in their unique way include: Mr and Mrs Caleb A. Yaro, Mr and Mrs Samuel Dalaky, Professor Yusufu Turaki, Rev Dr Bauta Motty, Professor Danfulani Kore, Rev Dwight Singer (the Deputy Provost of JETS), Dr Scott S. Cunningham, Professor Victor Cole who fanned into flame my interest in the New Testament's use of the Old Testament, Dr Mrs Theresa Adamu (the Registrar of JETS), Dr Mrs Rose Galadima, Mr and Mrs John Hunt, Rev Col S. K. Bargo, Rev Dr Barje Maigadi, Rev Dr Cephas Tushima, Rev Emmanuel Jatau and members of ECWA Seminary Church, Rev Dr Sunday Agang (the Academic Dean of JETS), Rev and Mrs Bello Misal, Rev and Mrs Nathan Chiroma (who made South Africa a home away from home for us), Rev David Kajom, Rev Dr Emmanuel Sule, Rev Bitrus Cobongs, Rev and Mrs Andrew Kolo, Byang Kato Research Library staff, JETS Cyber-Café staff, Dr Joshua Sule, Dr Musa Dankyau, Dr John Mandong, Mr Innocent Vwamdem, Mr and Mrs Douglas Hadiri, Rev Robert D. Sarma and Deacon and Mrs Moses A. Sarma. Thank you all.

I also cherish the role of my dependable prayer partners and friends like Rev Nuhu M. Guddal, Rev Dr Ibrahim Bakari, Rev and Mrs Michael Ijah, Mr and Mrs Elisha Ali, Mr and Mrs Silas Dokong, Mr and Mrs John Ajik, Rev Yonana Turba and Pastor and Mrs Dickson Ogidi. You are all my fellow-workers and *sunduloi* in the Lord Jesus Christ. I also thank each of the professors who taught at the PhD program and made significant impact in my life in one way or the other. Space will not permit me to say how each of you has contributed to the success of this work. The same goes for all the faculty, staff, and students of JETS. You are all special to me. I am grateful to you all.

It is impossible to forget many others who worked behind the scene but whose names cannot appear here because they are 'anonymous' supporters. These men and women cut across race, color, and geographical locations. They gave cheerfully for the sake of Christ and the kingdom of God. I am thankful to you all.

I am deeply thankful to Langham Partnership for promoting biblical literature in the majority world. I sincerely appreciate you all, and especially for the pains taken to publish this work. Worthy of mention is the publishing team within Langham Literature. Thank you for your vision 'to see churches in the majority world equipped for mission and growing to maturity in Christ through the ministry of pastors and leaders who believe, teach and live by the Word of God.' I pray for God's immense blessings as you continue in this labor of love.

Finally, this work would not have been successful without the sacrificial care and support of my wife, Sanatu, and our five children Esther, Grace, Rejoice, David, and Victoria, to whom the work is dedicated. From you I find significance, security, and acceptance. I owe you love and devotion. Thank you.

Abbreviations

AB	Anchor Bible
ABD	*The Anchor Bible Dictionary.* Edited by D. N. Freedman. 6 vols. New York, 1992
ACCS	Ancient Christian Commentary on Scripture
ACW	Ancient Christian Writers
AnaBib	Analecta Biblica
ANF	Ante-Nicene Fathers
ATLAS	American Theological Library Association
Bar	Baruch
BECNT	Baker Exegetical Commentary on the New Testament
BSac	*Bibliotheca sacra*
CBQ	*Catholic Biblical Quarterly*
CCL	Corpus Christiannorum, Series Latina
CurTM	*Currents in Theology and Mission*
DJD	Dictionary of Jesus and the Gospels
ERT	Evangelical Review of Theology
HTS	Harvard Theological Studies
ICC	International Critical Commentary
Int	*Interpretation*
JBL	*Journal of Biblical Literature*
JES	*Journal of Ecumenical Studies*
JET	*Journal of Ecumenical Theology*
JETS	*Journal of the Evangelical Theological Society*
JSNT	*Journal for the Study of the New Testament*
JSNTSup	Journal for the Study of the New Testament, Supplement Series
JSOT	*Journal for the Study of the Old Testament*

KJV	King James Version
LXX	Septuagint
Macc	Maccabees
MT	Masoretic Text
NAS	New American Standard Bible
Neot	*Neotestamentica*
NIDNTT	*New International Dictionary of New Testament Theology*. Edited by C. Brown. 4 vols. Grand Rapids, 1975–1985
NIGTC	New International Greek Testament Commentary
NIV	New International Version
NovT	*Novum Testamentum*
NSBT	New Studies in Biblical Theology
NT	New Testament
NTS	*New Testament Studies*
OT	Old Testament
Pss. of Sol.	*Psalms of Solomon*
RevExp	*Review and Expositor*
SBJT	*Southern Baptist Journal of Theology*
SBL	Society for Biblical Literature
SBLDS	Society for Biblical Literature Dissertation Series
SBLSM	Society of Biblical Literature Monograph Series
SBLSP	Society of Biblical Literature Seminar Papers
SJOT	*Scandinavian Journal of the Old Testament*
Sir	Sirach
SNTSMS	Society for New Testament Studies Monograph Series
TD	*Theology Digest*
Tob	Tobit
TS	*Theological Studies*
TDNT	*Theological Dictionary of the New Testament*. Edited by G. Kittel and G. Friedrich. Translated by G. W. Bromiley. 10 vols. Grand Rapids, 1964–1976
TynBul	*Tyndale Bulletin*
WBC	Word Biblical Commentary
ZNW	*Zeitschrift für die neutestamentliche Wissenschaft und die Kunde der älteren Kirche*

CHAPTER 1

Introduction

1.1 Purpose and Direction of the Study

The Gospel of Matthew is pivotal in scholarly discussion on the hermeneutical use of the Old Testament in the New Testament. Similarly, scholars who approach the Gospel from a missiological standpoint draw inspiration from passages such as Matthew 9:35–38 and 28:16–20. But they also wrestle with the perennial and overarching issue of particularity and universality[1] in the Gospel such as 10:5, 6 and 28:19.[2] Is there a connection between these spheres of interest? Does the Gospel of Matthew provide such a relationship? This work, therefore, is an investigation of the hermeneutics of mission in the Gospel of Matthew in relation to the central issue of mission to Israel and the nations. The investigation seeks to answer the question: What is the framework of Matthew's mission theology? The work is an attempt to explore how Matthew utilizes an OT viewpoint in his concept of mission.

---

1. These concepts refer to the tendency in Matthew where he seems to portray the mission of God as exclusive to the house of Israel on the one hand, and the mission of God as embracing the nations on the other hand.
2. Ferdinand Hahn points out, "The Gospel of Matthew is of the greatest importance for the question of mission in early Christianity" (Ferdinand Hahn, *Mission in the New Testament*, Studies in Biblical Theology 47 [Naperville: Alec R. Allenson, 1965], 120). David Bosch also notes, "The Gospel of Matthew reflects an important and distinct sub-paradigm of the early church's interpretation and experience of mission" (see David Bosch, *Transforming Mission: Paradigm Shift in Theology of Mission* [Maryknoll: Orbis Books, 1991], 56). But the issue in this study is how Matthew justifies the seemingly contradictory mission to Israel and the nations from the OT.

At this point, the writer offers a definition of how the term *mission* is to be understood in this work. *Mission* is used here as a conceptual idea[3] to describe God's activity and purpose in saving his people from sin (Matt 1:21).[4] The term is here distinguished from *missions* in the sense of calling or vocation or human endeavor. According to A. Scott Moreau, Gary R. Corwin, and Gary B. McGee, until the mid-1990s no distinction was made between the two. It was out of the work of the International Missionary Council that "came the recognition that biblical discussion of the idea of mission was not limited to what the church was doing, since God has always been active everywhere in the world."[5] This working definition views *mission* as primarily the work of God, namely, his divine initiative and execution of the work of salvation. But most definitions of *mission* stress its roots in the Latin verb *mitto* which means to send. As Christopher J. H. Wright observes, this understanding sees the primary significance of the concept "in the dynamic of sending or being sent."[6] While appreciating the importance of the theme within the Bible, Wright, however, sheds light on the inadequacy of limiting mission to sending and being sent as human endeavor. According to him, "if we define mission only in 'sending'

---

3. Although the word *mission* does not occur in the Gospel of Matthew, the concept runs throughout the entire narrative.

4. As the Gospel of Matthew unfolds, salvation is not limited to the Jews but extends to all the nations.

5. See A. Scott Moreau, Gary R. Corwin, and Gary B. McGee, *Introducing World Missions: A Biblical, Historical, and Practical Survey* (Grand Rapids: Baker Academic, 2004), 17. Similarly, Bosch says, "We have to distinguish between *mission* (singular) and missions (plural). The first refers primarily to the *missio Dei* (God's mission), that is, God's self-revelation as the one who loves the world, God's involvement in and with the world, and in which the church is privileged to participate. *Missio Dei* enunciates the good news that God is the 'God-for-people'. *Missions* (the *missiones ecclesiae*: the missionary ventures of the church), refer to particular forms, related to specific times, places, or needs, of participation in the *missio Dei*" (see Bosch, *Transforming Mission*, 10). The term *mission* is also to be distinguished from *missionary*, that is, someone sent to serve in a mission field, although missionary service is no longer limited to this understanding but embraces a wide range of services such as health workers, relief workers, and teachers, among others. Moreau, Corwin, and McGee say, "In one sense they all have the opportunity to work out the general call of God that all Christians share—the call to urge people to respond to Christ and to live lives reflecting his kingdom" (Moreau, Corwin, and McGee, *Introducing World Missions*, 17).

6. See Christopher J. H. Wright, *The Mission of God: Unlocking the Bible's Grand Narrative* (Downers Grove: IVP Academic Press, 2006), 23.

terms we necessarily exclude from our inventory of relevant resources many other aspects of biblical teaching that directly or indirectly affect our understanding of God's mission and practice of our own."[7] In Matthew's Gospel mission grows out of God's salvific purposes for humankind. He sees God working through the history of Israel, the nations, and even geographical locations as ongoing series that are divinely orchestrated toward the realization of salvation. He therefore quotes from the OT to justify God's mission to Israel and the nations.[8] Graham Stanton says, Matthew "is not simply concerned to underline purely incidental agreements between an Old Testament prophecy to interpret the passage to which it is attached, for he is convinced that the story of Jesus is very much at once with God's purposes."[9]

But before engaging with the theme of mission in Matthew it is worth noting that the study of Matthew's Gospel is saturated with wide-ranging issues.[10] One of such leading concerns is the purpose of the book. Most scholarly discussion on the purpose of the book of Matthew falls in the

---

7. Wright, *The Mission of God*, 23. In this work, the mission of the church, beginning with the disciples, is considered secondary, although essential, element that flows from the initiator—God of mission. God initiated mission and executed it through a long history in the biblical accounts culminating in the coming of Christ. He then enlists men and women and makes them his co-workers in carrying out the task of mission in the world. Human effort is accomplished only with God's initiative and help. It is based on this viewpoint that the writer prefers the working definition advanced above.

8. Jesus comes as king of the Jews in 21:5 as fulfillment of Zech 9:9. But he also proclaims justice to the nations in 12:18–21 as fulfillment of Isa 42:1–4.

9. Graham Stanton, *The Gospels and Jesus*, 2nd ed. (Oxford: Oxford University Press, 2002), 71. He emphasizes that "Matthew clearly believes in the continuing importance of the Old Testament for Christians. He strenuously resists the claim which may have been made by his Jewish opponents that Christians have abandoned the Old Testament."

10. R. T. France, *The Gospel of Matthew*, The New International Commentary on the New Testament (Grand Rapids: Eerdmans, 2007), 1. John Riches well notes that apart from the perennial questions in the discipline of NT studies, the discipline also undergoes shifts from one set of issues to another, "when certain methods and approaches gain favour" (John Riches, William R. Telford, and Christopher M. Tuckett, *The Synoptic Gospels: With an Introduction by Scot McKnight* [Sheffield: Sheffield Academic Press, 2001], 43–52). On our corpus in particular, the questions of setting, sources, structure and theology preoccupied Matthean studies in the 1960s and 1970s. The 1980s to the present saw a kind of paradigm shift from those earlier concerns to focus on the community of Matthew and interest in the composition of the Gospel as a narrative. Although Riches noted that the nature of shifts could be exaggerated, there is the need for scholars to note the change of emphasis and to avoid ossification because such inflexibility could cause stagnation, as "a discipline which never changed its mind would be one which was stagnant" (44).

realm of conjecture because he nowhere formally states his purpose for writing, unlike Luke (1:1–4) and John (20:30, 31).[11] In addition to this seeming lack of definite standpoint from which he wrote are the several motifs that run through the book which appear to defy attempt for a unifying theme or focus.[12] As D. A. Carson and Douglas J. Moo have noted, "Matthew's dominant themes are several, complex, and to some extent, disputed. Attempts to delineate a single narrow purpose are therefore doomed to failure."[13] This seems to suggest that identifying a single theme exhaustive of all dimensions in Matthew is impossible. And the search for themes and attempt for mergers in Matthew has continued to generate considerable interest.

In addition to this quest for theme(s) in the Gospel is its unique canonical placement and use of the OT that "is a subject of perennial interest and vast dimensions."[14] Some of these dimensions are "a number of

---

11. See Donald Guthrie, *New Testament Introduction,* (Leicester: Apollos, 1990), 32; see Walter A. Elwell and Robert W. Yarbrough, *Encountering the New Testament: A Historical and Theological Survey,* 2nd ed. (Grand Rapids: Baker Academic, 2005), 80. Those who approach the Gospel of Matthew from structuralist studies, however, believe that the organization of the book, and any of the biblical books, gives it meaning or intelligibility. For structuralism, a meaningful text must necessarily conform to a structure. It is for this reason that there is an upsurge of works on structuralism in literary studies, since the purpose of the book is thought to be inextricably connected with its structure. For examples of such works see, David R. Bauer, *The Structure of Matthew's Gospel: A Study in Literary Design* (Sheffield: Sheffield Academic Press, 1996); Jack Dean Kingsbury, *Matthew: Structure, Christology, Kingdom* (Philadelphia: Fortress Press, 1975).

12. Matthean scholars suggest variegated themes. France believes that the central theme of Matthew is "fulfillment" (see France, *The Gospel of Matthew,* 10). Others look at the exalted Christology in the book of Matthew as key to understanding its focus.

13. See D. A. Carson and Douglas J. Moo, *An Introduction to the New Testament,* 2nd ed. (Leicester: Apollos, 2005), 157. D. A. Carson devoted one of his books to the themes of Matthew (see D. A. Carson, *God with Us: Themes from Matthew* [Ventura: Regal Books, 1985]). Other introductions that point toward the multiplicity of themes in Matthew include Guthrie, *New Testament Introduction;* David A. deSilva, *An Introduction to the New Testament: Contexts, Methods & Ministry Formation* (Leicester: Apollos, 2004).

14. Richard Longenecker, *Biblical Exegesis in the Apostolic Period* (Grand Rapids: Eerdmans, 1975), 11. Among other issues in dealing with the relation between the two testaments are critical questions that include provenance of various writings, their purposes and theological perspectives, the nature of their literary structure, the identification of quotations and allusions within them, the specification of particular text-forms used by them, their procedures of interpretation, their development of biblical themes, and their employment of biblical phraseology. On the perennial nature of the issue see also John L. McKenzie, "Problems of Hermeneutics in Roman Catholic Exegesis," *JBL* 77 (September 1958): 200–201. He says, "The felt need of the theological interpretation of the Bible has

important theological issues as to the relation of the two testaments, the development of biblical religion, the nature of prophecy, and the meaning of fulfillment."[15]

On the relation of the two testaments and the meaning of fulfillment we may briefly trace this in Jewish hermeneutics of the Second Temple Judaism and where Matthew picks up from there. Richard N. Longenecker observes that Second Temple Jewish exegetes, especially in the first century, "viewed their task as primarily that of adapting, reinterpreting, extending, and so reapplying sacred Scripture to the present circumstances of God's people, both with respect to how they should live ('halakah') and how they should think ('haggadah')."[16] For these exegetes, interpretation is a "contemporizing exercise" in order to gain "new theological insights, attitudes, and speculations."[17] However, NT writers "used Scripture principally for different purpose."[18] Like the "Dead Sea covenanters and some of the other Jewish apocalyptic writers of the period, the New Testament writers used biblical materials, in the main, to highlight the theme of fulfillment."[19] Fulfillment is understood "in broader terms than just direct prediction and

---

centered since 1946 on the question of the unity of OT and NT. A mass of literature on the subject has risen, but the question is still open."

15. Longenecker, *Biblical Exegesis in the Apostolic Period*, 11. This 'perennial' interest is illustrated by Craig A. Evans who confirms the puzzle that faces the reader of New Testament accounts of prophecies and fulfillment, especially for beginning students. "Beginning students of biblical interpretation almost always are surprised to learn that New Testament writers and other Jewish and Christian writers of late antiquity often do not follow exegetical rules akin to those taught by modern interpreters. Original text, context and meaning are frequently ignored—or at least so it seems. Instead, key terms, catchwords and turns of phrases appear to provide the interpretive catalyst. The Hosean reminiscence, 'Out of Egypt have I called my son' (Hos 11.1), becomes for the Matthean evangelist a messianic prophecy fulfilled in Jesus' return to Israel (Matt 2:13–15). Indeed, Hosea's reference to Egypt itself may underlie the otherwise unattested tradition of the holy family's sojourn in that land. Matthew, furthermore, believes that Jesus' upbringing in Nazareth was surely foretold by prophets who said, in so many words, 'He shall be a Nazarene' (Matt 2.23; cf. Judg 13.5; Isa 11.1)." See Craig A. Evans, ed., "From Language to Exegesis," *The Interpretation of Scripture in Early Judaism and Christianity: Studies in Language and Tradition*, (London: T & T Clark International, 2004), 19.

16. Richard N. Longenecker, *Biblical Exegesis in the Apostolic Period*, 2nd ed. (Grand Rapids: Eerdmans, 1999), xxvi.

17. Longenecker, *Biblical Exegesis*, xxvi.

18. Ibid., xxvii.

19. Ibid.

explicit verification—that is, rather than viewing fulfillment as simply a linguistic or conceptual reenactment of an ancient prophecy, they understood it in a fuller and more personal manner."[20] Matthew's fulfillment story may be understood from this viewpoint.

In the early Christian self-definition, as argued by Randee O. Ijatuyi Morphe,

> "one need not look far in order to discover that NT authors were engaged in acts of *legitimation,* for instance, like their OT counterparts before them. What is significant for NT authors, like Luke, is that the *eschatological fulfillment* of God's promise of salvation, in the person and mission of Jesus becomes determinative of their stance toward the biblical tradition" (italics original).[21]

Therefore, it may be reasoned that the conceptual interpretative framework of Matthew and the rest of the NT is eschatological fulfillment made real through "the experience of messianic salvation in Jesus.[22] It is the argument of this writer, then, that the OT shapes Matthew's understanding of mission.[23] As David A. deSilva points out, "Matthew . . . seeks to demonstrate the complete continuity between the *ekklēsia* and the Jewish religious heritage, assuring the Christian communities that, far from being deviants

---

20. Ibid.
21. Randee O. Ijatuyi-Morphé, *Community and Self-Definition in the Book of Acts* (Bethesda: Academica Press, 2004), 7. In this work, Christianity is defined in the book of Acts in the broad context of Judaism, paganism, and God-fearism. Conversion-mission is the phenomenon that is used "to *legitimize a new Christian self* for the early Christians" (5). It is to be noted that these two basic elements are found in Matthew and the rest of the Gospels. Both John the Baptist and Jesus began their ministry by preaching repentance. Jesus engaged in mission and sent out his disciples for mission. In this regard, the Gospels become the blueprint for the model missionary work in Acts.
22. Ibid., 5.
23. In *The Gospels and Jesus* (New York: Oxford University Press, 2002), Stanton says, "In some cases Matthew's choice of an Old Testament verse as a comment on a particular tradition about Jesus seems odd to modern readers. But he is not simply concerned to underline purely incidental agreements between an Old Testament prophecy to *interpret* the passage to which it is attached, for he is convinced that the story of Jesus is very much at once with God's purposes" (71).

or heretics, they are the legitimate heirs of that heritage and stand at the center of God's plan of salvation."[24] Jesus, for Matthew, is "the focus and culmination of the Jewish scriptural hope."[25] Similarly, according to Bosch, Jesus "clearly and unequivocally understood his mission in terms of the authentic Old Testament tradition."[26] For Matthew, the OT is not only the Scripture for believers in Christ but also the foundation and basis of God's own initiative in mission to the Jews and the nations. He artistically frames his Gospel with the mission of the Triune God from the first chapter to the last. For him mission grows out of God's plan of salvation. Promise-fulfillment[27] is therefore the interpretative framework of Matthew's mission theology because "Matthew constantly refers to the Old Testament, illustrating how Jesus 'fulfilled' the promises given to Israel."[28] This framework has four basic elements: redemptive events and institutions, prophetic ministry, geography, and intertexual typology that Matthew presents as precursive to the life and mission of Christ. He sees God working through the history of Israel and the nations and places as an ongoing series divinely directed toward the realization of salvation in Christ. This concept has been described as *die Heilsgeschichte*.[29] God's salvific purposes are here to be

---

24. David A. deSilva, *An Introduction to the New Testament: Contexts, Methods and Ministry Formation* (Downers Grove: IVP Academic, 2004), 246.

25. Ibid. According to deSilva, "Matthew assures his Christian readers that they read the Scriptures correctly when they read them in light of Jesus' life and teaching."

26. Bosch, *Transforming Mission*, 20.

27. The word "promise" does not occur in the Gospel of Matthew. But the frequent use of "fulfillment" implies a prior promise. It is to be remembered also that Abraham and David as the key recipients of God's promises in the OT are mentioned in Matthew in connection with those promises. Observing the prevailing nature of the theme of promise amidst the diversity and variety of themes in the OT, some scholars identify promise-fulfillment as a major theme. Walter Kaiser sees the OT as the promise plan of God, a messianic primer, in which God's plan of salvation is revealed. See Kaiser, *Toward Rediscovering the Old Testament* (Grand Rapids: Zondervan, 1991); idem, *Toward Old Testament Theology* (Grand Rapids: Zondervan, 1978).

28. Donald Senior, *What are they saying about Matthew?* rev. and exp. ed. (New York: Paulist Press, 1996), 38.

29. The concept of *die Heilsgeschichte* ("salvation history") is usually defined as a divine economy in which God works out his salvific purposes from creation to the Christ and the "end of the age." This "divine economy" is considered hermeneutical key to understanding Matthew. Older works that use the term "salvation history" (*die Heilsgeschichte*) include John P. Meier, *Law and History in Matthew's Gospel*, AnaBib 71 (Rome: Biblical Institute Press, 1976); Oscar Cullmann, *Salvation in History* (Bloomsbury, London: SCM Press, 1967).

understood as an umbrella under which Matthew perceives people, events, and places as divinely ordered for the accomplishment of salvation through Christ the Messiah. In other words, Matthew understands Jesus' coming into the world from God's own mission to save humankind from sin. To this effect, one would posit that the purpose of God from his originally good creation to the salvation of fallen humanity is the grand narrative of the Bible from the very first book of Scripture to the last. This thought is well articulated by Wright:

> The full meaning of recognizing Jesus as Messiah then lies in recognizing also his role in relation to God's mission for Israel for the blessing of the nations. Hence, a messianic reading of the Old Testament has to flow unto a missional reading—which is precisely the connection that Jesus makes in Luke 24.[30]

This missional reading of the Bible suggests that "Mission is what the Bible is all about."[31] Paul M. van Buren well noted, "The Old Testament is the Scripture of Israel as the framework, context, and anticipation of the story of Christ."[32] He notes that although not every word points to Christ, the Scriptures as a whole, as the Emmaus story illustrates, points to him.

There are more recent works that retain the term "salvation history." These include: Walter C. Kaiser, Darrell L. Bock, and Peter Enns, *Three Views on the New Testament Use of the Old Testament*, eds. Stanley N. Gundry, Kenneth Berding, and Jonathan Lunde (Grand Rapids: Zondervan, 2008); Bosch, *Transforming Mission*; David B. Howell, *Matthew's Inclusive Story: A Story in Narrative Rhetoric of the First Gospel* JSNTSS 42 (Sheffield: JSOT Press, 1990), in which Howell discusses salvation history in chapter 2; Donald Senior and Carroll Stuhlmueller, *The Biblical Foundations for Mission* (Maryknoll: Orbis Books, 1983); James Mead, *Biblical Theology: Issues, Methods, and Themes* (Louisville, London: Westminster John Knox Press, 2007); John P. Meier, *The Vision of Matthew: Christ, Church, and Morality in the First Gospel* (New York: Crossroad, 1991); Willem VanGemeren, *The Progress of Redemption: The Story of Redemption from Creation to the New Jerusalem* (Grand Rapids: Baker Academic, 1988). In this work, however, "God's salvific purposes" is used as interchangeable term for "salvation history." The decision to use "God's salvific purposes" as alternative term is merely a matter of personal preference.

30. Wright, *The Mission of God*, 31.

31. Ibid., 29.

32. Paul M. van Buren, *According to the Scriptures: The Origin of the Gospels and of the Church's Old Testament* (Grand Rapids/Cambridge: Eerdmans, 1998), 94.

From the Christian perspective, then, the single most important event in history is Christ's redemptive act that finds its roots in the OT.

For this reason, the theme of fulfillment is, under the grand scheme of Matthew's narrative, inseparable from God's own mission in the world. Matthew's Gospel provides a biblical theology of mission that is rooted in the entire canon of Scripture and knitted in the work of the Triune God and the church. The Gospel of Matthew "affirms the inviolability of God's plan in history."[33] Similarly, Matthew's Gospel shows from the beginning that Jesus fulfills "Israel's destiny as the representative, paradigmatic Son of God, with the result that God's blessing to the nations, promised to Abraham, are to be fulfilled through Jesus and in the mission of his followers. It concludes with the Great Commission, which calls Jesus' followers to make disciples of the nations (28:18–20)."[34] In this sense Matthew, along with the rest of the Gospels, sets the stage for the message of the entire NT on both the theory and practice of mission.

Scholars recognize this mission motif in the Gospel.[35] However, this has never been clearly tied to the other themes such as Christology,[36] the kingdom of heaven,[37] ecclesiology, or eschatology. As a result the pursuit of

---

33. Craig S. Keener, *Matthew*, The IVP New Testament Commentary (Leicester: IVP, 1997), 70. As he notes, "In Jesus the anticipated salvation of God's people has begun."

34. See A. J. Köstenberger, "Mission," in *New Dictionary of Biblical Theology*, eds. T. D. Alexander, et al. (Leicester: IVP, 2000), 665. He says, "Matthew, like the other evangelists, portrays Jesus' mission as proceeding along salvation-historical lines: first to the Jews, then to the gentiles."

35. The term "evangelist" is a familiar one in scholarship. Unfortunately the mission motif in the Gospels is never brought to limelight in typical NT studies. Few scholars who are advocating for the missional reading of the Bible are most likely engaging scholarship toward the right direction.

36. In Matthew, Jesus is the 'Christ' or 'Messiah', the 'Immanuel', the 'Son of Man', the 'Son of God', the 'Son of David', and the 'Lord.'

37. W. D. Davies and Dale C. Allison see no significant distinction between the kingdom of God and the kingdom of heaven in Matthew. See W. D. Davies and Dale C. Allison, *The Gospel According to Matthew*, The New International Critical Commentary on the Holy Scriptures of the Old and New Testaments (London: T & T Clark, 1997), 3.187. Similarly, Keener says, "Some earlier dispensationalists contrasted the kingdom of heaven and the kingdom of God, but few hold this view today, and it is no longer a necessary part of modern dispensationalism" (Keener, *Matthew*, 41), but dispensationalism does not form part of the discussion of this work. Although Matthew's preferred rendering is the "kingdom of heaven," this study employs the two expressions as interchangeable terms. Robert H. Gundry, however, believes that Matthew's preferred term "heaven" is his expression of

individual themes with a dichotomizing tendency is sometimes the norm in scholarly discussion, a dichotomy which is probably not warranted, especially so through a careful reading of the text. Furthermore, through the pursuit of diverse themes, the prominence which the Gospel of Matthew places on the mission motif is never well stressed. In this view, the Gospel of Matthew, along with the other three Gospels, is probably the blueprint for the missionary character of Acts of the Apostles and the Letters. It is the gospel tradition that provided the scheme and impetus for "model missionary history"[38] of Acts and the rest of the letters. This work explores a tripartite mission motif as a unifying theme.[39] Although some scholars recognize a 'two-part' mission motif in the entire NT, namely, the mission of Jesus and the mission of Jesus' followers, it is observed that such approach leaves out the dominant pattern of the redemptive plan of the Triune God. It is suggested here that such approach lacks the needed stress on the prominence and progression of thought on God's plan of salvation from the particular (Israel) to the universal (all humankind) depicted in the NT, especially the Gospels.

While recognizing the quest of the dominant themes of the book such as the exalted Christology, the kingdom of heaven, *inter alia*, as legitimate, the limitation of such pursuit becomes apparent with the observation that the subject of the Gospel of Matthew is not in Jesus himself "but Jesus in his role as Savior and Lord,"[40] that is, in his mission to the world. It is suggested in this research that none of those themes should be studied in isolation from the primary focus of mission as though such a theme is an end in itself. Christ comes as a fulfillment of God's mission on earth. He is exalted

---

the *universality* of the dominion by Jesus and the Father (Robert H. Gundry *Matthew: A Commentary on His Literary and Theological Art* [Grand Rapids: Eerdmans, 1982], 8).

38. William J. Larkin Jr., "Introduction," in *Mission in the New Testament: An Evangelical Approach: An Evangelical Approach,* eds. William J. Larkin, Jr., and Joel F. Williams (Maryknoll: Orbis Books, 1998), 1.

39. I. Howard Marshall recognizes a two-part mission in the New Testament, namely, that of Jesus and that of his disciples. The New Testament documents are primarily documents on mission. See I. Howard Marshall, *New Testament Theology: Many Witnesses, One Gospel* (Downers Grove: IVP, 2004), 34.

40. Ibid.

because he is God's Son whom the Father sent to accomplish a mission.[41] Therefore we would probably agree that theology is essentially missionary theology.[42] In David J. Bosch's words, mission is the "mother of theology."[43] The presence of Jesus as the Messiah, his proclamation, his power, his suffering, his death, and his resurrection all point to the singular mission of God in the world.[44] For Matthew, God's promise of salvation in the Old Testament finds fulfillment in the mission of Christ. He writes from the perspective of eschatological fulfillment[45] of God's purposes for the world. In this sense there is both a continuity and discontinuity with the OT.

In summary, this work is an investigation of the hermeneutics of the mission of God in Matthew's Gospel. It looks at the particular importance of the OT to Matthew's notion of mission. The presupposition of this work is that the OT shapes Matthew's understanding of mission. The Gospel of

---

41. Senior also notes that Matthew's Christology undergirds his view of salvation history. "His conviction that Jesus of Nazareth was, in fact, the Christ, the Son of God, enables him to depict Jesus as the fulfillment of Jewish hopes embodied in the Scriptures. Through this fulfillment Jesus brings to completion the old age of anticipation. By the same token, because Jesus of Nazareth, crucified and risen, is proclaimed as exalted Son of God, as the awaited Son of Man, Matthew can depict him as the inaugurator of the new age, as one whose abiding presence will propel the community and its worldwide mission to the end of time and the final triumph of the kingdom" (Senior and Stuhlmueller, *The Biblical Foundations for Mission*, 241). Similarly, Harvey says that each of the titles of Jesus such as 'Christ', 'Son of David', 'Son of Abraham', introduces a major theme in Matthew's gospel, and "each has a significant connection to Jesus' mission" (Harvey, "Mission in Matthew," in *Mission in the New Testament*, 125).

42. Marshall, *New Testament Theology*, 34.

43. Bosch, *Transforming Mission*, 15.

44. deSilva, *Introduction to the New Testament*, 237, 8. Here deSilva speaks about the inclusion of the gentile believers into the body of Christ as fulfillment of the grand design of God.

45. See J. Behm, "*eschatos*" in *Theological Dictionary of the New Testament*, eds. Gerhard Kittel and Gerhard Friedrich (Grand Rapids: Eerdmans, 1985), 264. Apart from the general use as "last materially (Matt 5:26), spatially (Acts 1:8), or temporally (Matt 12:25)" the eschatological use of the term is from the prophetic "day of Yahweh" which began with Jesus coming (Heb 1:2) and is evidenced by the outpouring of the Holy Spirit in Acts 2:17. Other references about the last day are about the coming of scoffers and the antichrist. Yet the last day is awaited (Rev 15:1). In this work eschatology starts from the first coming of Christ until his second coming. Significant aspect in this time frame is the gathering of God's people in the kingdom as God's and (the church's) primary mission in the world in the last days.

Matthew stands in the context of God's redemptive plan.⁴⁶ It is a narrative of God's salvific purpose. In his hermeneutical scheme Matthew "purposes to show that major events in the life of Jesus took place in fulfillment of prophecy."⁴⁷

1.2 Contribution of the Study

The contribution this work hopes to make to scholarly discussion is threefold. First, the Great Commission appears to have given direction to missiological studies and scholarly discussion of mission in Matthew; but works that link this theme with similar themes and thoughts are rare. This work provides such a link, and especially brings the mission motif of the Gospel into the limelight in scholarly discussion. Second, although many significant works have been written on mission in the NT there is yet a dearth of comprehensive analysis, especially in a monograph form, on the Gospel of Matthew. This work fills this gap by providing such a monograph that is a synthetic articulation and presentation of the theme of mission in Matthew's thought with the OT as the foundation. Most of the scholarly works done in this field have consistently been too general, covering the entire NT and therefore lacking in-depth focus and analysis. This work therefore fills the void and offers to the scholarly community something handy on Matthew's Gospel. It is also hoped that the answers provided in treating the Gospel of Matthew will serve as guide and principles to be applied to other areas of mission in the light of prophecies and fulfillment in the entire NT. Third, in treating mission in the Gospels or Matthew in particular, most scholars look at the mission of Jesus and the mission of the disciples. This approach somewhat relegates the vital role the Trinity plays in mission. In addition, the focus on Jesus' and the disciples' mission

---

46. See Richard Beaton, "Isaiah in Matthew's Gospel," in *Isaiah and the New Testament,* eds. Steve Moyise and Maarten J. J. Menken (London: T & T Clark International, 2005), 63. According to him, "Matthew presents a symbolic world clearly shaped by the OT in his composition of document seeking to outline the significance of Jesus for future generations of followers."

47. Guthrie, *New Testament Introduction,* 32. Although Guthrie rightly says that Matthew is not alone in this understanding, such a motif is nowhere clearly expressed as in this Gospel.

in Matthew seems to ignore the ongoing discussion about one of the most important tensions in Matthew's Gospel, namely, mission to Israel and the nations.[48] This work is intended to fill this *lacuna*.

1.3 Methodology and Procedure of the Study

As an investigation of the nature of mission in Matthew's Gospel, the method adopted in this study is largely inductive—comparative and exegetical. Within the broader parameters of theological and missional reading of the Gospel of Matthew, the key texts examined do not necessarily follow the sequence of the evangelist's development of materials, namely, the progression of thought evidenced in the narrative structure from the first to the last chapter. Instead, these texts appear to be a web that is interwoven in the whole Gospel. It is for this reason that the exegesis requires going back and forth in the major subtitles.

The study consists of five chapters. Chapter 1 is the general introduction of the research. The chapter covers preliminary matters such as the statement of purpose and direction of study, contribution of the research, and research methodology.

Chapter 2 is an inductive survey that provides general background for the rest of the work. Some of the major issues raised in this chapter are the bedrock of discussion in chapters 3 and 4. The redemptive history, emplotted in Matthew's narrative, sees the Triune God at work. God is mentioned as the Father and Jesus as the Son in several places in the Gospel of Matthew (3:17; 11:25–27). The sending role of the Father is highlighted. God sent the prophets as messengers to communicate his salvific purposes beforehand (1:22; 12:17–21). He also sent angels in the birth and infancy narrative of Jesus and the time of his temptation. Jesus is the one sent as mediator of salvation, in order to save his people from their sins (1:21; cf. 15:24). Matthew portrays the Holy Spirit as God's agent in the miraculous

---

48. Bernard Combrink, "Teaching and living the good news: Mission according to Matthew," in *Missionary Perspectives in the New Testament: Pictures from Chosen New Testament Literature*, eds. Johann du Plessis, Eddie Orsmond, and Hennie van Deventer (Wellington: Bible Media, 2009), 82.

conception (1:18, 20), leading Jesus before the temptation (4:1), and empowering him for ministry (12:18–32). The Holy Spirit is also present at Jesus' baptism and in the baptism formula (28:19, 20) alongside the Father and the Son (3:16; 28:19–20). To this effect, an axis of communication in the Gospel of Matthew may be used as a paradigm for interpreting his mission theology. God is the *sender*. The purpose or object of sending Jesus is salvation from sin. Jesus is the *mediator* of salvation. The Holy Spirit is an *agent* in the work of salvation. The *recipients* of salvation are the house of Israel and the nations.[49]

The chapter is therefore divided into three subheadings, stressing the work of the Father, the Son, and the Holy Spirit in mission. The writer believes that scholarly discussion has not paid enough attention to the role of the Triune God in Matthew's mission theology. In answering the question, "Who is Jesus?" Lesslie Newbigin says, "He is the Son, sent by the Father and anointed by the Spirit to be the bearer of God's kingdom to the nations."[50] For Newbigin, the three persons of the Godhead are all involved in mission. As Bosch also points out, the term *mission* was used

---

49. This model is a modified version of Rollin G. Grams' narrative theory of the underlying narrative in Isaiah in which he provides an intertextual and narrative reading of Isaiah's and Matthew's mission theology, on the premise that Matthew's mission theology is thoroughly based on his reading of Isaiah (see his "Narrative Dynamics in Isaiah's and Matthew's Mission Theology," *Transformation* 2, no. 4 [October 2004]: 238–255). Grams sees Isaiah not as a collection of oracles or as first, second, and third Isaiah, but rather as a unified whole involving an underlying narrative. That is, the text is divided into substructures and follows topical sequences. The oracles are read in the light of this narrative framework (240). The 'axis' of communication is always in three parts: there is the *sender* who sets up the task, contract, mandate, etc.; the *object* is what the subject wishes to deliver or accomplish; and the *receiver*, that is, the recipients of the object which the subject wishes to deliver. With this theory applied to the book of Isaiah, God is seen as the Sender and the object is either God's glory or salvation and the recipients are Israel and the nations. The 'axis of conflict' is called 'Help': that is, God's presence and power. The 'subject' in this axis is either the Servant or Israel. And the 'opponent' is Israel's sin. Thus the sender, the object, the receiver, the help, the subject, and the opponent are called the six *actants* that constitute the spheres of action, sometimes referred to as characters. Grams applies this to Isaiah and Matthew, especially on the object actant or mission thus: "The mission in Isaiah and Matthew involves (a) God's glory or coming reign as King; (b) the redemption of Israel; (c) the redemption of the nations; (d) a reign of compassion, reconciliation, justice, righteousness and peace on earth" (243). The receivers actant Israel and the nations, the opponent is sin, the help is God's forgiveness and his presence, the subject actant is Jesus, who is God's servant (248–250).

50. Lesslie Newbigin, *The Open Secret: An Introduction to the Theology of Mission* (Grand Rapids: Eerdmans, 1995), 23. This concept of anointing is found in Matt 12:17, 18 and Luke 4:18–19 as fulfillment of Isa 42:1; 61:1–2.

with reference to the work of the Triune God before the sixteenth century.⁵¹ The work of the Triune God in Matthew's Gospel in the plan and execution of the work of salvation is given careful attention. As noted earlier, God the Father is the sender in mission. Jesus is the one sent.⁵² The Holy Spirit empowers for mission. The Triune God is seen both at the baptism and the transfiguration of Jesus. The baptism formula also provides evidence of the Triune God's involvement in the work of salvation. The focus is the kingdom of God in redemptive history that has come to fulfillment in Matthew's narrative. ⁵³ The dominant pattern of divine redemptive plan that is common in both Testaments is fully seen in Matthew's Gospel. As Richard Bauckham says, "God identifies himself as the God of Abraham, Israel and Jesus in order to be the God of all people and the Lord of all things."⁵⁴ The Holy Spirit's active participation in the life and ministry of Jesus is also examined. This leads to the next chapter on mission to Israel in the Gospel of Matthew.

Chapter 3 treats Matthew and Jewish mission. The writer selects key texts from Matthew for exegesis, especially those with OT foundations and motifs. Where there are more than two passages on a given issue, the researcher limits himself to one or two that he deems as representative texts and most relevant to the focus of the study. The literary context of

---

51. See Bosch, *Transforming Mission,* 1. He says, "Until the sixteenth century the term was used exclusively with reference to the doctrine of the Trinity, that is, of the sending of the Son by the Father and of the Holy Spirit by the Father and the Son." It was the Jesuits, he says, who first began to use the term for the spreading of the Christian faith to all unbelievers and Protestants as well.

52. According to Warren Carter "Jesus has little significance in Matthew's Gospel apart from God's perspective and actions. It is God who initiates his conception (1:18–25), who names him, and who commissions him for his life's work of saving people (1:21–23). It is God who declares Jesus' identity at his baptism and transfiguration, 'my Son, the Beloved, with whom I am well pleased' (3:13–17; 17:5). Jesus makes it clear that he exists in intimate relationship with God (11:25–27) and that he is concerned with doing God's will (4:1–11; 26:42). Hence any discussion of Jesus in Matthew should begin with God and God's purposes". See Warren Carter, *Matthew and Empire: Initial Explorations* (Harrisburg: Trinity Press International, 2001), 60.

53. See Köstenberger, "Mission," *New Dictionary of Biblical Theology,* 668. He says, "God takes the initiative in mission, for the effecting of salvation through Christ. The Abrahamic promises, the Davidic kingship, and the Isaianic Servant of Yahweh are major motifs that culminate in Jesus' coming and mission."

54. Richard Bauckham, *Bible and Mission: Christian Witness in a Postmodern World* (Grand Rapids: Baker Academic, 2003), 13.

every text is given special attention. Grammatical and syntactical analyses are also given where necessary. Similarly, the OT text Matthew cites or alludes to is analyzed. The writer examines the function of the OT text in its NT context. The writer also highlights the hermeneutical method used by Matthew, and the theological and the missional significance of the text(s). Although the researcher gives priority to the primary sources, he interacts with and evaluates secondary sources based on the evidence of the text(s). This interaction and evaluation comes after the evidence of the exegetical analysis. The researcher draws tentative conclusion(s) based on the evidence of the text(s).

Key interpretive issues discussed in this chapter that are also applied to the next chapter include: redemptive events and institutions, prophecy, geography and intertextual typology. In the redemptive events and institutions, the thrust is the continuity of God's work of salvation. Paul J. Achtemeier, Joel B. Green, and Marianne Meye Thompson say, "One of the pressing issues for the community that gathered around Jesus and persisted beyond his death was continuity."[55] This issue of continuity has two dimensions. The first has to do with the relationship between the earthly life of Jesus and the church that continued after him. The second, and directly related to this work, "is the relation of the earthly life and ministry of Jesus to the activity of God and faith of Israel prior to Jesus' birth."[56] It is this "activity of God and the faith of Israel" that is here understood as God's salvific purpose and the basis upon which Matthew uses the OT. The birth of Jesus, in Matthew's view, is the fulfillment of God's covenant promises. Therefore, Matthew's presuppositions about the OT are here highlighted as reasons for his legitimizing of references from the OT.[57] The study of the conceptual and theological framework that shaped Matthew's

---

55. Paul J. Achtemeier, Joel B. Green, and Marianne Meye Thompson, *Introducing the New Testament: Its Literature and Theology* (Grand Rapids/Cambridge: Eerdmans, 2001): 89.

56. Achtemeier, Green, and Thompson, *Introducing the New Testament,* 89. As they rightly observe, "The first book of the NT does not circumvent these central questions, but begins to address them forthrightly, and immediately in its opening chapters."

57. Guthrie suggests that although fulfillment motif is to be found in all the New Testament, it is nowhere clearly stated as in the Gospel of Matthew (see his *New Testament Introduction,* 32).

presuppositions and exegetical practice is deemed necessary for proper understanding of the discussion that follows in the succeeding chapters.

Similarly, God sends the prophets as messengers to communicate his salvific purposes. In this regard, prophecy-fulfillment and typology are viewed as vehicles through which God communicates his plan of salvation. The concepts of πορεύομαι and ἀποστέλλω (חָלַךְ and שָׁלַח) are examined as key terms in God's mission from the prophets to the Christ and his disciples. It is for this reason that gaining proper insight into the historical, theological, and exegetical framework of the NT's use of the OT regarding prophecy and fulfillment is essential for discerning the heart of the NT and for avoiding interpreting the Bible in what is believed to be inconsistent interpretation with the original sense of Scripture.[58] This premise informs the renewed search in the scholarly circles for the interpretative method of prophecies and their fulfillment in the NT. G. K. Beale agrees: "The question of the NT's use of the OT is a thorny one . . ."[59] The thorny issue, according to him, is the degree of continuity and discontinuity in both theology and interpretative method between Christians and Jews. Beale points out, "One widely held position is that Jesus and the writers of the NT used non-contextual and atomistic hermeneutical methods such as were used by their Jewish contemporaries. We today would regard such methods as illegitimate."[60] Jeremy Punt describes this as a 'face value' reading of the Bible such that the way the OT is interpreted or used by the NT authors "seemingly harbors on misinterpretation or abuse."[61] On the other hand,

---

58. R. Kendall Soulen, "The Believer and the Historian: Theological Interpretation and the Historical Investigation," *Interpretation: A Journal of Bible and Theology* 57 (April 2003): 175.

59. G. K. Beale, "Did Jesus and his Followers Preach the Right Doctrine from the Wrong Texts? An Examination of the Presuppositions of the Apostles' Exegetical Method," *Themelios* 14 (April 1989): 89.

60. Ibid.

61. Jeremy Punt, "Paul, Hermeneutics and the Scriptures of Israel," *Neot* 30, no. 2 (1996): 378. According to him, the NT authors "do not always quote the literal text, often quote a text out of its context—seemingly without any regard for its original sense—while some authors quote the same text but with different interpretations of it—sometimes it is not even clear whether it is a quote or allusion at all" (378).

some perceive clear unity in both Testaments under the rubric of promise-fulfillment, type-antitype, and salvation-history.[62]

But the underlying presupposition of those who challenge the interpretative 'method' of the NT writers is that their method is *flawed*. Among such scholars are those who suggest that although the methodology of the NT writers is flawed, they may still be accepted because they should be judged according to their time, presuppositions, and worldview.[63] Others believe that their method should be discarded and the biblical accounts should not be trusted. But C. A. Evans says,

> One of the most important assumptions underlying the NT's use of the OT is that of fulfillment and continuity. NT usage of the OT cannot be reduced to mere proof-texting and apologetic. The purpose, structure, and content of OT theology lie behind the major theological themes of the NT. Beliefs in and about the only God and Creator, who establishes a covenant with a chosen people and who promises redemption and salvation, are the beliefs presupposed in the NT theology and its exegesis of specific OT passages.[64]

Therefore we will focus on the underlying theological and missional motifs governing Matthew's use of the OT. Finally, we will treat geography and intertextual typology as other key elements in Matthew's concept of mission. For it has been noted that nearly half of Matthew's fulfillment quotations focus on geography (Bethlehem, Egypt, Ramah, Nazareth,

---

62. C. L. Blomberg says, "The most common examples of perceived unity in both Testaments combined can be described under the headings of promise-fulfillment, type-antitype, salvation-history, a relationship with the living God, intertextuality and Christology". See "The Unity and Diversity of Scripture," in *New Dictionary of Biblical Theology*, eds. T. Desmond Alexander and Brian S. Rosner (Downers Grove: IVP, 2000), 66.

63. One of the leading figures in this direction is M. D. Goulder whose book *Midrash and Lection in Matthew: The Speakers Lectures in Biblical Studies, 1968–71* (London: SPCK, 1974) describes Matthew's work as Midrash according to the Midrashic method of the time which is characterized by creativity. He was followed by others like Gundry, *Matthew*.

64. C. A. Evans, "New Testament Use of the Old Testament," in *New Dictionary of Biblical Theology*, 79.

and Capernaum).⁶⁵ These fulfillment quotations, echoes, and allusions by Matthew make his Gospel stand out uniquely linked with the OT concerning God's salvific purposes realized in Christ Jesus. Similarly, Matthew uses persons, objects, and places such as Jonah, stone, the wilderness, and mountain with typological significance and salvific purposes. These are also explored in this study.

Chapter 4 focuses on the universal character of the Gospel of Matthew. The writer looks at redemptive events and institutions, prophecy, geography, and intertextual typology through the prism of God's purposes for both Jews and the nations. It is argued here that although for the most part references to mission to the nations in the Gospel of Matthew are rather anticipatory, Jesus engaged in mission to the nations. Such references to mission to the nations are given careful examination, rooted in the promise of God in the OT to bless all the nations of the earth through one man, Abraham, and to make the Servant of the Lord the light of the nations. The thrust of the chapter is that salvation flows from Israel to all nations. The choice of Jesus' disciples is particularly important in this direction, namely, that the inaugurated kingdom of God is to be spread through them. Jesus commissioned these disciples to be witnesses to the ends of the earth. Jesus' mission becomes the disciples' (and of the church's) mission. These are all tied to the one mission of God. This, then, leads to the conclusions and recommendations in chapter 5.

Chapter 5 is conclusions and recommendations. The conclusions will include a brief trajectory of Matthean studies in recent times and the way forward and synthesis of findings based upon the key elements in the mission theology of the Gospel of Matthew, namely, mission of the Triune God, redemptive events and institutions, prophecy, geography and intertextual typology. It will be argued that in Matthew all of these elements point to the Immanuel (1:23) who fulfills OT messianic expectations and also embodies the presence of God as one sent from him as the savior from sins. The writer submits that in Immanuel,⁶⁶ God brings together

---

65. Moyise, *The Old Testament in the New*, 39. These include Jesus' birth place, his sojourn in Egypt, the wailing in Ramah, Jesus' home in Nazareth, and his dwelling in Capernaum.
66. For the treatment of Immanuel, see David Kupp, *Matthew's Emmanuel: Divine Presence and God's People in the First Gospel*, SNTSMS 90 (Cambridge: Cambridge University

both Israel and the nations in a new community called the *ekklēsia* through which he extends his reign. The new community or the *ekklēsia*, though not the totality of the kingdom of heaven, is an extension of the reign or kingdom of heaven.[67] According to Bruce Chilton, "The kingdom of heaven lies at the center of Jesus' message both as a fact and as a mystery."[68] Similarly, Schnabel says, "Jesus' proclamation focused on the kingdom of God."[69] However, this motif is sometimes treated as though it is only a theological theme without a missional import, hence the scholarly confusion on the meaning of the kingdom for hundreds of years.[70] On the con-

---

Press, 1996).

67. See Bosch, *Transforming Mission*, 31. He stresses that the reign of God is central to Jesus' entire ministry. The kingdom of heaven is, as announced by John and Jesus Christ, the reign of God that came through the coming of Christ. Cyprian, for example, says that when believers pray, "your kingdom come" it is "the very kingdom acquired by the blood and passion of Christ." See Manlio Simonetti (ed.), *Matthew 1–3*, Ancient Christian Commentary on Scripture (Downers Grove: IVP, 2001), 133, citing Cyprian *Treatise on the Lord's Prayers* in CCL 3a: 97 and ANF 5:450–51. Augustine explains that the kingdom of God may come does not mean that such kingdom of God does not already exist. "Come" is to be interpreted in the sense that the kingdom may be made manifest to humanity. (Augustine, *Sermon on the Mount*, 2.6.20). Origen says, "Every saint, being ruled by God as king and obedient to the spiritual laws of God, as it were, dwells within this kingdom as in a well-ordered city. The Father is present to such a one, and Christ reigns with the Father in the soul that is maturing. This is in accord with the promise that 'we will come to him and make our abode with him,'" (Origen on Prayer, *GCS* 3:356–57; *ACW* 19:84–85). Similarly Tim Dearborn sees the kingdom of God as "mission's integrating theme" (Tim Dearborn, *Perspectives on the World Christian Movement*, eds. Ralph D. Winter and Steven C. Hawthorne [Pasadena: William Carey Library, 1999], 44). Since the messages of both John the Baptist, Jesus, and the disciples centered on the kingdom of heaven, then the mission of God is undoubtedly in some way connected with that kingdom.

68. Bruce Chilton, *Pure Kingdom: Jesus' Vision of God* (Grand Rapids: Eerdmans, 1996), ix. See also Jack Dean Kingsbury, *Matthew: Structure, Christology, Kingdom* (Philadelphia: Fortress Press, 1975). He says, "The single most comprehensive concept in the first Gospel is without doubt that of the kingdom of Heaven. It touches on every major facet of the Gospel, whether it be theological, christological, or ecclesiological in nature" (128). He also points out: "Whether Matthew's document is described as 'liturgical,' 'apologetic,' 'catechetical,' 'didactic,' 'a manual,' a 'book,' the term either tends to be one-sidedly paraenetic in connotation or does not do justice to Matthew's own summary of the contents of his work as 'the Gospel of the Kingdom'" (5).

69. Eckhard J. Schnabel, *Early Christian Mission*, vol. 1, *Jesus and the Twelve* (Leicester: Apollos, 2004), 211. See also Richard R. De Ridder, *Discipling the Nations* (Grand Rapids: Baker Book House, 1971). His chapter 3 dwells considerably on the kingdom of God.

70. Bosch, *Transforming Mission*, 31. He says, "The fact, recognized by everyone from the first disciples of Jesus to the most skeptical of scholars, is that Jesus preached that the kingdom was at hand. The mystery debated perennially by those inside and outside the church, concerns what precisely Jesus meant when he spoke of the God's kingdom. The

trary, the kingdom of God is the key to understanding the mission of God in both the OT and the NT. In the mission motif of Matthew the kingdom of God is strategic.[71]

Finally, this new community that Jesus inaugurated and brought together into the kingdom of God through faith in him pursues one mission—the discipling of the nations (Matt 28:19–20). Disciple making is therefore the method by which the kingdom of heaven is realized and expanded by Jesus' disciples. The writer then makes some recommendations to the scholarly community and the church in Africa based upon the observations drawn from the study.

---

past hundred years have witnessed especially intense scholarly discussion concerning the kingdom of God."

71. Some scholars share in the understanding that the kingdom of God is connected with mission. See Moreau, Corwin, and McGee, *Introducing World Mission*, 17. According to them, mission is a broad term that refers "to everything the church is doing that points toward the kingdom of God."

CHAPTER 2

Mission in Matthew: The Role of the Triune God

2.1 Introduction

This chapter examines the role of the Triune God in Matthew's concept of mission.[1] Tad Dunne noted, "From its earliest reflections on the Trinity, the Christian community has been convinced that we cannot understand what 'divinity' means outside of understanding what God—Father, Son, and

---

[1]. It has been argued in chapter 1 that scholarly discussion has not paid enough attention to the role of the Triune God in Matthew's mission theology. But "if mission is essentially God's mission, then the Trinity is foundational for the theology of mission." See M. Accad and J. Corrie, "Trinity," in *Dictionary of Mission Theology: Evangelical Foundations,* ed. John Corrie, et al. (Nottingham: IVP, 2007), 397. Although a great deal of general works has been written in the recent past on Trinity and mission, the writer does not intend to summarize this general literature or trace its development. I do not intend to trace the trajectory of interpretation or explain the doctrine of the Trinity in the church's later Trinitarian thought. Rather, the primary goal of this chapter is to present a model, inductively, of the Triune God's mission in Matthew's narrative. For the general works on Trinity and misssion, see Newbigin, *The Open Secret,* 23; Tad Dunne, "Trinity and History," *Theological Studies* 45 (1984): 139–152; Kevin Daugherty, "*Missio Dei*: The Trinity and Christian Mission," *ERT* 31, no. 2 (2007): 151–168; Ajith Fernando, "Grounding Our Reflections in Scripture: Biblical Trinitarianism," in *Global Missiology for the 21ˢᵗ Century: The Iguassu Dialogue,* ed. William D. Taylor (Grand Rapids: Baker Academic, 2000); Alan Roxburgh, "Rethinking Trinitarian Missiology," in *Global Missiology for the 21ˢᵗ Century;* John F. Hoffmeyer, "The Missional Trinity," *Dialog: A Journal of Theology* 40, no. 2 (Summer 2001): 108–111; John S. Connor, "Toward a Trinitarian Theology of Mission," *Missiology: An International Review* 9, no. 2 (April 1981): 155–169; S. Mark Heim, "Witness to Communion: A Trinitarian Perspective on Mission and Religious Pluralism," *Missiology: An International Review* 33, no. 2 (2005): 192–199. What is significant about all of these missiological studies is that they emphasize the role of the Triune God in mission.

Spirit—is doing with humanity."[2] What God is doing with humanity in the Christian community's "primary belief" is "sharing the divine life with flesh and blood, and, in doing so, 'saves' what is most in need of saving."[3] Therefore, it is in the context of "salvific experiences" that Trinitarian theology developed. But as already mentioned, although so much scholarly work has been done in the general direction, no significant work has appeared that has critically examined Matthew's gospel with respect to the role of the Triune God in mission.

The thrust of this chapter is that mission to Israel and mission to the nations in the Gospel of Matthew flow from the mission of the Triune God. This paradigm shift[4] from the anthropocentric and ecclesiocentric to the theocentric is considered a significant shift for laying a better foundation for mission praxis. Therefore, it is argued in this chapter that the three persons of the Godhead—the Father, the Son, and the Holy Spirit—are active participants in the work of mission in Matthew's narrative. To this effect, an axis of communication in the Gospel of Matthew may be used as a paradigm for interpreting his mission theology. God the Father is explicitly the *sender*,[5] "the acting subject in mission"[6] in addition to other redemptive roles. The purpose or object of sending Jesus is salvation from sin. The Father also sends the angels and the prophets. Broadly speaking, Jesus is sent as the *mediator* of salvation.[7] But as the Father sends, Jesus also

---

2. Dunne, "Trinity and History," 139. The focus on the individual roles of the Father, Son, and Holy Spirit for mission is noted by Daugherty, (see Daugherty, *Missio Dei*, 151).

3. Ibid., 45. The imparting of "the divine life with flesh and blood" is reminiscent of the incarnation.

4. Although not a new shift as noted in this work, the freshness appears in the application of the concept to a gospel that is considered important in mission study.

5. In the redemptive work of the Father crafted in Matthew, *sending* is more pronounced. This sending is not limited to Jesus, as the study shows, but the angels as well. However, we also notice the aspect of revealing the Son (11:25). According to Accad and Corrie, "mission is rooted in the sending activity of God as the continuing movement of his Trinitarian life, from the Father who sends his Son into the world" (Accad and Corrie, "Trinity," 397).

6. See J. Verkuyl, *Contemporary Missiology: An Introduction*, trans. and ed. Dale Cooper (Grand Rapids: Eerdmans, 1978), 3.

7. The word *mediator* as used here is by inference, suggesting that the concept is derived from a reading of the whole gospel as Jesus' mediating character is seen from the fact that he came to save by giving his life as a ransom (1:22; 20:28). Jesus is primarily the one sent by God. He reveals the Father by virtue of his distinctive relationship with him. But Jesus also sends his disciples for mission and the angels at the eschaton.

sends the angels and the disciples.[8] The Holy Spirit is an *agent* in the work of salvation. The Spirit brings into being what is not as in the miraculous birth of Christ such that he might be considered the creative power of God. He also anoints Jesus, empowers him, as well as speaks through the disciples (10:19, 20). The *recipients* of salvation are the house of Israel and the nations. In this regard, Matthew shows that the Christian Trinitarian God—Father, Son, and Holy Spirit—fully participates in the salvific work of God.[9]

2.2 The Father's Redemptive Role in Mission

This section reinforces the thesis that mission is the corporate work of the Triune God.[10] God the Father is the one who *sends* for mission. The issue of sending (πορεύομαι and ἀποστέλλω, used in Matt 10:5, 6; 28:19) highlighted in the introductory chapter is given further clarification here. The fact that the Father is the *sender* in mission is explicitly expressed in relation to Jesus the Son. These concepts of *sender* and *one sent* are fundamental to mission discussion. Ferris L. McDaniel writes:

> Jesus was raised from death and promised an empowerment to the disciples for mission. His commission reduces to this: God sends. The question must arise, Is there any anticipation

---

8. See Verkuyl, *Contemporary Missiology*, 3.

9. When placed in the social context of the first century AD patron-client relations, God may be seen as the benefactor, Jesus and the Holy Spirit are the mediators or brokers, while Israel and the nations are the beneficiaries. See, for example, Halvor Moxnes, "Patron-Client Relations and the New Community in Luke-Acts," in *The Social World of Luke-Acts: Models for Interpretation*, ed. Jerome H. Neyrey (Peabody: Hendrickson, 1991), 241–268.

10. The line of thought is that human mission praxis is derived from the mission of the Triune God. Therefore, human beings are agents who participate in mission through a delegated authority (Matt 28:16–20). As Thomas R. Schreiner says, since "we tend to look past what constantly stands in front of us," it is easy "to screen out what the NT says about God himself." It is probably due to this looking "past what constantly stands before us" that discussion on mission in the NT, and particularly in Matthew, has often ignored the role of God the Father. Schreiner sees most scholars investigating themes such as justification, reconciliation, redemptive history, and new creation, while God is "shoved to the side". See T. R. Schreiner, *New Testament Theology: Magnifying God in Christ* (Nottingham: Apollos, 2008), 119. But this writer has not surveyed the works on this area.

of this action or any informing theology in the OT for the action of God sending?[11]

In his lexical study of the concepts of ἀποστέλλω and שָׁלַח as the link between the testaments, McDaniel looks at שָׁלַח from the secular and divine sending. He comes to the important conclusion that "More frequently than any other use, however, is the association between God sending and the office of the prophet."[12] Not only did God send the prophets with the message of judgment, he also sent them with "the message of salvation and hope leading to repentance and fellowship."[13] This salvation and hope would include the entire earth, as "people from far nations will worship Israel's God."[14] McDaniel's major argument is that divine sending is a recurring theme in the prophetic writings. This work builds on this divine sending as Matthew shows that God sends the angels, the prophets, the workers into the harvest field, and the Son. Jesus also sends the disciples and the angels at the end of the age.

According to John D. Harvey, the Father takes the initiative in mission, as illustrated in several ways in the Synoptic Gospels. Jesus sees himself as a steward (Matt 11:25–27); the Father assumes the role of a shepherd who leaves ninety-nine sheep in search for one (Luke 15:3–7; cf. Matt 18:12–14); the Father is like a woman who searches for a lost coin (Luke 15:8–10); and as a Father who runs to meet his son who was lost (Luke 15:11–32). Moreover, the Father is seen as the king who sends out his servants to invite people for the banquet of his son (Matt 22:1–4; Luke 14:16–24). Harvey concludes that the Father's initiative is clearly in view in each of these instances.[15] Regarding Jesus' mission, the Father's several specific functions include sending his angel to Joseph with information

---

11. Ferris L. McDaniel, "Mission in the Old Testament," in *Mission in the New Testament: An Evangelical Approach*, ed. William J. Larkin Jr. and Joel F. Williams (Maryknoll: Orbis Books, 1998), 11.

12. McDaniel, "Mission in the Old Testament," 19.

13. Ibid., 20. See Isa 66:19; 19:18–25.

14. Ibid.

15. John D. Harvey, "Mission in Jesus' Teaching," in *Mission in the New Testament: An Evangelical Approach*, ed. William J. Larkin Jr. and Joel F. Williams (Maryknoll: Orbis Books, 1998), 32.

and instructions (1:20; 2:13, 19); sending John the Baptist to prepare the way for the Lord (3:3); commissioning Jesus for mission by sending the Holy Spirit at the baptism (3:16); and confirming Jesus' sonship and mission through audible speeches (3:16; 17:5). These are examined in greater detail in subsequent discussions.

The sending role of the Father is explicated as follows.

2.2.1 He Sends the Angels

The *angel of the Lord* as God's messenger plays a prominent role in the discussion about the *sending* aspect of the redemptive mission of God in Matthew. From the nativity narrative to the resurrection of Christ, the angelic announcements advance the kingdom of God. The term ἄγγελος occurs 19 times in Matthew.[16] Some of these references are explored in this chapter in relationship to angelic advancement of God's salvific purposes. In the first pericope of Matthew, the angel of the Lord appears first to Joseph in a dream[17] (1:20). His mission here is to give revelatory information to Joseph and to encourage him to rescind from his decision to divorce Mary, his betrothed.[18] The identity of the angel of the Lord is not disclosed. However, in Luke 1:26 he is identified as Gabriel. He was, according to Luke, sent (ἀπεστάλη) from God.

Joseph obeys the voice of the angel of the Lord (1:24). He woke up from sleep and did as the angel of the Lord commanded (προσέταξεν) him. The angel of the Lord allayed Joseph's doubts and fears. But this is absent in Luke's account; rather, it is Mary who questions the angel of the Lord, Πῶς

---

16. See Matt 1:20, 24; 2:13, 19; 4:6, 11; 13:39, 41, 49; 16:27; 18:10; 22:30; 24:31, 36; 25:31, 41; 26:53; 28:2, 5.

17. It is to be noted that key elements in the birth and nativity narrative are linked with the Holy Spirit, angelic appearances, and dreams. Joseph restrains himself from divorcing his wife because an *angel* asked him not to. He goes to Egypt according to angelic instruction in a *dream*. He also returns from Egypt according to *angelic* instruction in a *dream*. France says, "Divine guidance both by dreams and by the appearance of angels is of course a regular feature of OT spirituality, and would need no explanation. The point of their concentration in these chapters is to emphasize the initiative of God in guiding Joseph's actions through this crucial period" (France, *The Gospel of Matthew*, 52).

18. Matthew's use of ἐνθυμηθέντος (Matt 1:20) suggests that his mind had been made up already concerning Mary his betrothed (see also France, *The Gospel of Matthew*, 52).

ἔσται τοῦτο, ἐπεὶ ἄνδρα οὐ γινώσκω; (Luke 1:34). And she is assured that this would take place through the Holy Spirit.[19]

In 2:13–15 God protects Jesus' family from the brutality of Herod.[20] The target of Herod's fury is the baby Jesus. Joseph's flight to Egypt takes place after he is instructed by an angel of the Lord who appears in a dream as in the previous instance. Here Joseph is commanded to take the child Jesus and his mother Mary and flee to Egypt and to be there until the same angel (ἕως ἂν εἴπω σοι) comes with another message.[21] "Until I speak" is indicative of one angel of the Lord speaking now as well as in the next encounter.

In 4:11, after the temptation in the wilderness, angels came and ministered to him. This ministry of the angels seems to have taken place throughout the period of testing as recorded by Mark (1:12, 13), while it is omitted in Luke altogether. Here the mission of the angels is specified as service (διακόνος). The motif of angel ministering to Jesus is understood to have a Jewish background.[22] This ministry of angels is beyond meeting physical needs such as food and water which he had to endure for the period of forty days in the wilderness. The angels came "to call special attention to the victory of the obedient Son," therefore symbolizing the true identity of the Son, and also to underline "God's faithfulness to the obedient."[23]

The angels are also associated with the end of the age when God will send them in order to serve as harvesters. This is evident in Matthew 13: 41; 24: 31; cf. Mark 13: 27. This will be examined in the subheading dealing with Jesus sending the angels. Meanwhile, the prophets are examined in God's redemptive mission.

---

19. The importance of ἐκ πνεύματος ἁγίου (Matt 1:21) is discussed in the section on the Holy Spirit.

20. Here commentators note some parallels with the story of Moses (see Craig S. Keener, *A Commentary on the Gospel of Matthew,* [Grand Rapids: Eerdmans, 1999], 107).

21. Ibid. According to Keener, ancient literature is full of "stories of divine children overcoming superhuman opposition as well as of other babies miraculously preserved by fate for their future destiny" (107).

22. Donald A. Hagner, *Matthew 1–13,* Word Biblical Commentary, vol. 33 (Nashville: Thomas Nelson, 1993), 33.69.

23. Hagner, *Matthew 1–13,* 33.69.

2.2.2 He Sends the Prophets

The word *prophet* occurs more frequently in the Gospel of Matthew than any of the Synoptic Gospels.[24] This underscores the concept of promise-fulfillment in Matthew.[25] It is the OT prophets who are given prominent place in the Gospel, although John the Baptist and Jesus are also regarded as prophets (11:9–13; 14:5; 21:11, 46). In giving an account of Jesus' miraculous conception Matthew sums up the narrative in this first pericope thus: "All this took place to fulfill what the Lord had said through the prophets" (1:22). This marks the beginning of the significant role the prophets play in the entire Gospel of Matthew regarding God's salvific scheme. In 23:37 Jerusalem is denounced as one who kills the prophets and "stone those sent to you." The "servants" in the parable of the vineyard (21:34–37) and the wedding banquet (22:2–14) may be understood as the prophets God had sent in preparation for the coming of Jesus such that the "eschatological component" of the prophet's mission is prominent.[26] In this regard, it is believed that "exile and restoration provided the focal moment in history for Israel's prophetic ministry."[27] The "restoration" is linked with the coming messiah. For this reason *restoration from exile* provides "a valid and

---

24. It occurs 37 times as against Mark's 6 times and Luke's 30 times (Harvey, "Mission in Matthew," 123).

25. The Hebrew נָבִיא (spokesman, speaker, prophet) means one called "having a special commission directly from God" (Douglas Stuart, "The Old Testament Prophets' Self Understanding of their Prophecy," *Themelios* 6 [September 1980], 10). All genuine prophets experienced a divine call and they spoke God's word and not their own. For this reason, there is the frequent use of "Thus says the Lord" (כֹּה אָמַר יְהוָה). An example of call and commissioning from God is Jer 1:5 where God tells the young prophet Jeremiah that before he was formed in the womb he had been set apart and appointed as a prophet to the nations.

26. Harvey, "Mission in Matthew," 123.

27. O. Palmer Robertson, *The Christ of the Prophets* (Phillipsburg: P&R Publishing, 2004), 453. See also See also VanGemeren, *The Progress of Redemption*, 284); Craig A. Evans, "Jesus and the Continuing Exile of Israel," in *Jesus and the Restoration of Israel: A Critical Assessment of N. T. Wright's Jesus and the Victory of God*, ed. Carey C. Newman (Carlisle: Paternoster, 1999), 77–100. For Evans, exile theology in Jesus' teaching and actions include the appointment of the twelve disciples as symbolic reconstruction of the twelve tribes of Israel; the request of a sign (cf. 1Q27 frag. 1, 1:5–8); driving out the merchants from the temple by appealing to Isa 56:7; Jesus' allusion to Zech 2:6, a passage that envisions the gathering of the exiles; Jesus' prophetic threats to Israel's leaders (Matt 11:21–23; Luke 10:13–15); and traces of exile theology and motifs in the NT and early Christian writings such as Matt 1:11–12, 17 (91–99).

valuable hermeneutical prism for the interpretation of Matthew's gospel."[28] Similarly, Axel von Dobbeler connects Matthew 10:5, 6 and 28:18–20 with the restoration of Israel and the inclusion of the nations.[29] This matter is taken up in the next chapter as the restoration is significant for Matthew's messianic age.

This decisive prophetic ministry is taken up in the next two chapters. Meanwhile, God's sending of workers into his harvest field will be considered.

2.2.3 He Sends out Workers into His Harvest Field

What is the *harvest*[30] and who are the *workers* that God sends out into his harvest field in Matthew 9:35–38?[31] In this text, Jesus goes through all the towns and villages. He teaches in their synagogues and preaches the good news of the kingdom, accompanied by miracles of healing. "When he saw the crowds, he had compassion on them, because they were harassed and helpless, like sheep without a shepherd" (9:36, NIV).[32] The situation here is reminiscent of Ezekiel 34:5 and Zechariah 10:2 where the people are likened to sheep without a shepherd.[33] Israel's condition is also like harvest without enough workers.

---

28. Mervyn Eloff, "From the Exile to the Christ: Exile, Restoration and the Interpretation of Matthew's Gospel," (Doctor of Theology dissertation presented to the University of Stellenbosch, December 2002), iii.
29. Axel von Dobbeler, "Die Restitution Israels und die Bekehrung der Heiden: Das Verhältnis von Mt 10, 5b.6 und Mt 28, 18–20 unter dem Aspekt der Komplementarität— Erwägungen zum Standort des Matthäusevangeliums," *ZNW* 91 (2000), 18–44.
30. For Matthew's harvest imagery, see 3:8–10, 12; 6:26; 13:30, 39; 21:34; 25:24, 26; 20:1–16.
31. Matthew 9:35–38 marks a transition between the miracle stories that began from 8:1–9:34. This pericope introduces the mission discourse that follows in chapter 10. It begins with a summary of the works of Jesus as in 4:23. The identical summaries are said to "serve as an *inclusio*, bookends that bracket the two 'books' of Jesus' words and deeds within a missional perspective." See David L. Turner, *Matthew*, Baker Exegetical Commentary of the New Testament (Grand Rapids, Mich.: Baker Academic, 2008), 262. See John Nolland, *The Gospel of Matthew*, NIGTC (Grand Rapids, Mich./Cambridge, U.K.: Eerdmans, 2005), 406.
32. See Matt 14:14; 15:32; 18:33; 20:34 in which Jesus is moved by compassion because of the people's problems.
33. Compare also Num 27:17; 1 Kgs 12:17; 2 Chr 18:16.

When Jesus speaks of the readiness of the *harvest* he might have in mind the work of the prophets, the exile experience, the work of John the Baptist, even his own work to this point. According to Davies and Allison, the harvest in the OT and other Jewish sources is frequently associated with eschatological themes, and the connection is maintained in the NT such that this text needs to be read within an eschatological context.[34] This harvest is believed to be "an image of the eschatological calling of people into the kingdom of God," and not eschatological judgment.[35] It is therefore to be understood as part of eschatological blessings.[36] In Matthew 9:38 Jesus uses the imagery of God as owner of a farmland who employs laborers for harvest. Although the commissioning of the twelve suggests that they were part of the harvest, the need for prayer indicates that they were not enough for this ripe harvest.[37] God is the one who casts (ἐκβάλῃ) workers into the harvest field. Their work would include shepherding the people that were harassed and helpless, like sheep without a shepherd.

But he also sends the Son. The sending of the Son is a key component in the understanding of mission in Matthew as is discussed below.

2.2.4 He Sends the Son

Matthew views the life and ministry of Jesus as fulfillment of God's promises through the prophets.[38] The concept that every mission involves a sender

---

34. W. D. Davies and Dale C. Allison, Jr., *A Critical and Exegetical Commentary on the Gospel According to Saint Matthew*, The International Critical Commentary (Edinburgh; London; New York: T & T Clark, 2001), 2.149. As Davies and Allison point out, the mission of the twelve disciples and the believers "of the post-Easter church belongs to the latter days. It is not simply a prelude to the end but itself part of the complex of events that make up the end. This means that the evangelist and his community perceived their own time as eschatological time" (149).

35. Nolland, *The Gospel of Matthew*, 408.

36. Blaine Charette, "A Harvest for the People? An Interpretation of Matthew 9:37f," *JSNT* 38 (1990), 32.

37. According to Davies and Allison, the workers, in Matthew's mind, are the missionaries of the post-Easter period. Therefore, those missionaries existed as answer to the prayers of the disciples. "Which is to say: not only is the post-Easter mission grounded in the activities of Jesus and the twelve, it is also grounded in the prayer request of Christ the Lord" (*A Critical and Exegetical Commentary,* 2.149–50).

38. As Chrysostom says, "The nativity is best understood in relation to the coming salvation and its prophetic expectation, which had been already promised by the Lord

and a sent one[39] has been underscored. In Matthew 10:40 (cf. Mark 9:37; Luke 9:48) he who received Jesus received the one who sent him. How this *sending* agrees with the שָׁלַח motif in Judaism is considered in the redemptive mission of the Son as he sends the disciples. Meanwhile, in Matthew 15:24 Jesus understood himself as one sent by God "to gather the lost sheep of the house of Israel" (cf. Luke 4:43). Jesus' frequent references to the "Father" and the affirmation of his sonship at his baptism and the transfiguration are indicative that the sender is God the Father.[40]

But why did God send the Son? From the first pericope after the genealogy the task of Jesus' mission is announced (1:21). He is the Messiah who saves his people from their sins.[41] For Jesus' Davidic kingship implies that he will save his people as shown in his given name "Jesus".[42] R. H. Gundry points out that in 1:21 Matthew is quoting Psalm 130:8, but replaces "will redeem" with "will save" in order to draw a link with the meaning of the name Jesus.[43] It is noteworthy here that the "redemptive nature of that mission is a significant concept for Matthew."[44] He came to seek the lost (Matt 18:12–14; cf. Luke 15: 3–10), and to give his life as a ransom for many (Matt 20:28; Mark 10:45). Jesus' use of λύτρον "fixes this firmly within the

---

speaking through Isaiah." See Manlio Simonetti, (ed.) *Matthew 1–13*, Ancient Christian Commentary on Scripture (Downers Grove: IVP, 2001), 11.

39. Harvey, "Mission in Jesus' Teaching," 31.

40. Harvey says that although the concept of the Father sending the Son into the world is particularly Johannine and is less prominent in the Synoptics, "Father" remains a characteristic way of Jesus addressing and referring to God in the Synoptics. He notes 45 occurrences in Matthew alone; 5 in Mark; and 16 in Luke (Harvey, "Mission in Jesus' Teaching," 32).

41. Harvey, "Mission in Matthew," 125. In its OT context, calling someone Messiah does not necessarily connote divinity, but that the person so called is anointed by God for a particular task. The development of the concept may be traced to the description of David and his descendants as the anointed of the Lord (see 1 Sam 16:12–13; 2 Sam 2:4, 7; 3:39; 5:3, 17; 12:7; 1 Kgs 1:34, 39, 45; 5:1; Ps 89:20, 38, 51; 130:10, 17). Matthew links this Messiah with Jesus from the first verse of his Gospel so that the promise made to David becomes God's purpose that is made for the whole world. And the Messiah in Matthew is a deliverer from sins, and not only a political or economic liberator as thought by some Jews in Jesus' day, although Luke 4:18–19 probably has political and economic implications.

42. Gundry, *Matthew*, 23.

43. Ibid.

44. Harvey, "Mission in Matthew," 126.

sphere of redemptive activity, for the OT background is one of obtaining deliverance by paying a price."[45]

As confirmation that the Father sent the Son he testifies about him in the baptism and the transfiguration (3:17; 17:5; cf. Mark 1:11; 9:7; Luke 3:21, 22). In the baptism accounts Jesus is referred to as "my beloved Son."[46] This is believed to be an allusion to Psalm 2:7.[47] The Psalm, "originally an enthronement psalm, is here used to announce in advance Jesus' messianic enthronement."[48] This christological title "Son of God" is distinguished from the "Messiah" who is understood as the anointed Son of David in order "to establish the Kingdom of God in power."[49] G. E. Ladd sees the sonship as "the prior ground and the basis of Jesus' election to fulfill his messianic office" and therefore not synonymous with the messianic status.[50] For Ladd, this "sonship involves a supernatural element."[51]

---

45. Harvey, "Mission in the Teaching of Jesus," 35.

46. On the question, "To whom does the Matthean voice speak?" most scholars believe that the voice is God's public affirmation that is directed to the crowds standing by (see Nolland, *The Gospel of Matthew*, 156). But Nolland thinks that the voice is intended for the heavenly court as God acclaims Jesus as his Son while Jesus is "privileged to overhear the heavenly conversation" (156–57).

47. G. E. Ladd, *A Theology of the New Testament*, rev. ed. Donald A. Hagner (Grand Rapids: Eerdmans, 1993), 163.

48. Keener, *Matthew*, 86.

49. Ladd, *A Theology of the New Testament*, 162. This christological title is explained in the section on the redemptive role of the Son.

50. Ibid., 164.

51. Ibid. But Stanton says the term "may well be synonymous with a Jewish messianic term 'the Chosen.'" And since "most scholars agree that the Aramaic or Hebrew word behind 'son' is 'servant' the voice from heaven is believed to be an echo of Isa 42:1 (see Stanton, *The Gospels and Jesus*, 245). But considering the miraculous conception in the birth narrative of Jesus, Ladd's position appears plausible. Jesus is the Son of God in a unique way. His messianic task begins with his anointing as the Son of God. As the Son of God he is the mediator of salvation. And when the account of the first pericope (1:18–25) is given due attention, Jesus came as Son of David and God with us and therefore qualifies as both Israel's Messiah and Son of God. However, Yigal Levin treats Jesus as "Son of God" and "Son of David" from the influence of Roman concept of legal adoption since "adoption was unknown in Jewish law of the period". See Yigal Levin, "Jesus, 'Son of God' and 'Son of David': The 'Adoption' of Jesus into the Davidic Line," *JSNT* 24, no. 4 (2006): 415. According to Levin, "both Matthew and Luke, faced with the dual traditions of both Jesus' Davidic Messianity and his Divine Sonship, dealt with the obvious contradiction in the only way that would have seemed natural to a subject of the Julio-Claudian and Flavian Principate: by assuming that Jesus, Son of God, could have been adopted into the royal line of Israel, all the while retaining his status as θεοῦ υἱός" (434).

The mountain motif is a prominent feature in Matthew.[52] The transfiguration event (Matt 17:1–5; Mark 9:1–7; Luke 9:28–26) takes place six days after the confession of Peter and Jesus' prediction of his death (Matthew and Mark) and about eight days after that confession (Luke). The account has strong OT motifs as it takes the reader back to two of the most important figures in the OT, namely Moses and Elijah. It is also reminiscent of the cloud that led the people of Israel after they were delivered from Egypt and the cloud that settled on Mount Sinai as well as the glory that radiated from the face of Moses (Exod 24:16).[53] It is also a reminder of the glory and power of God manifested in the life of the prophet Elijah, especially the Mount Carmel experience (2 Kgs 18:16–46). The symbolic appearance of Moses and Elijah in a conversation with Jesus relates to Jesus' and John the Baptist's ministries "as occupying the eschatological role of Elijah and the strong Matthean affirmation that Jesus came to fulfill the Law."[54] So while Moses is seen as predecessor of Jesus, Elijah is seen as his precursor.[55]

Significant for this discussion is the voice from heaven that affirms Jesus' sonship. The voice is preceded by a cloud from heaven, a sign of God's "hidden presence."[56] This voice is connected with the baptism of Jesus (3:17) as it repeats what has been said there. These are the only two occasions such a voice is heard in the Gospel of Matthew. This time the voice speaks explicitly to the disciples, and "listen to him" is said to be a likely

---

52. Gundry says, "Matthew's repeated paralleling of Moses and Jesus justifies the supposition that he looks on 'the high mountain' as a new Sinai and on Jesus' going up it after six days as a repetition of Moses' going up Sinai after six days (i.e. on the seventh) (Exodus 24:16)". Gundry, *Matthew*, 342.

53. Stephen Williams, "The Transfiguration of Jesus," *Themelios* 28 (Autumn 2002): 22. Walter L. Liefeld notes exodus pattern in the transfiguration such as the significance of the time, the cloud motif, Moses and Elijah, the proposal to build a tabernacle, and the voice from heaven. See Walter L. Liefeld, "Theological Motifs in the Transfiguration Narrative," in *New Dimensions in New Testament Study*, ed. Richard L. Longenecker and Merrill C. Tenney (Grand Rapids: Zondervan, 1974), 162–179.

54. Nolland, *The Gospel of Matthew*, 701–702.

55. Ibid., 702. By "predecessor" and "precursor," Nolland probably means that Jesus succeeds Moses, namely, that Moses precedes Jesus in office or position as leader or lawgiver while Elijah is a sign of what is to follow. Elijah, therefore, anticipates the approach of Jesus or points to his coming.

56. Ibid., 703.

echo of Deuteronomy 18:5.⁵⁷ Here Jesus anticipates suffering as Son of God, not in his Father's glory as in 16:28.

From the work of the Father the redemptive role of the Son is explored. The Gospel of Matthew shows that "the whole coming, the whole appearance and activity of Jesus" is seen in the light of sending.⁵⁸ This is treated below.

2.3 The Son's Redemptive Role in Mission

What redemptive roles does Jesus play in Matthew? In the Gospel of Matthew, Jesus is the Son of God.⁵⁹ More importantly, "He is the Son, sent

---

57. Ibid., 704.

58. Jürgen Moltmann, *The Trinity and the Kingdom*, (New York: HarperCollins Publishers, 1991), 71.

59. This sonship is understood in three important ways, according to Schreiner. First, "If we open the Synoptic Gospels with the OT background in mind, the theme that Jesus is the true Son of God—the true Israel—emerges." An example of this is Matthew's use of Hos 11:1. Second, the title also signifies that Jesus is the one anointed by God to rule over Israel. In this sense, Jesus is the fulfillment of the promises made to David. He is therefore the true Messiah, that is, "the one to whom the covenantal promises given to David pointed." According to Willard M. Swartley, "Messiah-Christ and Son of David are the most prominent titles which, like Son of God, bear directly upon Matthew's portrait of Jesus as king". See Willard M. Swartley, *Israel's Faith Traditions and the Synoptic Gospels: Story Shaping Story* (Peabody: Hendrickson Publishers, 1994), 220. Third, the gospel writers look at the meaning of the Son of God from the perspective that Jesus "shares a unique and special relation with God" (see Schreiner, *New Testament Theology*, 236–37). Moltmann describes this relationship in "an absolute sense" in which Jesus is "the Son" and not merely as corporate Israel or the Davidic king (see Moltmann, *The Trinity and the Kingdom*, 65). In Matthew Jesus fulfills all of these as corporate Israel, as fulfillment of the promise made to David, but in a profound way as a unique Son of God. As Schreiner points out, while Matthew's use of "Son" or "Son of God" may refer to true Israel or Messiah, "what must be emphasized, however, is that Matthew typically uses the phrase to denote Jesus' special and unique relation to God" (237–38). As such "Matthew wants readers to see all the 'Son of God' statements in light of the full revelation that has come after Jesus' death and resurrection. Jesus is not simply the Messiah; he stands in a special relationship with the Father and, like the Father, is divine" (240). This uniqueness is depicted by the miraculous conception and the name given to him as Immanuel. Bultmann thinks that the title Son of God in the Gospels is rooted in "Hellenistic way of thinking" where, in Greek mythology, the "idea of being begotten by a god to men" was prevalent (Rudolf Bultmann, *Theology of the New Testament*, 2 vols. [New York: Scribner's, 1951, 1955], 1:130). For a good treatment of "Son of God" see Kingsbury, *Matthew: Structure, Christology, Kingdom* and Martin Hengel, *The Cross of the Son of God: Containing the Son of God, Crucifixion, the Atonement* (London: SCM Press, 1986) in which Hengel explores the meaning of the

by the Father and anointed by the Spirit to be the bearer of God's kingdom to the nations."[60] Let us then examine the redemptive role of the Son in relation to God.

2.3.1 He Saves[61] from Sins

As 1:21 provides the foundation upon which the whole narrative is based, critical questions include: the identity of "his people" or the saved, what salvation consists of, and how the people are saved.[62] While the genealogical record fixes Jesus in his OT roots, this first pericope provides the manner and purpose of his coming. This purpose is provided in Matthew 1:21[63] which is also tied to Isaiah 7:14 as Matthew 1:22–23 suggest. His name represents his character and destiny. As Powell notes, "In literary-critical terms, the intrusive comments of the narrator in this verse establishes the frame of representation within which the character of Jesus is to be understood in the narrative that follows."[64] By this Powell means that the use of

---

son of God from the history-of-religions school. In chapter 5 Hengel looks at the OT and then considers Greek and Hellenistic parallels such as mysteries, dying and the rising sons of God and the ruler cult, the divine men, the Gnostic redeemer myth, and the sending of the redeemer into the world and other related conceptions. On this sonship of Jesus, the difference is usually between the history and religions school of thought and those who believe in the supernatural and the historicity of the Gospels (see Keener, *Commentary of the Gospel of Matthew*, 131–135 on the Father's attestation of the baptism narrative).

60. Newbigin, *The Open Secret*, 23. This concept of anointing is found in Matt 12:17, 18 and Luke 4:18–19 as fulfillment of Isa 42:1; 61:1–2.

61. Martin Karrer believes that the understanding of Jesus as Savior is largely due to the encounter between Hellenism and Christianity. See Martin Karrer, "Jesus, der Retter (*Sôtêr*): Zur Aufnahme eines hellenistischen Prädikats im Neuen Testament," *ZNW* 93 (2000), 153–176. But this cannot be pursued here.

62. See Robert H. Gundry, "Salvation in Matthew," *SBLSP* 39 (November 2000): 402–407.

63. Luke also portrays Jesus as Savior from sins both of Israel and nations (1:67–79; 2:11, 30–32; 3:6).

64. Mark Allan Powell also sees this as a summary of the mission of Jesus as is evidently shown by the name given to him. See Mark Allan Powell, *God With Us: A Pastoral Theology of Matthew's Gospel* (Minneapolis: Fortress, 1995), 3. Nolland observes that in the OT "heaven-given names always have etymological significance" (Nolland, *The Gospel of Matthew*, 98). Morris also says that Jesus' destiny is "expressed in the meaning of the name" given to him. See Leon Morris, *New Testament Theology* (Grand Rapids: Zondervan, 1986, 1990), 29. Kingsbury says that the focus of 1:18–25 is on the names of Jesus (Kingsbury, "The Birth Narrative of Matthew," in *The Gospel of Matthew in Current Studies*, 161). The significance of the name Jesus from its OT roots is treated in this chapter concerning the redemptive role of the Son.

the proper name Jesus in the narrative which occurs 150 times "serves as a subtle reminder to the readers that this is the person who has come to save his people from their sins."[65]

But who are *his people* and what *salvation* is in view? Some think that the *people* refers to Israel or Christians,[66] Israel,[67] or "national-political salvation involving deliverance from the Roman occupation."[68] While each of these may find valid support from reading particular references from the Gospel of Matthew, a "broader designation" seems more ideal from reading the entire gospel. Powell suggests that his people comprise "the lost sheep of Israel" to whom Jesus is initially sent (15:24) as well as some among the 'world' (24:14) where the gospel is to be preached (24:14) and the 'nations' where disciples are to be made (28:19).[69] Perhaps a more plausible interpretation is that which takes the whole gospel into consideration while at the same time recognizing the passages that indicate particularism. So while "his people" may initially mean Israel, Matthew and his readers must have given a deeper meaning such that the "people" are now equated with the ἐκκλησία.[70]

What salvation consists of is understood from the phrase "from their sins." Jesus saves *his people* from their sins. The OT concept of cleansing from sin is well known (Lev 16:1–34; cf. Ps 51:7). While outward ceremonies provide *atonement* for sins, God is the one who ultimately forgives and cleanses his people from their sins (Ps 51; 103). Some scholars think that Matthew might have Psalm 130:8 in mind here.[71] In Matthew confession of

---

65. Powell, *God With Us*, 3, 5. Chris Wright's *Salvation Belongs to Our God: Celebrating the Bible's Central Story* (Nottingham: IVP, 2008) is written to show that although salvation in the Bible may be understood in a variety of ways, salvation from sin is the Bible's central story.
66. Morris, *The Gospel According to Matthew*, 30.
67. Keener, *A Commentary on the Gospel of Matthew*, 97.
68. Hagner, *Matthew 1–13*, 19.
69. Powell, *God With Us*, 5. The following additional references express the diversity of the people in view: 7:14; 9:13; 10:14, 42; 13:43; 16:18; 18:16, 17; 20:28; 25:34; 28:19. They are therefore the few who find their way to life, the sinners, and the righteous for whom the kingdom is prepared, the disciples, the little ones, and the church. This broader understanding of the identity of those who are saved is shared by Gundry (see Gundry, "Salvation in Matthew", 405–406).
70. Hagner, *Matthew 1–13*, 19–20.
71. See Nolland, *The Gospel of Matthew*, 99; Hagner, *Matthew 1–13*, 19.

sins marks the ministry of John the Baptist. Powell suggests that ἁμαρτιῶν (plural) means Matthew is concerned about individual offenses rather than the condition of fallen humanity.[72] This position is shared by Gundry who says that the use of the plural implies "that Matthew does not conceive of sin as an external power that has enslaved its victims so as to make them sin against their will" so that "the blame for sinning" lies "on the sinners themselves."[73] While Powell's and Gundry's suggestions appear reasonable based on semantics, the narrative may suggest a broader application. The death of Jesus provides the forgiveness of *sin* and *sins* through his shed blood (20:28; 26:28).[74] It is most likely, therefore, that the universal condition of fallen humanity is in view rather than individual offenses.

On how the people are saved, Matthew provides various ways through which the salvation offered by Jesus is received. First, there is the requirement for confession, repentance from sins, producing fruit in keeping with repentance, and baptism (3:6–10; 7:16–20; 12:33–35; 21:43; 28:19). Second, one must believe in Jesus as God's sent Messiah (18:6) by confessing him in public (10:32–33).[75]

2.3.2 He Heals Sicknesses

What is the significance of Jesus' healing ministry in Matthew? From the beginning of Jesus' ministry, Matthew's Messiah is depicted as one who heals[76] (4:23–24). This healing ministry fulfills God's promises in Israel's Scripture (8:16–17; cf. Isa 53:4) and in direct conformity with the expectations of the time (11:2–6). The healing ministry of Jesus is not only a

---

72. Powell, *God With Us*, 6.
73. Gundry, "Salvation in Matthew," 402.
74. See Nolland, *The Gospel of Matthew*, 99.
75. Gundry, "Salvation in Matthew," 406–09.
76. Lidija Novakovic, *Messiah, Healer of the Sick: A Study of Jesus as the Son of David in the Gospel of Matthew* (Tübingen: Mohr Siebeck, 2003). In chapter 2, Novakovic argues extensively on the origin of Jesus the son of David from God's promise to David and the Davidic Messiah from biblical and early Jewish writings. In chapters 3and 4 he argues that Jesus' healing ministry is part of the messianic activity. Similarly, Giuseppe Buono says that Jesus' miracles are the *signs* of his messianic character. See Giuseppe Buono, *Missiology: Theology and Praxis* (Nairobi: Paulines Publications Africa, 2002), 93. For more on Jesus' healing ministry in Matthew, see Jack Dean Kingsbury, "A Profile of a Ministry of Healing," *ATLAS* (n.d.), 102–107.

demonstration of the power of God at work in the new kingdom but also a part of the restoration of humanity to its original wholeness in God's salvific scheme.[77] It involved exorcism and delivering people from physical sicknesses.[78]

In the healing of the blind and mute, a demon-possessed man (12:22–23), the question raised by the people as to whether Jesus could be the Son of David suggests that the idea that Davidic Messiah would heal the sick as this was one of the prevailing notions in the messianic expectation of the time.[79] This healing, according to Jesus, is an assurance that the kingdom of God has come upon the people. It means that God's rule extends to the sick, the unclean, the demonized, and the dead.[80]

But the Son not only heals the sick; he also leads his people as shepherd-king. This is also one of the crucial redemptive roles of the Son as examined below.

2.3.3 He Restores and Leads Israel as Shepherd-King

Some passages in Matthew such as 1:17; 2:5–6; 8:17;[81] 12:23; 21:1–12 are to be read in the light of first-century restoration hopes.[82] This restoration is linked with the Davidic Messiah and king whom Matthew portrays as shepherd. Expectation of the Davidic Messiah is among "the greater glory of the future acts of God" for Israel.[83] The Qumran community interprets 2 Samuel 7:12–17 along with Amos 9:11 as the branch of David who will

---

77. The theme of restoration is treated further in chapter 3.
78. Keener, *A Commentary on the Gospel of Matthew*, 155.
79. Novakovic, *Messiah, Healer of the Sick*.
80. Vern S. Poythress, *The Shadow of Christ in the Law of Moses* (Phillipsburg: P&R Publishing, 1991), 275.
81. France connects the miracles of healing of Matt 8:1–17 with restoration of the distressed and excluded (see France, *The Gospel of Matthew*, 302–22). One of the major works on restoration is E. P. Sander's *Jesus and Judaism* (Philadelphia: Fortress Press, 1985). In part 1 of his book, Sanders focuses on restoration of Israel, precisely on Jesus and the temple, restoration in Jewish literature, and other indications of restoration eschatology.
82. See the question of the disciples in Acts 1:6. See also Jones, "Subverting the Textuality of Davidic Messianism," 264, who shows that the birth of Jesus symbolizes Israel's redemption from exile.
83. Francis Foulkes, "The Acts of God: A Study of the Basis of Typology in the Old Testament," in *The Right Doctrines from the Wrong Texts? Essays on the Use of the Old Testament in the New* ed. G. K. Beale (Grand Rapids: Baker Academic, 1994), 356–57.

rise up in Zion in the last days. He comes to deliver Israel.[84] This shepherd-king motif is explicit in Matthew 2:1–6; 21:1–5; 26:31. He is born as shepherd king, the ruler of God's people Israel (2:6). The first acknowledgment of Jesus as king comes from the Magi from the East. But the chief priest and the teachers of the law knew also that this king, who was to be born in Bethlehem, is also the Christ. In Micah's prophecy, the one born in Bethlehem is a ruler, a shepherd of the people of Israel (Mic 5:2). As David is appointed to be the ruler and shepherd of the people of Israel (2 Sam 5:2), so also Jesus is born as a ruler and shepherd of the people of Israel. Jesus enters Jerusalem as a humble and gentle king of Israel (21:1–5). And he dies as a shepherd struck (26:31), all in fulfillment of God's salvifiv purpose.

The themes of restoration and the Davidic kingship are taken up in chapter 3. But not only does he lead his people as shepherd-king, he also fulfills the *Torah*. This is one of the crucial redemptive roles of the Son of David as highlighted here and treated in-depth in chapter 3.

2.3.4 He Fulfills the Torah

Matthew 5:17–20 is one of the significant passages about the mission of Jesus. It is the Torah that defined the identity of Israel as a nation.[85] And now Jesus comes to fulfill it according to God's salvific purpose for the world.[86] Scripturally, the law points upward to the character of God as a holy God (Lev 19:2). But it also points backward to God's redemptive acts in Egypt (Exod 20:2; Deut 5:15) as the people of Israel are constantly reminded that they have been rescued from a land of bondage so they might be free to serve the only true God. In addition, the Torah stipulates the vertical and horizontal relationship of the people of God, that is, relationship with God and fellow mankind. But the law also points forward to its final

---

84. 4QFlorilegium 1–3:1:10–19 (see Florentino García Martínez, *The Dead Sea Scrolls Translated*, 2nd ed. trans. Wilfred G. E. Watson [Leiden: Brill, 1996], 136).
85. Nolland, *The Gospel of Matthew*, 218.
86. Some have understood the passage as a polemic in view of the Jews who saw Christianity "as an upstart religion seeking to overturn the ancestral Law of the Jews" (see Nolland, *The Gospel of Matthew*, 218). More is said about this in chapter 3.

embodiment and fulfillment in Christ as "perfect sacrifice for sin."[87] This fulfillment of the law is taken up in the next chapters as it is significant in the redemptive purposes of God, especially with Jesus as the fulfillment of the Torah.

Apart from fulfilling the Torah, Jesus also mediates the knowledge of the Father. This is also one of the crucial redemptive roles of the Son as examined below.

2.3.5 He Mediates the Knowledge of the Father

What is the knowledge of God and how does Jesus mediate it in Matthew? Matthew 11:25–27 (cf. Luke 10:21–22; John 1:18; 10:15) is a significant text about Jesus' unique relationship with the Father.[88] This relationship "is exclusive and mutual."[89] Matthew 11:27[90] has been especially considered as "the corner stone for other attempts to penetrate back to Jesus' self-consciousness."[91] It is also deemed as "the most important passage for the study of synoptic Christology.[92] He is conscious of his unique relationship with God as "the recipient and mediator"[93] of the mystery of the knowledge of God.

In Matthew, the knowledge of God seems to be the disclosure of God's nature, character, and will. Jesus is *Immanuel*, "God with us." He himself

---

87. Poythress, *The Shadow of Christ*, 98.

88. The Gospel of Matthew is replete with references to πατήρ. Schreiner confirms that the majority of Jesus' use of the term "my Father," or "my heavenly Father" in the Gospels are found in Matthew (see his *New Testament Theology*, 129). He emphasizes the uniqueness of Jesus' relationship to the Father. It is also replete with υἱός. What is the meaning of πατήρ in God's relation to Jesus? And what does υἱός mean for Jesus in relation to πατήρ? James D. G. Dunn sees Matt 11:27 as "a verse of particular importance" in the sense which Jesus' use of the term designates distinctive relationship with the Father. See James D. G. Dunn, *Jesus and the Spirit: A Study of the Religious and Charismatic Experience of Jesus and the First Christians as Reflected in the New Testament* (Grand Rapids: Eerdmans, 1975), 26–40.

89. Schreiner, *New Testament Theology*, 130.

90. See Paul Winter for an extensive discussion on the development of this verse (Paul Winter, "Matthew 11:27 and Luke 10:22 from the First to the Fifth Century: Reflections on the Development of the Text," *NovT* 1, no. 2 [April 1956]: 112–148).

91. Dunn, *Jesus and the Spirit*, 27.

92. Ladd, *A Theology of the New Testament*, 164.

93. Ibid., 39; see also Schreiner, *New Testament Theology*, 238.

is the embodiment of the character and power of God.[94] This knowledge is mediated through preaching, teaching, and healing ministry that reveal God. In addition, some specific statements Jesus makes concerning God such as his perfection (5:48) and his care for his children (6:32) constitute the means by which God is known. All this is derived from Jesus' activities from the commencement of his ministry to this point where he praises his Father, the Lord of heaven and earth who chose to hide "these things" from the wise and learned, and to reveal them to little children (11:25). According to Craig L. Blomberg, Matthew 11:25 underscores God's sovereign purposes in the universe. For this reason, even the "increasingly polarized response to Jesus" is part of God's eternal plan. Therefore, God in his sovereign will, hides "these things" which are "the overall significance of Jesus' mission." But the language of free will is also apparent in verses 20–24 and verses 28–30 in which people are either judged for rejecting Jesus or offered salvation for accepting him. The text shows how divine sovereignty and human responsibility are usually juxtaposed (e.g. Gen 50:19–20; Lev 20:7–8; Jer 29:10–14; Joel 2:32; Phil 2:12–13).[95] Therefore, "hiding these things from the wise and the learned" does not contradict God's universal mission to all people.

In this text, Jesus denounces the cities in which most of his *miracles* had been performed (11:20–24). The reason is that they failed to recognize Jesus in his connection with God, evidenced by the power to perform miracles. In Matthew 11:27, therefore, Jesus affirms "his unique messianic status as the exclusive revelator of the Father."[96] "All things have been committed to me by my Father" anticipates of 28:18. While this text has πάντα μοι παρεδόθη ("all things have been handed over to me"), 28:18 says, Ἐδόθη μοι πᾶσα ἐξουσία ("all authority has been given to me"). The passives, "have been handed over," "have been given" suggest that Jesus is the recipient of "all things" and "all authority" through God's good pleasure.

---

94. In the Gospel of John, to know Jesus is to know the Father (14:5–11), and to have eternal life is to know God as the only true God and Jesus Christ, whom he has sent (17:3).

95. Craig L. Blomberg, *Matthew*, The New American Commentary (Nashville: Broadman Press, 1992), 192–193.

96. William Hendriksen, *Exposition of the Gospel According to Matthew*, New Testament Commentary (Grand Rapids: Baker Book House, 1973), 303.

The sense of πάντα ("all things") here is understood in two ways as either meaning "the transmission of knowledge or the granting of full authority to Jesus."[97] In Matthew 11:27 Jesus presents himself as the "mediator of revelation"[98] from God to man. This is the mission of the Son. The Father is unknowable except by the special revelation that comes through the Son as he chooses to reveal the Father.

2.3.6 He sows the seed of the Kingdom[99]

What is sowing the seed and why is this salvific? Sowing is a dominant metaphor in the first three parables of the kingdom in Matthew 13. In Matthew 13:3, a farmer goes out to *sow* his seed. Similarly, in Matthew 13:24, a man *sowed* good seed in his field. In Matthew 13:31 a man also *sowed* mustard seed in his field. An aspect of Jesus' mediation of the knowledge of God is teaching and preaching the good news of the kingdom (4:23; 9:35). Both Hahn and Harvey agreed that preaching and teaching τὸ εὐαγγέλιον τῆς βασιλείας is prominent in Matthew as an aspect of Jesus' mission.[100]

Jesus is the sower of 13:3 and 13:24,[101] for "the one who sowed the good seed is the Son of Man" (13:36–43).[102] Therefore, "The mysterious 'Son of Man' of Daniel's prophecy (7:14), to whom, according to Daniel's vision, was to be given 'dominion and glory and royal power' was now a

---

97. Nolland, *The Gospel of Matthew*, 471.

98. Dunn, *Jesus and the Spirit*, 31.

99. See Maren Bohlen, "Die Einlasssprüche in der Reich-Gottes-Verkündigung Jesu, " *ZNW* 99 (2008): 167–184.

100. Hahn, *Mission in the New Testament*, 120; Harvey, "Mission in Matthew," 127. Hahn notes how "Matthew has consistently distinguished between κηρύσσειν and διδάσκειν, the first relating to the message of God's reign and the second to the exposition of the law" (Hahn, *Mission in the New Testament*, 121).

101. Hagner, *Matthew 1–13*, 393.

102. In "Messias order Menschensohn?" Ethelbert Stauffer discusses the problem of the combination of titles "Messiah" and "Son of Man" for Jesus and says that these are two fundamentally different concepts with completely different history. He says that Jesus was never addressed as the Messiah in the Gospels. But the merger came as a result of messianic hopes of the Jewish people, especially the resistance movement. The idea of Jesus as Messiah gradually gained acceptance as theological polemic of the Middle Ages. See E. Stauffer, "Messias order Menschensohn?" *NovT* 1, no. 2 (April 1956): 81–102.

humble sower."[103] The preaching of the kingdom of heaven[104] is the primary medium through which both Jesus and John the Baptist announced the ushering in of the kingdom of heaven (3:1, 2; 4:17). Repentance and bearing fruit is the right response as the seed is sown (4:17; 21:43). The enemy who sows the bad seed aims at ensuring that the good seed is either destroyed or made fruitless.[105]

2.3.7 He Sends for Mission

Whom does Jesus *send* for mission? Why does he *send* for mission and how does this *sending* relate to the Father's *sending*? The concept of sending is a significant component in the redemptive purposes of God in the Gospel of Matthew.[106] God sends Jesus for mission. But Jesus also sends those through whom God's mission would continue. Although the primary work of giving his life as a ransom for many was his alone, the proclamation of this salvific work continues through the disciple until the gospel of the kingdom is preached to all the nations.

First, he sends his disciples, and by so doing he presents himself as the Messiah of Israel (10:6) and of the world (28:18–19).[107] Part of Jesus' messianic mission was to proclaim the message of the kingdom. It was for this mission that he called the twelve disciples (Matt 4:18–22; cf. Mark 3:13–19; 6:7–13; Luke 9:1–6). He sent out his disciples twice (10:1–15; cf. Mark 6:7–13; Luke 9:2–5; 10:1–12) "to practice the ministry he had

---

103. Hendriksen, *Matthew*, 571. See notes on "Son of Man" as used in the OT and in Daniel in the section below on Jesus' authority to forgive sins.

104. Since the usage "kingdom of heaven" is rather Matthean, it appears that Matthew represents OT dualism in his gospel such as "heaven" in contrast to "world." For the polarization of the concept of heaven and earth in Matthew, see Kari Syreeni, "Between Heaven and Earth: On the Structure of Matthew's Symbolic Universe," *JSNT* 40 (1990): 3–13.

105. Nolland, *The Gospel of Matthew*, 559.

106. For mission in the Gospel of John, see Andreas Köstenberger, *The Mission of Jesus and the Disciples According to the Fourth Gospel* (Grand Rapids: Eerdmans, 1998); idem, *John*, Baker Exegetical Commentary on the New Testament (Grand Rapids: Baker Academic, 2004), 573–574, n13; Okure T., "The Significance of Jesus' Commission to Mary Magdalene," *International Review of Mission*, 81 (1992): 177–188.

107. Harvey says that Jesus did not assume the role of sending for mission until after his resurrection (see Harvey, "Mission in Jesus' Teaching," 44). But this is hardly correct in view of Matthew 10 and Luke 9, 10.

modeled for them,"¹⁰⁸ although the mission of the twelve and the seventy-two (Luke 10:1–12) is said to be conflated.¹⁰⁹ He instructed them that when persecuted in one place, they should flee to another with the assurance that they would not finish going through the cities of Israel before the Son of Man comes.¹¹⁰ But what Jesus says in 10:17–23 goes beyond the mission of the twelve disciples and the limitation of mission to the house of Israel to include mission to the nations.¹¹¹ The modeling nature of this sending as suggested by Harvey is also mentioned by Keener who says that by sending the disciples Jesus "provides a relevant model for his appointed agents in subsequent generations (whether they are 'apostles' in the narrower sense of the word or not)."¹¹²

In the final commission (28:16–20)¹¹³ Jesus sends the disciples with the authority (ἐξουσία) that has been given to him by the Father. The *sent one* now assumes the role of a *sender*. He sends them out to make disciples of all nations, baptizing and teaching them. To make disciples (μαθητεύειν) of all nations is the primary responsibility of the disciples as sent ones. But

---

108. Harvey, "Mission in Jesus' Teaching", 42.
109. See Gundry, *Matthew*, 183–84.
110. See Dom Jacques Dupont, "Vous n'aurez pas achevé les villes d'Israël avant que le fils de l'homme ne vienne" (Matt 10:23)," *NovT* 2.3/4 (October, 1958): 228–244.
111. D. A. Carson, "Matthew," in *Expositor's Bible Commentary*, abr. ed. Kenneth L. Barker and John Kohlenberger III (Grand Rapids: Zondervan, 1994), 48.
112. Keener, *A Commentary on the Gospel of Matthew*, 313. Matthew 10 is placed in the "agent background" from the "early and broad Mediterranean parallels" (314). It is arguable that "the language used here for 'sending' probably connotes commissioning agents with delegated authority" (313). (See also Davies and Allison, *A Critical and Exegetical Commentary*, 1.153; Hagner, *Matthew 1–13*, 256; Gundry, *Matthew*, 184). As agents go with specific instructions, so the disciples were given instructions where "the word *instructing* has a military ring about it" (see Morris, *The Gospel According to Matthew*, 245). Jesus' practice here recalls the OT era in which the prophets were commissioned. In the OT the prophets were God's agents. The language of *sending* and *going* prominent in the work of the OT prophets (Jer 1:7) is also reflected in commissioning of the disciples. God commanded Jeremiah saying, "I will send you, you will go" (אֶשְׁלָחֲךָ תֵּלֵךְ). Jesus also "sent" (ἀπέστειλεν) the disciples and commanded them to "go" (πορεύεσθε). Therefore "the connection in this text between Jesus' commissioned messengers and prophets should not be overlooked" (Keener, *A Commentary on the Gospel of Matthew*, 314). The OT prophetic commissioning is here reenacted. Cf. Matt 22:3; 23:34, 37; 21:34, 36; 23:37.
113. Matt 10 and 28 seem to suggest that there are two commissionings. Matt 10 is commission to Israel and Matt 28 is commission to the nations. But as noted in chapter 4, some scholars think that Matt 10 anticipates Matt 28.

πορευθέντες precedes the main verb μαθητευειν. The disciples proclaim the message of the kingdom as they go into the world.[114]

Second, he sends prophets, wise men, and teachers (23:34).[115] The context of the verse is the vehement invectives against the teachers of the law and the Pharisees who, although they sit in Moses' seat, do not practice what they preach. In Matthew 23:29–32, these "brood of vipers" testify against themselves that they are descendants of those who murdered the prophets God sent to the nation Israel. In the same way they will reject and even murder the prophets that Jesus is sending to them (23:34). But Jesus goes ahead to send his prophets.[116] The verse also shows that just as the Father sends for mission, so does the Son.

Third, he sends the angels at the end of the age. Two passages (13:36–43; 24:30–31) provide evidence for the sending role of the Son at the end of the age. At the end of the age[117] the Son of Man sends and gathers out of his kingdom everything that causes to stumble and lawlessness (13:41). Therefore, the angels would serve as "agents who implement the divine judgment."[118] But Matthew shows that the harvest is not only for judgment. It is a time when the righteous shine like the sun in the kingdom (13:43). Similarly, he sends his angels with a loud trumpet and gathers the elect from the four corners of the heavens (24:31; cf. Rev 14:14–20).

---

114. For the use of the attendance circumstance participle (aorist participle + aorist imperative constructions) πορευθέντες in Matt 28:19, see Daniel B. Wallace, *Greek Grammar Beyond the Basics: An Exegetical Syntax of the New Testament* (Grand Rapids: Zondervan, 1996), 642. Wallace does not subscribe to the reading "having gone," or "as you are going." The participle would then be rightly translated simply as "go". Davies and Allison note similar construction in Matt 2:8; 9:13; 10:6–7; 17:27 (Davies and Allison, *A Critical and Exegetical Commentary*, 3.683–684). The aorist participle πορευθέντες ("go") modifies the aorist imperative and reinforces the action of the main verb μαθητεύσατε (see Köstenberger and O'Brien, *Salvation to the Ends of the Earth*, 103–104).

115. Prophets were people who received direct revelatory message from God and passed on the same message to the people. He also sends wise men. It appears that the wise men differed from the prophets because they did not receive a direct revelation from the Lord as the latter, but were, instead, diligent students of Scriptures who could instruct their generation as a result of their knowledge of the sacred writings. Finally, Jesus also sends scribes who are learned in Scripture and could teach and write.

116. Morris, *The Gospel According Matthew*, 588.

117. Nolland, *The Gospel of Matthew*, 560. Of the gospel writers this phrase is found only in the Gospel of Matthew, but is frequently used in apocalyptic literature (e.g. Dan 12:4, 13).

118. France, *The Gospel of Matthew*, 535.

2.3.8 He Forgives Sins

What is the significance of Jesus' authority to forgive sins in God's salvific purpose? The forgiveness of sins is a prominent theme in Matthew.[119] Jesus forgives the sins of a paralytic (9:1–8; cf. Mark 2:1–12; Luke 5:17–26).[120] Since the forgiveness of sins is believed to be the prerogative of God the Father (9:3; Mark 2:7; cf. Matt 6:12, 14, 15), the response of the scribes when Jesus pronounced the paralytic forgiven in Matthew 9:3 is Οὗτος βλασφημεῖ ("This is blasphemy"). In the OT a priest could pronounce a person forgiven of his sins on the basis of repentance, restitution, and sacrifice (Lev 4; 5; 16; 17:11); but here Jesus claims the ability to forgive sins as God does. This pronouncement by Jesus was seen as a conceited act of blasphemy because the forgiveness of sins is God's sole prerogative. This was a very grave sin in the Law, hence the reaction of the scribes. Conflict with the authorities ensues. Jesus knew in his spirit what they were thinking (cf. John 2:23–25).

Furthermore, he shows that both forgiveness and healing come from God. In response to their unbelief, he says that the Son of Man[121] has authority to do both. Son of Man is here used christologically.[122] Although

---

119. Davies and Allison, *A Critical and Exegetical Commentary*, 2.89). They cite 1:21; 20:28; and 26:28. They believe that this theme might have come to prominence after AD 70 with the temple, center of sacrificial system through which Israel reconciles with God, now gone. The religious Jews must have now begun to think "anew about the atonement, and at such a time it might have been opportune to preach that God, in Jesus, had dealt with sins once and for all" (89–90).

120. The third person passive (ἀφίενται) in Matt 9:2 is considered "a divine passive" (Davies and Allison, *A Critical and Exegetical Commentary*, 2.89). On the basis of the passive voice some think that it is God who has forgiven the man's sins, and Jesus only declares what God had done. But as Davies and Allison say, "verse 6 disallows this interpretation" (89).

121. The title "Son of Man" is found primarily in the gospels and is only used by Jesus. The title occurs more frequently than "Messiah" or "Son of God." But as Stanton says, "scholars accept that the Son of Man sayings are the single most intractable paragraphs facing serious students of the New Testament writings" (see Stanton, *The Gospels and Jesus,* 247). However, these sayings fall into three categories. There are those that refer to the earthly activity of Jesus, those that refer to his suffering and death, and those that refer to his future glory. (See also Ladd, *A Theology of the New Testament,* 147–49, who gives the same categories of the "Son of Man" sayings). For more on this, see Hagner, *Matthew 1–13,* 214.

122. How is this title used in the OT and later Jewish writings? Stanton provides a good summary. It is thought that the "son of man" who sits at God's right hand is the background for Jesus' answer to the high priest (26:64; Mark 14:62). Ezekiel's usage, occurring 93 times, "underlines the humanity of the prophet." Daniel 7:13–27, the one "like a Son of Man" provides the background of the three categories of uses mentioned earlier. Not only does

the title is used in Ezekiel merely as son of humanity and mortality, in Daniel 7:14 the title is used for someone with everlasting authority from

---

one "like a Son of Man" come with the clouds of heaven and is presented to the ancient of Days (God), he "is linked with the saints of the Most High who suffer" and whose obedience "leads through suffering to vindication and to a role as a judge" (249). In 1 Enoch 37–71 the "Son of Man" is a recurring title. This Son of Man is seen (62:2) "seated with the Lord of the Spirits (God) on the throne of judgment" (249). He is also "the elect one who has been hidden from the beginning and is revealed on that day (of judgment) to the elect (61:1, 6–7, 13)" (249). It is noted that 1 Enoch's portrait of "Son of Man" is similar to Dan 7:13–27. This has developed into a divine being as is encountered in the gospels (247). However, Bultmann rejects the common opinion that in Jesus' self-consciousness "he actually did consider himself to be the Messiah, or the Son of Man" (see Bultmann, *Theology of the New Testament*, 26). He thinks such opinion "is burdened with serious difficulties." First, it is thought that though the opinion agrees "with the evangelists' point of view" the "question is whether they themselves have not superimposed upon the traditional material their own belief in the messiahship of Jesus" (26). Second, those who argue that the church's belief in Jesus as the Messiah or Son of Man "is comprehensible only if Jesus was conscious of being the Messiah and actually represents himself as such—at least to the disciples" must consider that stories such as Jesus' baptism, Peter's confession, the transfiguration, Easter stories are "projected backward into Jesus' life-time" (26). These stories are told, "in the interest not of biography but of faith" (26). Therefore, "the acknowledgment of Jesus as the one whom God's word decisively encounters man, whatever title be given him—"Messiah (Christ)," "Son of Man," "Lord"—is a pure act of faith independent of the answer to the historical question whether or not Jesus considered himself the Messiah" (26). For more on the Son of Man, see I. H. Marshall, "The Synoptic Son of Man Sayings in Recent Discussion," *NTS* 12 (1965–66): 327–51; P. M. Casey, *The Son of Man: The Interpretation and Influence of Daniel 7* (London: SPK, 1979); W. Horbury, "The Messianic Associations of The Son of Man," *JTS* 36 (1985): 34–55; and J. J. Collins, "The Son of Man in First Century Judaism," *NTS* 38 (1992): 448–86. In spite of the intractable nature the subject at hand, one would suggest that Jesus uses the "Son of Man" for his earthly ministry, death, and coming back in glory as portrayed by the gospels.

God.[123] Here Jesus is acting for God as his authority is always derived from him (Matt 28:18, 19).[124]

Not only does Jesus forgive sins, he symbolically cleanses the temple.

2.3.9 He Cleanses the Temple

Jesus' action in the temple in Matthew 21:12–17, recorded by all the four Gospels (Mark 11:15–18; Luke 19:45–46; cf. John 2:13–17),[125] is significant in the life and ministry of Jesus in fulfillment of God's salvific purpose. The significance of this action is reinforced by the citation of two OT passages (Isa 56:7; Jer 7:11) in support of Jesus' action. Jesus' symbolic action is understood because the temple is at the heart of Israel's religious worship

---

123. See Graham Twelftree, *Jesus the Miracle Worker* (Downers Grove, Illinois: IVP, 1999), 65. But Wright thinks that "Daniel 7 has long suffered from being read in isolation from chapters 1–6" with the common themes of call of the Jews to compromise their faith and their refusal to do so (N. T. Wright, *The New Testament and the People of God* [London: SPCK, 1992], 293). He therefore suggests a "literary representation" whereby he sees the son of man as a human figure who "functions as a symbol for Israel" rather than an individual human or a divine being (291–92). For him the monsters are literary representations of pagan nations that wage war against the nation Israel. He believes that the imagery in Dan 7 "is obviously pregnant with the meaning of Genesis 2, evoking the idea of the people of God as the true humanity and the pagan nations as the animals" (292). He reasons that no one in Daniel's time would imagine that the monsters represented in the vision would appear on earth as actual monsters from the sea and attack the son of man. And if the son of man "represents Israel within the logic of the vision-genre" then it would be incorrect to jump from this literary representation "to a metaphysical representation whereby the 'son of man' becomes a transcendent heavenly being existing in another realm" (292). Wright sees saints of the most high in 18, 25, 27 as Israel and not angels. He thinks that a contextual reading of Dan 7 in the first century would locate "its meaning first and foremost in terms of vindication of Israel after her suffering at the hands of the pagans" (292). This understanding of the son of man in Daniel notwithstanding, still Matthew presents the Son of Man as one with authority to forgive sins and to heal the sick. For a good treatment on the Son of Man, see Walter Wink, *The Human Being: Jesus and the Enigma of the Son of the Man* (Minneapolis: Augsburg Fortress, 2002). In summary, Wink redefines divinity and presents a Christology from below and argues that such a Christology was created by Jesus in his teaching on the Son of Man. For Wink, Jesus' objective seems to have been to help human beings to become, not something they are not—divine—but what they really are—human. The difference between Wright and Wink is that Wright focuses on the people of God while Wink focuses on the person of Christ as representative of true humanity.

124. See Keener, *A Commentary on the Gospel of Matthew*, 290.

125. Carson notes that the cleansing of the temple in Matthew is the second time following that of John 2:12–22. The Synoptics, however, have not recorded the one in John because they omit Jesus' early Judean ministry (Carson, "Matthew," 95).

(Jer 7:2). But the critical issue here is on the symbolic meaning of this cleansing, and specifically toward what purpose Jesus' action is directed.[126] If Jesus, the Davidic Messiah king, restores Israel, then this restoration is connected to Israel's center of worship—the temple. Carson says that "purification of Jerusalem and the temple was part of Jewish messianic expectation."[127] Since he fulfills the law, his function reaches the temple cultus. He discloses his identity and authority over Israel's Holy Place.[128] But his significance extends to the nations as well. Wright believes that the "prophetic sign in the temple" indicates gentile inclusion in the mission of Jesus.[129] The writer will discuss further Jesus' action in the temple in chapters 3 and 4.

Meanwhile, Jesus' eschatological mission as judge is examined.

2.3.10 He Judges the Nations at the end of the Age

What is the essence of the final judgment in Matthew 25:31–46? The coming of the eschatological kingdom that Jesus "constantly looked forward to" would bring about the final judgment when there would be *separation of the righteous from the wicked* based on their *response* to the proclamation of kingdom and its ethics.[130] Although the audience of 25:31–46 is the disciples (24:1–3), the context is the invectives against the religious leaders of Israel began in that began in 23:1.[131] In Matthew 25:31–46 "the OT imagery continues with the gathering of all nations for judgment, as in Joel 3:1–12 with a likely verbal echo of Joel 3:2."[132] Some scholars think

---

126. For a comprehensive work on this, see Alexander J. M. Wedderburn, "Jesus' Action in the Temple: A Key or a Puzzle?" *ZNW* 97 (2006): 1–18. The issue he raises is: "from what must the temple be cleansed—commercialization, abuse real or assumed, or as preparation for an eschatological role?" (1).

127. Carson, "Matthew", 95.

128. Ibid.

129. Wright, *The Mission of God*, 509.

130. Ladd, *A Theology of the New Testament*, 181.

131. David E. Garland, *Reading Matthew: A Literary and Theological Commentary* (Macon, Ga.: Smyth & Helwys Publishing, 2001), 240.

132. France, *The Gospel of Matthew,* 961. In the *Pss. of Sol.* 17:26, the Davidic Messiah would judge his people. But as Craig A. Evans points out, this is not punitive judgment but "judging in the sense of the judges of old Israel" whose task was "to enforce the Law and protect the people" (see Evans, "Jesus and Justice: We Can't Have One without the Other," *Sapienta Logos* 1, no. 2 [2009]: 217).

that the "judgment scene is set in language largely drawn from Daniel 7:13–14 and its wider setting."[133] The term "throne" and the accompanying angels are likely derived from Daniel 10:9, 10. It is noteworthy that the Son of Man who stands as the judge[134] is also a king. And this is understood as "the culmination of the process throughout this gospel whereby the kingdom of God/heaven becomes embodied in the kingship of the Son of Man."[135] Accordingly, "all the angels with him" echoes Daniel 7:10 and Zechariah 14:5, especially the last clause in Zechariah's passage where God's eschatological coming is depicted. "In this climatic vision, then, the OT expectation of the eschatological visitation of God in judgment and salvation finds its fulfillment in Jesus the Son of Man, who sits on his glorious throne and pronounces judgment."[136]

Finally, the writer will discuss the redemptive role of the Holy Spirit. The work of the Holy Spirit begins prior to the post-Easter experience in the account of Matthew. This becomes the foundation upon which the Easter experience is built.

2.4 The Holy Spirit's Redemptive Role in Mission

What is the significance and role of the Holy Spirit in Matthew? Blaine Charette rightly argues that scholars have paid little attention to Matthew's theology of the Spirit. According to him, this neglect is regrettable because Matthew shows that the eschatological restoration he describes in his book is the direct result of the work of the Holy Spirit.[137] But this restoration that Jesus brings is on a "spiritual rather than a political plane."[138] Charette observes that the Holy Spirit not only anoints Jesus for ministry

---

133. Ibid., 960.
134. Davies and Allison say, "The Son of Man"—Matthew's favorite christological title—is chosen because it is in this role that Jesus will act as judge in the final day" (Davies and Allison, *A Critical and Exegetical Commentary* 2.427).
135. France, *The Gospel of Matthew*, 960. See Matthew 13:41; 16:28; 20:21.
136. Ibid., 961.
137. Blaine Charette, *Restoring Presence: The Spirit in Matthew's Gospel*, JPTSup 18 (Sheffield: Sheffield Academic Press, 2000), 11–13.
138. Charette, *Restoring Presence*, 39.

in fulfillment of OT prophetic expectation, but he is also present in all of Jesus' work of redemption such as forgiveness of sins, conflict with Satan, exorcism, commissioning of the disciples, Jesus' death, and the abiding presence in Matthew's community.[139] Therefore, "the spirit is the very essence of the Messiah and of the redemptive work associated with him."[140] However, most scholars look at the work of the Holy Spirit from the post-Easter experience of the church. This writer argues that such approach ignores the vital background that the Gospels provide for the understanding of the mission of the Holy Spirit. The opening pericope of the Gospel of Matthew provides the perspective from which the rest of the book is to be viewed, namely, that the Holy Spirit is involved in the salvific purposes of God. In that pericope "Jesus' deity" is highlighted because "Mary bore a divine child as a result of generation by the Holy Spirit."[141]

This discussion of the role of the Holy Spirit in Matthew is based on the premise that Matthew looks back to the promises made in the OT about the Spirit (Matt 12:18; cf. Isa 42:1).[142] Similarly, "There had already been a history of revelatory events in which God's Spirit was encountered,

---

139. Ibid., chapters 1–3.
140. Ibid., 57.
141. Gundry, *Matthew*, 20.
142. See John R. Levison, *The Spirit in Early Judaism*, (Leiden: Brill, 1997, reprint), 181. Levison identifies the spirit and wisdom as in Isa 11:1–9 and asserts that 42:1b–c is a later variation of the same spirit in which "wisdom is supplanted by justice." He adds, "Although wisdom is eclipsed by justice in the Isaiah corpus, early Jewish authors rekindled the original association of the spirit with wisdom in their appropriations of Isaiah 11." (238). Yet, Levison well notes that Isa 61:1–7 "claims justice rather than wisdom as the fundamental project of his calling" (238). The anticipated Messiah is believed to be a deliverer, and justice marks the life of such a one as evident in Isa 11:1–9; 42:1–4; 61:1–3; cf. Luke 4:18–19). See also Charette, *Restoring Presence*, 27–30.

welcomed, and waited for."¹⁴³ He is part of the irrevocable "covenant promise" of God (cf. Joel 2:28f).¹⁴⁴

2.4.1 He is the Agent in Jesus' Miraculous Conception[145]

In Matthew, Jesus' relationship to the Holy Spirit begins with his conception (1:18).[146] What is the significance of Jesus' conception through the Holy Spirit? The words of Matthew εὑρέθη ἐν γαστρὶ ἔχουσα ἐκ πνεύματος ἁγίου of 1:18 "anticipate the quotation of Isaiah 7.14."[147] According to Gundry, "'Virgin' clears the way not only for a miraculous conception and birth, but also for the incarnation of God himself."[148]

The miraculous and virginal conception "is something that is taken for granted by Matthew and dealt with as a problem for Jesus' lineage that

---

143. Dunne, "Trinity and History," 143. The Hebrew words קֹדֶשׁ (holy, sacred) and רוּחַ (wind, spirit, breath) have their Greek equivalents as ἅγιος (holy, sacred) and πνεῦμα (spirit) respectively. The word "holy" and the verb "to sanctify," "to set apart," "to consecrate" in biblical Hebrew have the idea of a place (Exod 3:5; 26:33), an object (Exod 29:37), or a person (Judg 13:5) set apart or consecrated. The word "spirit" in the OT, as distinguished from wind or breath, is used for the most part for the "Spirit of the Lord" or the "Spirit of God." The first encounter in the OT is Genesis where the Spirit of God (רוּחַ אֱלֹהִים) "was hovering over the waters" in the creation account. The Spirit of God gradually came to be understood as the "manifestation of divine presence and power" (see F. W. Horn, "Holy Spirit," in *Anchor Bible Dictionary* [New York: Doubleday, 1992], 3.261) and could fill people for special tasks such as in the case of Bezalel (Exod 31:3) and "especially in prophetic inspiration" (261). The Spirit of God also came upon the judges of Israel (Judg 6:34) and the kings of Israel (1 Sam 10:6, 10). Therefore, in the period of the exodus, the judges, and the kings, the Spirit of God appears as source of divine presence and power, giving God's people the energy to perform special task, while in later prophetic era he is seen as the author of divine revelation and inspiration (Isa 61:1; Ezek 2:2; Mic 3:8; Zech 7:12; 9:30).

144. E. Kamlah, "Spirit, Holy Spirit," in *New International Dictionary of New Testament Theology* (Grand Rapids: Zondervan, 1986), 3:692. The period of the exodus, a time of great salvation, saw the gift of the Spirit to Moses. "The post-exilic prophets see this promise fulfilled in the re-establishment of Israel in Jerusalem." (692). See Hag 2:5; Zech 4:6.

145. Some scholars see the biblical foundation for the virgin birth in Matthew 1 from the account of Gen 5:1–6:4. See Reik Heckl, "Der biblische Begründungsrahmen für die Jungfrauengeburt bei Matthäus: Zur Reception von Gen 5, 1 in Mt 1," *ZNW* 95 (2004): 161–180.

146. Schreiner, *New Testament Theology*, 435.

147. Davies and Allison, *A Critical and Exegetical Commentary*, 1.200. For the question of "how" it happened, John Chrysostom says, "neither Gabriel nor Matthew has explained, nor is it possible" (Simonetti [ed.], *Matthew 1–13*, ACCS, 12).

148. Gundry, *Matthew*, 24.

is surmounted only by a direct angelic intervention."[149] This "angelic intervention" provides the solution as to "how Jesus, who had no physical, human father, could be the son of David."[150] That there was a problem demanding an explanation from an angel of the Lord is seen in Joseph's contemplation to divorce Mary secretly. Joseph appears to have been embarrassed by Mary's sudden pregnancy, therefore the angel of the Lord intervenes to save an embarrassing situation.

2.4.2 He is the Agent at Jesus' Baptism

What baptism does Matthew refer to in 3:11–12 (cf. Mark 1:7–8; Luke 3:16–18)? In the text, contrast between John's and Jesus' baptism is highlighted by the use of μὲν . . . δ.[151] As John preaches the message of repentance he also announces the coming of the Messiah who would act as a judge in fulfillment of God's salvific scheme. In the Isaianic texts, the Spirit would rest on the Messiah (11:1–2; 42:1; 66:1). And this would not be a prerogative of mortal man. That is why in 3:11, John the Baptist makes a contrast between himself and Jesus, probably because many people were already drawing the conclusion that he was the Christ (cf. Luke 3:15; John 1:19, 20; 3:25–36).[152] That the one coming behind him would baptize with the Holy Spirit and fire instead of water highlights the degree of difference between the two.[153] But the question is whether the baptism by the Holy Spirit and fire are to be reduced to a single activity or separate activities. Nolland suggests that they are separate activities since the "fire" would mean judgment.[154] Similarly, Keener believes that the mention of fire in this context must be interpreted as judgment,[155] hence a separation of the two baptisms. But Hendriksen thinks that they are a single event. Jesus would cause the Spirit to come upon the believers as in Acts 1:8. The men-

---

149. Garland, *Reading Matthew*, 21.
150. Ibid.
151. See Gundry, *Matthew*, 49.
152. Hendriksen, *Matthew*, 108.
153. According to Blomberg, water baptism is "the outward sign of an inward change (cf. John 4:1–2), but only Jesus will baptize with the Holy Spirit and fire" (Blomberg, *Matthew*, 79.
154. Nolland, *The Gospel of Matthew*, 146–147.
155. Keener, *Matthew*, 83.

tion of fire along with the Holy Spirit is reminiscent of the Pentecost event (Acts 2:3).[156] "The flame illumines. Fire cleanses. The Spirit does both."[157] But except in John 3:26 and 4:1, 2 where it is said that Jesus was baptizing, or rather his disciples, Matthew does not mention where Jesus baptized anyone. For this reason, and in the light of the church's later experience, this baptism may rather be regarded as the baptism of the Holy Spirit.[158]

2.4.3 He Anoints and Empowers Jesus for Mission

The discussion focuses on the nature of Jesus' anointing.[159] In the OT, the Spirit is "the living power of God, giving life to all and empowering men to perform special service or to receive special revelation."[160] The role of the Holy Spirit is essential in Matthew (12:18–21; Isa 42:1–4). His arrival represents the power of God and "functions as an eschatological marker of the times of the Messiah (12: 28). It serves to demonstrate that the long-awaited time has arrived and that Jesus is the Messiah."[161]

The Holy Spirit rested on Jesus at his baptism as a sign of his anointing.[162] This anointing empowers him; for immediately after this event, he is led[163] into the wilderness (4:1–11 cf. Mark 1:12–13; Luke 1:1–13) by the same Holy Spirit to be tempted by the devil.[164] Jesus is conceived by the Spirit. He is also anointed by the Spirit. Now he is led (ἀνήχθη) by the Spirit to be tempted by the devil (Matt 4:1). Therefore, the presence and guidance

---

156. According to Blomberg, "Acts 1–2 demonstrates that John's prediction was fulfilled at Pentecost" (Blomberg, *Matthew*, 79).

157. Hendriksen, *Matthew*, 108.

158. On the question of "when" this baptism takes place and the meaning of the phrase "Baptism of the Holy Spirit" see Craig Keener's comments on Matt 3:11 in his *Gift and Giver: The Holy Spirit for Today* (Grand Rapids: Baker, 2001), 143–146).

159. See Charette, *Restoring Presence*, 27–30.

160. Newbigin, *The Open Secret*, 23.

161. Ibid.

162. Davies and Allison see this baptism as the new exodus (see Davies and Allison, *A Critical and Exegetical Commentary*, 1.352).

163. For debates on the nature of this leading, see Keener, *Matthew*, 136; Hendriksen, *Matthew*, 222. Keener believes those who dismiss the account as myth base their assumption cultural grounds (Keener, *Matthew*, 136). But the researcher does not intend to engage in this debate).

164. According to Ladd, "The chief function of Satan in the Gospels is to oppose the redemptive purposes of God" (Ladd, *A Theology of the New Testament*, 47).

of the Holy Spirit in the life of Jesus is explicit.[165] Moreover, some scholars view the temptation of Jesus as a "reflection" on Deuteronomy 6–8 such that "Jesus, the Son of God, is repeating the experience of Israel in the desert."[166] His forty days of fasting "being analogous to Israel's forty years of wandering."[167] Here the exodus is reenacted in which Jesus as corporate Israel goes through the desert experience, but emerges victorious. These wilderness and exodus motifs are treated in the next two chapters. In addition, not only does this leading reflect "a common biblical motif of God leading his people in the wilderness" but it also "underlines the biblical principle that God's calling must be tested" as God's servants and the leaders of his people such as Abraham, Joseph, Moses, David, and Job were all tested.[168] The difference is that while some of the leaders failed at some points, Jesus did not fail his tests.

The empowering is manifest in Jesus' ministry, and particularly his miracles and healings (cf. Matt 12:22–32; Mark 3:19–30; Luke 11:14–23; 12:10). While some of the people wonder if Jesus could be the awaited Son of David,"[169] the Pharisees saw Jesus' action as manifestation of the power of Beelzebub, the prince of demons. On the contrary, Jesus implicitly tells them that he drove demons by the Spirit of God, which is evidence that the kingdom of God had come upon them. The Spirit in the life of Jesus (Matt 12:18–21) gave him the power to drive out demons.

2.4.4 He Speaks through the Disciples

In fulfillment of God's salvific purpose, Jesus sends out the twelve (Matt 10:1–42) but warns them that they would encounter personal threats even to their lives. From 10:16 he explains some of the specific dangers that lay

---

165. Keener, *Matthew*, 137. See Ps 107:7; Isa 63:14. This leading is a common motif in the Bible, especially "of God guiding his people in the wilderness" (137). According to Nolland, there is a strong link between 4:1–11 and 3:13–17. For him, "The role of the Spirit leading Jesus here should be taken as paradigmatic for the whole of the ministry to come" (Nolland, *The Gospel of Matthew*, 162).

166. Davies and Allison, *A Critical and Exegetical Commentary*, 1.352.

167. Ibid.

168. Keener, *Matthew*, 88.

169. Hendriksen, *Matthew*, 524. Compare Matt 20:21; 23: 37–39; Luke 19:41, 42; Acts 1:6; John 6:15, 35–42. For Hendriksen, "The messianic conception of many of the people, including some of Christ's own disciples, was distinctly materialistic, earthly, Judaistic," 524.

ahead of their mission because he was sending them out like sheep among wolves. In 10:17 Jesus says that men would hand the disciples over to the local councils. The persecutors at this point are the Jews because the flogging takes place in the synagogues. At such prospect, the thought would be on how "to extricate oneself from this place of personal danger" by "a carefully prepared legal defense"[170] in view of the legal suits that their enemies may institute against them (17–18). These stern warnings give just cause for *anxiety*. Yet Jesus encourages them and gives them hope (10:19–20). When they are handed over to the authorities in order to make their defense, they need not be anxious of what to say because it will be given (δοθήσεται) to them what to say (Matt 10:19).[171] At this time it is the Spirit who will speak through the disciples. The πνεῦμα τοῦ πατρὸς ὑμῶν (Matt 10:20) is a familiar concept in the OT as in Exodus 4:12.[172] This is the "notion of Spirit-inspired utterances in special circumstances.[173] The role of the Holy Spirit is crucial here as the one who instructs them on the right things to say as they defend their cause.

2.4.5 He is the Spirit of Prophetic Inspiration

The focus is the meaning of Matthew 22:41–46 (cf. Mark 12:35–37; Luke 20:41–44). Jesus uses Psalm 110:1 to respond to his opponents. The issue for this discussion is about David speaking through the Spirit. Of particular importance for this discussion is the place of the text (Ps 110:1) in Jesus' use of the OT. According to Davies and Allison, Psalm 110 has a trajectory of messianic interpretation by pre-Christian Jews.[174] The psalm begins with a superscript that attributes the psalm to David according to Jewish tradition. Jesus accepts the superscription of the psalm as authentic. The validity of this text is derived from the inspiration of the wordings by the Spirit because the citation "assumes the Spirit's moving David to write

---

170. Nolland, *The Gospel of Matthew*, 424.
171. Hagner, *Matthew 1–13*, 277. The δοθήσεται "is a divine passive wherein God is understood as the acting subject" (277).
172. Ibid.
173. Ibid., 227.
174. Davies and Allison, *Matthew*, 384.

it."[175] For in Matthew 22:43 Δαυὶδ ἐν πνεύματι καλεῖ αὐτὸν κύριον λέγων ("David speaking by the Spirit calls him Lord") is an indication of divine inspiration.[176] Matthew "does not elsewhere link the Holy Spirit with the production of the wording of Scripture."[177] However, Matthew's τὸ ῥηθὲν ὑπὸ κυρίου διὰ τοῦ προφήτου (Matt 1:22) may be understood from the standpoint of the Holy Spirit's involvement in making known the mind of God to the prophets. According to Matthew, the Spirit of prophetic inspiration points to the coming of Christ the Savior of the world.

2.5 Summary and Conclusion

This chapter reveals that the works of the three persons of the Godhead in Matthew converge upon the one salvific purpose of God, namely, saving his people from their sins. The Father is primarily the *sender*. He sends the angels, the prophets, the workers into his harvest, and the Son. But he also *reveals* hidden things to the little ones who express faith in Jesus. The Son is the one sent by the Father to save his people from their sins. However, the Son also takes on the responsibility of the Father as he also sends for mission (cf. John 20:21). In addition to this sending, the Son sows the seed of the kingdom, heals the sick, forgives sins, mediates the knowledge of the Father, and judges the nations. The Son plays the role of the Father in sending and *mediates* the knowledge of the Father because he is *Immanuel,* "God with us." The Holy Spirit has the special responsibility as the agent in Jesus's miraculous conception. In addition, he anoints Jesus and leads him. He also empowers him for mission. But the Holy Spirit also empowers the disciples by speaking through them, and acts as the Spirit of inspiration. Therefore, Matthew presents mutual interdependence in the Godhead as each person's role is dependent on the others.

But there are particularly significant issues that the writer observed in the chapter that require further exploration, especially OT citations and

---

175. Turner, *Matthew,* 540. For the inspiration of the wordings of Ps 110, see also Hendriksen, *Matthew,* 812.
176. Hagner, *Matthew 14–28,* 650.
177. Nolland, *The Gospel of Matthew,* 915.

allusions that fill up Matthew's gospel. These include: interpretation of prophecy, the Torah, the temple, David, exile and restoration, and typology. First is how Matthew perceives and interprets prophecy in his gospel. Matthew portrays that God communicated his salvific purpose through the prophets including all the events in the life of Jesus and even geographical locations surrounding him. Matthew 2:13–15 quotes Hosea 11:1 to show that a fulfillment has taken place. The primary issue is how Matthew uses such texts in his fulfillment citations. Second is the Torah in the teaching of Jesus. Although Jesus says that he came to fulfill the Torah (5:17), the meaning of this fulfillment has ever remained a subject of interest and discussion among scholars. Third is Jesus' action in the temple. From what does he cleanse the temple and what symbolic meaning does he convey? Fourth is the place of David in the Gospel of Matthew. How does Matthew make a connection between the OT Davidic king and the identity of Jesus? Fifth is Matthew's view of exile and restoration. Does Matthew seem to suggest that the restoration of the nation Israel has found fulfillment in the coming of Christ? And sixth is Matthew's typological use of places, objects, and people such as wilderness, mountain, stone, and Jonah. How do these all fit into Matthew's mission theology?

Since Matthew shows that Jesus fulfills God's intention to save the whole world, the redemptive work of the Son (from his saving name) as the one sent by the Father is the key for understanding the missional character of Matthew's gospel and, therefore, provides the discussion of the next two chapters. The discussion in chapters 3 and 4 centers on the *field* or *scope* of mission in Matthew, that is, the house of Israel ("his people") and the nations. Tension exists in this crucial area as the Gospel of Matthew exhibits both particularistic and universalistic tendencies. This is one of the existing conundrums in Matthean studies, sometimes referred to as the "contradictions in Matthew." The next two chapters would suggest that it is probably helpful to keep in mind that the Gospel of Matthew is a whole and should be studied as a narrative that sees both aspects of mission as legitimate program of God. And Matthew projects this view by the framework of promise-fulfillment. A careful reading suggests that the Gospel of Matthew engages the gentile world from the beginning and the theme is interwoven throughout the narrative, as the gentile mission is also substantiated by OT references.

The preliminary conclusion drawn from the above points is that Matthew views mission as work of the Triune God. God initiates the work of salvation as recorded in the second pericope of the gospel (1:18–25). The events in the life of Jesus all fulfill God's salvific purposes as indicated by fulfillment quotations. The disciples of Jesus are sent out as agents of the Triune God for mission to Israel and the nations.

CHAPTER 3

Mission to Israel: Foundations and Framework

3.1 Introduction

The primary objective of this chapter is to examine mission to Israel using OT foundations and framework of redemptive events and institutions, prophetic ministry, geographical locations, and intertextual typology. The writer examines this OT fabric in the light of Matthew's theme of promise-fulfillment. This approach looks at the entire Gospel of Matthew rather than narrowly investigating what is usually considered Matthean missionary texts (9:35–10:42; 15:24 and 28:16–20).[1] The writer believes that a fragmentary reading of the Gospel of Matthew might be responsible for the notion that the rejection of the Messiah by Israel means that

---

1. Kyung Soon Na's position is a significant shift away from the way scholars approach mission in Matthew. See his "Understanding the Great Commission Against the Background of Matthew's Gospel as a Whole" (a Doctor of Theology Dissertation submitted to the University of Stellenbosch, August 1998). He argues that Matthew as a whole should be read from a missionary perspective with 28:16–20 as the interpretative key. Cf. Daniel W. Ulrich, "The Missional Audience of the Gospel of Matthew," *CBQ* 69 (January 2007) who seems to lean toward the missionary texts.

God rejected Israel,[2] τὸν λαὸν αὐτοῦ[3] of 1:21, and there is no future for it.[4]

---

2. The "anti-Jewishness" of the Gospel of Matthew might explain K. W. Clark's proposal that the Gospel of Matthew could not have been written by a Jew. See K. W. Clark, "The Gentile Bias in Matthew," *JBL* 66 (1947): 165–172. Other scholars who followed similarly include L. Gaston, "The Messiah of Israel As Teacher of the Gentiles: The Setting of Matthew's Christology," *Int* 29 (1975): 24–40; G. Strecker, *Der Weg der Gerechtigkeit* (Göttingen: Vandenhoeck & Ruprecht, 1962), 15–35; N. Nepper Christensen, *Das Matthäusevangelium: ein juden-christliches Evangelium?* (Aarhus: Universitetsforlaget, 1958).

3. Hahn believes that the issue of the people of God is primarily that of contrast between those who believe and those who do not believe the message of Jesus and that of his disciples. For Hahn, the Gospel of Matthew portrays Israel as largely unrepentant, and even calling judgment upon itself, but "the evangelist and his church regarded themselves inwardly and outwardly tied to Israel. The commissioning words of chapter 10 strongly emphasize the inalienable task of preaching the gospel to God's ancient people. It is Israel that is offered the Kingdom of God, which has now drawn near, and it is therefore the Israelites who are called in 8:12 'sons of the kingdom.' Matthew lets it be seen particularly clearly that the Church regards itself primarily as the band of disciples from the Jews, as the lost sheep of Israel to whom Jesus has come" (see Hahn, *Mission in the New Testament*, 125-126).

4. Such view posits that only gentile mission remains. According to G. W. E. Nickelsburg, the Gospel of Matthew presents a triple paradox. It proclaims the good news about Jesus as the promised Messiah king of the Jews, but at the same time transmits "the bad news that the Jews as a nation have rejected him and have lost their status as God's people" thereby resulting in a sharp schism between the people of Israel and the gentile church. The second paradox, for Nickelsburg, is that although Matthew passes a strong judgmental word of rejection on Israel, he holds to the faith traditions of Israel for the expression of his message. And, finally, "because of its interwoven good news and bad news, this gospel has helped to foster less-than-Christian attitudes and actions toward the Jews over the centuries" (see George W. E. Nickelsburg, "Good News/Bad News: The Messiah and God's Fractured Community," *ATLAS* [n.d.]: 324). While Nickelsburg's third observation about the "less-than-Christian attitudes and actions toward the Jews over the centuries" as rooted in the understanding of Matthew is correct, it must be noted that such understanding is probably based on improper exegesis of the message of Matthew. It is probably true that most scholars see Matthew "prejudiced and polemically narrow in his view toward Judaism (not ancient Israel) because of the post-70 CE historical situation" (Rudolf Schnackenburg, "Matthew's Gospel as Test Case for Hermeneutical Reflections," trans. Ronald D. Witherup, in *Treasures New and Old: Recent Contributions to Matthean Studies*, ed. David R. Bauer and Mark Allan Powell [Atlanta: Scholars Press, 1996], 263). The invectives poured on Israel's leaders such as in Matt 23 notwithstanding; it is probably helpful to make some distinctions here. In this regard, David R. Bauer's classification of Israel into two groups, namely, the crowds and the religious leaders is helpful (See Bauer, "The Major Characters of Matthew's Story: Their Functions and Significance," *ATLAS* (n.d.): 363. In Matthew the crowd generally responds to message of Jesus with amazement and is seen as sheep without a shepherd, while the religious leaders are characterized by doubts, antagonism, and open rejection of his message. The religious leaders might have persuaded the crowd to reject Jesus at last, but the distinction made here needs to be kept in mind in dealing with the issue of the rejection of Israel. Contrary to Nickelsburg's position that there is no future for Jewish mission, Garland says, "The mission to Israel is to continue until the Son of Man comes" (see Garland, *Reading Matthew*, 112). Nickelsburg's view is challenged in the section dealing with the "stone" motif in chapter 4.

But rather than depicting Israel as rejected by God as Nickelsburg does, Amy-Jill Levine's point that Matthew does not divide the world into "good Gentiles" and "bad Jews" but that "the principal division" is "between those who bear good fruit and those who corrupt,"[5] is important in understanding mission to Israel and mission to the nations.[6] Therefore, instead of a fragmentary reading, we will examine the entire Gospel of Matthew for a good understanding of mission to Israel and the nations.

From the general foundation laid in chapter 2, what Jesus does or represents is understood in the light of God who sends and the Holy Spirit who empowers. Jesus' primary work is mission to Israel and the nations. The significant issues the writer treats in this chapter, as highlighted in chapter 2, include: Matthew's theological and missional interpretation of prophecy, fulfillment of the *Torah,* the cleansing of the temple, the Davidic kingship, exile and restoration, and typology. The writer focuses on these themes from the entire Gospel of Matthew and analyses selected fulfillment quotations and other relevant texts. Where necessary, he examines the textual background of those OT texts and how Matthew uses them to achieve his theological and missional purposes. In the textual analysis only significant changes are highlighted and treated. The writer then evaluates

---

5. See Amy-Jill Levine, "Matthew and Anti-Judaism," *CurTM* 34.6 (December 2007), 410. See also Hahn, *Mission in the New Testament,* 125. Hahn believes that the issue of the people of God is primarily that of contrast between those who believe and those who do not believe the message of Jesus and that of his disciples. For Hahn, the Gospel of Matthew portrays Israel as largely unrepentant, and even calling judgment upon itself, but "the evangelist and his church regarded themselves inwardly and outwardly tied to Israel. The commissioning words of chapter 10 strongly emphasize the inalienable task of preaching the gospel to God's ancient people. It is Israel that is offered the Kingdom of God, which has now drawn near, and it is therefore the Israelites who are called in 8:12 'sons of the kingdom.' Matthew lets it be seen particularly clearly that the church regards itself primarily as the band of disciples from the Jews, as the lost sheep of Israel to whom Jesus has come" (see Hahn, *Mission in the New Testament,* 125–126).

6. For more on ancient and modern issues concerning the Gospel of Matthew and the nation Israel, see Gabriella Gelardini, "Religion and Ethnicity; Toying with Two Related Concepts in 19th and 20th Century German Jesus Scholarship: A Socio-historical Analysis," *Sapienta Logos* 1, no. 2 (2009): 162–193. See also Donald Senior, "Between Two Worlds: Gentiles and Jewish Christians in Matthew's Gospel," *CBQ* 61 (1999): 2. Senior sees the Holocaust as "a powerful underlying motivation" for the renewed interest in the social setting of the NT and the Jewish background of Matthew, "since traditional interpretation of Matthew's gospel has often fueled a negative and prejudicial view of Judaism" (2). While this modern debate is noted, its discussion is outside the scope of this study.

the selected secondary sources dealing with these key issues in the light of the evidence of Matthew's text(s). The interaction with and evaluation of secondary sources in this chapter and the next is also intended to fill up the *lacuna* of literature review not carried out as a separate chapter in this work.

3.2 Redemptive Events, Institutions, and Mission[7]

The argument of this section is that, like Jesus,[8] Matthew sees the OT as the major witness to God's salvific purposes. But what are the OT redemptive events and institutions that shaped Matthew's mission concept? [9] And

---

7. Significant works in this general direction include Swartley's *Israel's Scripture Traditions*. Swartley's thesis is that key OT theological traditions provided the framework for the structure and theology of the Synoptic Gospels. In other words, "early Christian understanding of Jesus reflects, at a fundamental level, motifs and structures of thought that testify to a Christian self-identification with Israel" (16). The "older events" that gave meaning to the "new events" include the exodus-Sinai traditions; Israel's way-conquest traditions; the temple traditions; and Israel's kingship traditions. Each of the Synoptic Gospels shows a significant use of these traditions. The gospel writers, by way of reflection and transformation, interpreted the life and ministry of Jesus in the light of the "older events." Donald J. Verseput's "The Davidic Messiah and Matthew's Jewish Christianity," *SLBSP* (1995): 102–116, is a good treatment on expectations of the Messiah in Second Temple Judaism as reflected in the Gospel of Matthew. Robertson's *The Christ of the Prophets* treats Israel's saving events in his introduction and exile and restoration in chapter 14. Saving events for Robertson include the exodus, the covenant at Mount Sinai, the establishment of the monarchy, among others. Evans' article, "Jesus and the Continuing Exile of Israel," is critical assessment of N. T. Wright's *Jesus and the Victory of God, Christian Origins and the Question of God*, vol. 2 (Minnesota: Fortress, 1996). Evans examines, from Wright's perspective, how the Second Temple Jews saw themselves as still in exile. This exile and redemption theology underlie Jesus' teaching and actions.

8. See Richard B. Hays and Joel B. Green, "The Use of the Old Testament by New Testament Writers," in *Hearing the New Testament: Strategies for Interpretation*, ed. Joel B. Green (Carlisle: The Paternoster Press, 1995), 222. See also C. H. Dodd, *According to the Scriptures: The Sub-Structure of New Testament Theology* (London: Nisbet, 1952). Jesus' attitude toward the OT is that he regarded it "as a divinely directed and inspired movement, as having arrived at its goal in himself" so that "the Old Testament would lose its purpose and significance" if he were taken away (Geerhardus Vos, *Biblical Theology: Old and New Testaments* [Edinburgh: Banner of Truth Trust, 1975], 358). It is evidently this attitude that Matthew and the rest of the NT writers adopt in their use of the OT.

9. Many scholars use salvation history as a framework for interpreting mission in Matthew (see, Donald Senior and Carroll Stuhlmueller, *The Biblical Foundations for Mission* [Maryknoll, New York: Orbis Books, 1983] 238). But due to its diverse meanings, the researcher prefers the concept of "redemptive events" in its place for clarity and identifiable actions of God that constitute these *redemptive events*. Some of the problems associated with the use of the phrase "salvation-history" are highlighted by Oscar Cullmann. See Oscar

what makes these events and institutions *redemptive*?[10] These redemptive events and institutions are the acts of God in Israel's history, "the heritage of Judaism,"[11] which were recorded for Israel's (and the world's) future. Table 1 illustrates Matthew's interpretative approach. Particularly significant on the table is exile and restoration. Israel is assumed to be in exile until the coming of Christ. Matthew reasons along the line of his predecessors and contemporaries. For even after the return from the Babylonian captivity, Ezra and Nehemiah still see the nation as in exile. Similarly, the expectation of redemption runs through the centuries that in the first century BC the *Pss. of Sol.* 8:28 says, "Bring together the dispersed of Israel with mercy and goodness, for your faithfulness is with us."[12]

Culmann, *Salvation in History* (London: SCM Press, 1967), 11. For more on salvation-history in Matthew see John P. Meier, *The Vision of Matthew: Christ, Church, and Morality in the First Gospel* (New York: Crossroad, 1979), 30; idem, *Law and History in Matthew's Gospel: A Redactional Study of Matt 5:17–48* (Rome: Biblical Institute Press, 1976), 30–31. But concepts and themes like salvation history and redaction criticism are only noted here and not pursued in this work because they do not constitute the focus of the study.

10. The criteria for including some events as *redemptive* are probably best summed up in Swartley's "major streams of Israel's traditions" (Swartley, *Israel's Scripture Traditions,* 289). They are the saving acts of God and regarded as the heritage of Judaism or "their faith traditions." They gave Israel her identity as a nation. Matthew and the other Synoptics echo these saving acts prominently in their gospels.

11. Senior and Stuhlmueller, *The Biblical Foundations for Mission*, 238.

12. See Evans, "Jesus and the Continuing Exile of Israel," 85, 88. But by his genealogy, Matthew suggests that the exile had come to an end with the coming of Christ. According to Keener, "Matthew's Genealogy unifies the defining periods of Israel's history and points them to Jesus," (Keener, *A Commentary on the Gospel of Matthew,* 78). The exile and restoration issue is taken up later in this chapter.

Table 1: *OT "faith traditions" Fulfilled*[13]

OT Event and Institution	Matthew's Interpretation
The Exodus: God calls his son out of Egypt (Hos 11:1)	Jesus-Israel typology: God calls his Son out of Egypt (Matt 2:13–15)
The Torah seals God's covenant with Israel (Ex 25:27–28)	Jesus comes to fulfill the Torah (Matt 5:17)
The exile and restoration: "Israel still in exile" (Neh 9:36; Ez 9:8–9)	"From the exile to the Christ": Jesus restores Israel (Matt 1:17)
The Davidic king is born in Bethlehem (Mic 5:2)	Davidic shepherd-king born in Bethlehem (Matt 2:5, 6)
The temple is a house of prayer for all nations (Isa 56:7)	Jesus is one greater than the temple; the temple is house of prayer [for all nations] (Matt 12:1–8; 21:13)

The key verse in understanding how Matthew interprets the OT, using his framework of promise-fulfillment, is what Jesus says at the end of his teaching on the parables of the kingdom of God in Matthew 13:52, found only in the Gospel of Matthew. In several places in his narrative, Matthew is like "every teacher of the law who has been instructed [μαθητευθεὶς] about the kingdom of heaven" and therefore "brings out [casts out] of his storeroom [things] new and old." Jesus does not do away with the old (teaching of the OT),[14] but the new teachings "are the key to understanding them."[15] The gospel of the kingdom Jesus proclaimed is "a blend of continuity and discontinuity with the old" because "at its heart the gospel

---

13. This is Swartley's description of the events and institutions that shaped Matthew's gospel which he also calls "theological traditions" (Swartley, *Israel's Scripture Traditions*).

14. Gundry understands the "new things" to mean the new understanding gained through the parables while the "old things" represent the old understanding the disciples had before the parabolic teaching (Gundry, *Matthew*, 281). But since Jesus refers to the teachers of the law, one would suggest that the "old things" and the "new things" probably refer to old and new understanding regarding the things of the law.

15. Morris, *The Gospel According to Matthew*, 363; see also Keener, *A Commentary on the Gospel of Matthew*, 393–94; Peter Phillips, "Casting out the Treasure: A New Reading of Matthew 13:52," *JNST* 13.1 (2008): 3–24. Although Phillips argues that the verb ἐκβάλλει is used consistently in terms of "disposal" or "expulsion" rather than "bring forth" or "bring out from," this does not seem to be the only way Matthew uses the word (e.g. Matthew 12:35; cf. John 10:4).

consists of new things."[16] Matthew draws, therefore, from the key elements of Israel's faith recorded for future generations and reflects upon them and reinterprets them in the light of Christ. According to Robertson,

> These mighty, formative acts of God in behalf of his chosen covenant people were carefully recorded and their abiding significance preserved in writing for the generations to come. Consequently every future age is able to confirm for itself the intent of God in forming this people in the processes of human history and join with Israel in the covenant that was intended to make them a blessing to all the nations of the world.[17]

The key here is God's *formative acts* on behalf of Israel. God himself instructed the people to record what he did on their behalf, especially his mighty hand in liberating them from Egypt because of its significance. This is intended for the generations (see Ps 78 where the dual focus of God's dealings with Israel is evident: judgment and salvation).[18]

The issue of joining with Israel as stated by Robertson echoes Israel's covenant blessings that extend to the rest of humankind (Gen 12:1–3). Matthew seems to have reflected on these "great saving events in Israel's history" and skillfully interwoven them into his narrative. These key redemptive events and institutions include the exodus, the divine covenant initiated at Mount Sinai, the establishment of Davidic dynasty as "the apex of redemptive history in its progress under the old covenant," the temple, and exile and restoration.[19] Similarly, Swartley sees four themes of "divine re-

---

16. Hagner, *Matthew 1–13*, 402. In the words of Blomberg, Matthew may have Jesus' disciples in mind who, like other scribes, are "endowed with wisdom, authority, the right understanding of the law, and perhaps some measure of prophetic inspiration". Therefore, "in light of v. 35, Jesus probably means that as his disciples teach God's will, they will be drawing out the meaning of the Hebrew Scriptures ('things old'), while showing how they are fulfilled and apply in the kingdom age ('things new')." See Blomberg, *Matthew*, 225.

17. Robertson, *The Christ of the Prophets*, 3.

18. See Kenneth L. Barker and John R. Kohlenberger III, *The Expositor's Bible Commentary*, abridged ed. (Grand Rapids: Zondervan, 1994), 879–881.

19. Robertson, *The Christ of the Prophets*, 2. See John Riches in *The Synoptic Gospels: With an Introduction by Scot McKnight*, by John Riches, William R. Telford, and Christopher M.

demptive activity" namely, exodus, way-conquest, temple, and kingship as having a formative influence on the structure and theology of the Synoptic Gospels.[20] Robertson and Swartley write from different perspectives. While Robertson examines prophecy from a christological viewpoint, Swartley looks at the OT faith traditions that shaped the structure and theology of the Synoptic Gospels. Both authors, however, converge upon the identification of some key events which are deemed salvific in Israel's history and that have shaped the message of the NT. Swartley restricts his work to elements of Israel's faith traditions from Exodus 15, while Robertson considers prophecy in the entire OT. This explains the addition of exile and restoration in Robertson as one of the key redemptive events in Israel. In the same vein, Jacob Neusner refers to the redemption from Egypt, the exile and the return, as salvific acts of God. For him, therefore, "*many salvations*, not only one, are recorded for Israel, all of them conforming to a single pattern, which imparts its definition upon the final act of salvation as well, the one that comes with personal resurrection and all Israel's entry into the world to come"[21] (emphasis added). This section examines how five redemptive events are viewed in the Gospel of Matthew.

3.2.1 The Exodus

The writer referred to the echoes of the exodus in chapter 2, especially in the wilderness and transfiguration narratives in the Gospel of Matthew.

Tuckett (Sheffield: Sheffield Academic Press, 2001). He says, "Israel's history of exodus, wanderings in the desert and revelation on the mountain is mirrored in Jesus' story in Matthew" (114).

20. See Swartley, *Israel's Scripture Traditions*, 32. For Swartley, the OT faith traditions shape both the content and structure of the Synoptic Gospels. According to him, the common structure of the Synoptic Gospels as distinct from the Gospel of John is better understood in light of their dependence on the OT faith traditions (32). Swartley structures his work on the song of deliverance in Exod 15. In this song the Lord's salvation at the Sea, the Lord's conquest of the Egyptians, the Lord's bringing them to the sanctuary, and the Lord's reign over the nation, are celebrated. These key themes, developed throughout the OT, are believed to be the faith traditions that shaped the Synoptic Gospels (33).

21. Jacob Neusner, *Recovering Judaism: The Universal Dimension of Judaism* [Minneapolis: Fortress Press, 2001], 111–112. Both Robertson and Neusner are not writing particularly on Matthew. They are mentioned here because of what they identify as Israel's redemptive events, which are the interest of this section of the study.

He now focuses on this exodus motif in Matthew 2:15. The texts read as follows:

Table 2:[22] *Jesus and the New Exodus*

MT	LXX	NT
Hos 11:1 כִּי נַעַר יִשְׂרָאֵל וָאֹהֲבֵהוּ וּמִמִּצְרַיִם קָרָאתִי לִבְנִי׃	**Hos 11:1** διότι νήπιος Ισραηλ καὶ ἐγὼ ἠγάπησα αὐτὸν καὶ ἐξ Αἰγύπτου μετεκάλεσα τὰ τέκνα αὐτοῦ	**Matt 2:15** ἵνα πληρωθῇ τὸ ῥηθὲν ὑπὸ κυρίου διὰ τοῦ προφήτου λέγοντος, Ἐξ Αἰγύπτου ἐκάλεσα τὸν υἱόν μου.
"When Israel was a child, I loved him, **and out of Egypt I called my son.**"	"When Israel was a child, I loved him, **and out of Egypt I called his children.**"	"And so was fulfilled what the Lord had said through the prophet: **"Out of Egypt I called my son."**

Attention is on Matthew 2:13–15 in which the exodus motif is probably most explicit.[23] But the textual background of the citation is examined first because Joseph's obedience to the angel of the Lord, and, especially, his going into Egypt, now fulfills Hosea 11:1. The exegetical question is what Hosea means by מִמִּצְרַיִם קָרָאתִי לִבְנִי and how Matthew reinterprets this. In wording his text, Matthew follows the MT in this quotation. He differs from the LXX by changing the compound aorist μετεκάλεσα to ἐκάλεσα.[24] But the most important difference Matthew makes to the LXX is that while God calls his children (τὰ τέκνα αὐτοῦ), Matthew has God

---

22. Except where indicated, the Scripture quotations in the tables are from the *New International Version* 1979, 1984 by International Bible Society.

23. According to France, this pericope portrays Jesus both as the new Moses (because it was in Egypt that Moses escaped the infanticide of Pharaoh and in the same Egypt fled to escape Pharaoh's anger but returned eventually after Pharaoh died) and the new Israel, God's son. But as France says, typology does not depend on exact correspondences (see France, *The Gospel of Matthew*, 77–78).

24. According to Craig L. Blomberg, this may be Matthew's "independent, literal translation of the Hebrew". See Craig L. Blomberg, "Matthew," in *Commentary on the New Testament Use of the Old Testament*, ed. G. K. Beale and D. A. Carson (Grand Rapids: Baker Academic, 2007), 8; cf. Davies and Allison, *A Critical and Exegeical Commentary*, 1.161.

call "my son" (ἐκάλεσα τὸν υἱόν μου) from Egypt.²⁵ Matthew's attraction to the MT is the sonship of Jesus.²⁶ His citation of the last clause closely follows "I loved him" of both the MT and the LXX in the first clause but differs from the LXX in the final clause. We will argue here that Matthew has a new exodus in view. Meanwhile, in Matthew's narrative the event in 2:13–15 takes place immediately after the visit of the Magi from the East. Their coming and their inquiry about the birth of the *king of the Jews*²⁷ disturbed Herod "and all Jerusalem with him" (2:3). In its literary context, the pericope flows as a natural sequence from the agitation caused by the news brought by the Magi from the East concerning the birth of the king of the Jews. It fits into the series of events surrounding the life of Jesus as narrated by Matthew. As in the second pericope (1:18–25), Matthew narrates this story from the viewpoint that all the events are orchestrated by God. God communicates his purposes and actions by the appearance of the angel of the Lord to Joseph in a dream. In chapter 2 of this work, God is primarily the sender in mission and among his agents are the angels. Here (2:13), the angel of the Lord appears to Joseph in a dream. The exact wordings used in 1:20 are used here except that the aorist passive ἐφάνη now becomes φαίνεται present middle or passive in 2:13. These may be compared as follows: Matt 1:20: ἰδοὺ ἄγγελος κυρίου κατ' ὄναρ ἐφάνη αὐτῷ λέγων; Matt 2:13: ἰδοὺ ἄγγελος κυρίου φαίνεται κατ' ὄναρ τῷ Ἰωσὴφ λέγων. The change of tenses, however, presents no significant difference.²⁸

---

25. A general consensus among scholars is that Matthew's fulfillment quotations are a mixed text form that blends LXX, Hebrew and Aramaic elements and some unique translations. But this mixed text form characterizes the other Gospels as well. "What makes the Old Testament quotations in Matthew's gospel unique is not their textual form but the way the evangelist applies these quotations to the life of Jesus" (see Senior, *What are they saying about Matthew?* 58).
26. See Turner, *Matthew*, 90.
27. This is the first address of Jesus as king of the Jews. And this recognition runs throughout the Gospel of Matthew, culminating in Jesus' crucifixion because, according to his accusers, he claimed to be king of the Jews.
28. For the historic present φαίνεται, see Matt 3:1 Ἐν δὲ ταῖς ἡμέραις ἐκείναις παραγίνεται Ἰωάννης ὁ βαπτιστής; Matt 3:13 Τότε παραγίνεται ὁ Ἰησοῦς ἀπὸ τῆς Γαλιλαίας ἐπὶ τὸν Ἰορδάνην πρὸς τὸν Ἰωάννην τοῦ βαπτισθῆναι ὑπ' αὐτοῦ. The historic present adds vividness to the narrative. See William Varner, "A Discourse Analysis of Matthew's Nativity Narrative," *TynBul* 58.2 (2007), 221; Ernest De Witt Burton, *Syntax of the Moods and Tenses in New Testament Greek* (Grand Rapids: Kregel Publications, 1976), 9.

This time, as in 1:20, Matthew draws attention to the angelic appearance to Joseph with a special message. But in lieu of the good news in that first pericope, the angel of the Lord comes with a caveat and a command to Joseph: Ἐγερθεὶς παράλαβε τὸ παιδίον καὶ τὴν μητέρα αὐτοῦ καὶ φεῦγε.[29] Joseph is commanded to take the newborn ruler and shepherd (2:6), and his mother, and flee to Egypt because Herod was now threatening to kill the baby. With φεῦγε Matthew begins his exploitation of the motif of flight from persecution, a motif he uses in several places in the gospel (12:15). Gundry thinks that this motif is the reason why Matthew changes Luke's going up to Jerusalem (2:22) into flight into Egypt.[30]

But the most important aspect of this fleeing for Matthew is the place Joseph goes with the baby Jesus. The angel of the Lord specifies the place—φεῦγε εἰς Αἴγυπτον ("flee into Egypt"). The textual analysis gave some clue about the significance of Egypt for Matthew. This is examined shortly. According to 2:14 Joseph arose and took the child and his mother by night. Matthew uses νυκτὸς (by night) probably to underscore the fact that Joseph treated the angelic command with a sense of urgency and seriousness.[31] He departs for Egypt as the angel of the Lord commanded him.

In Matthew 2:15 Joseph stays in Egypt with Mary and the child ἕως τῆς τελευτῆς Ἡρώδου. This stay in Egypt, for Matthew, happened ἵνα πληρωθῇ τὸ ῥηθὲν ὑπὸ κυρίου διὰ τοῦ προφήτου. The expression of purpose with ἵνα (+ subjunctive) demonstrates that God orchestrated this event toward a desired end. ἵνα πληρωθῇ occupies a special place in Matthew's

---

29. While the aorist participle ἐγερθεὶς before the imperative παράλαβε could render the translation literally as "after arising, take the child and his mother and flee," Daniel B. Wallace says that this would mean that Joseph could decide when to arise. "It was only that once he did arise, he was to obey the angelic command" (see Wallace, *Greek Grammar Beyond the Basics*, 641). The participle ἐγερθεὶς is therefore considered part of the imperative παράλαβε which is also in 2:14.

30. Gundry believes that the story is Matthew's creation as a *Midrash* to Luke's pericope of the visit to Jerusalem (Gundry, *Matthew*, 32). But the issue of Midrash in Matthew's narrative is not pursued in this work. For a contrary opinion with Gundry on this particular pericope see Turner, *Matthew*, 89. For objections on Matthew as midrashic, see Scott Cunningham and Darrel L. Bock, "Is Matthew Midrash?" *BSac* 144 (April–June, 1987): 157–180. See also Varner, "A Discourse Analysis of Matthew's Nativity Narrative," 227. Keener says that although there is no concrete historical support for the slaughter of the infants, the story fits Herod's character (see Keener, *A Commentary on the Gospel of Mattthew*, 110).

31. See also Wallace, *Greek Grammar Beyond the Basics*, 641.

narrative. Although ἵνα may express result, the ἵνα clause in Matthew usually expresses purpose. He uses ἵνα interchangeably with ὅπως.[32] The ἵνα and ὅπως clauses are significant in Matthew's expression of events in the life of Jesus as fulfillment of God's purposes. As in Matthew 1:22, the Lord is the personal agent (ὑπὸ κυρίου) in giving his prophetic word through the prophet (διὰ τοῦ προφήτου). Matthew's theological viewpoint is that God communicated his word through human writers.[33] This is the theological viewpoint he employs in treating OT passages concerning the life of Jesus. And this prophetic word is Ἐξ Αἰγύπτου ἐκάλεσα τὸν υἱόν μου, citing Hosea 11:1.

In this short pericope Matthew mentions Egypt three times. And in the last mention, Matthew ties Egypt with the exodus of the people of Israel. But what is the significance of the exodus in the Gospel of Matthew and what interpretative method does Matthew use to determine its meaning?[34] The exodus is described as God's model of redemption.[35] The word *exodus* does not occur in the Gospel of Matthew,[36] but allusions to the event are made in several places such as John the Baptist's ministry in the wilderness (Matt 3:1–12) and Jesus' temptation in the wilderness (Matt 4:1–11), which the writer highlighted in chapter 2.[37] Other events that recall the

---

32. Matt 1:22; 2:15; 2:23; 8:17 (see Burton, *Syntax of the Moods and Tenses in New*, 94).

33. See Buist Fanning, "Theological Analysis: Building Biblical Theology," in *Interpreting the New Testament Text: Introduction to the Art and Science of Exegesis,* ed. Darrell L. Bock and Buist M. Fanning (Wheaton: Crossway Books, 2006), 277.

34. It is "because God so willed that the Exodus redemption led by Moses be consummated in the Exodus of the Prophet who, like Moses, must suffer and die to effect new deliverance for the people" (Swartley, *Israel's Scripture Traditions,* 19; citing D. P. Moessner, *Lord of the Banquet: The Literary and Theological Significance of the Lukan Travel Narrative* (Minneapolis: Augsburg/Fortress, 1989), 323.

35. Wright, *The Mission of God,* 265–288, using Exod 15:13 as key; see also David L. Baker, *Two Testaments, One Bible: The Theological Relationship Between the Old and the New Testaments,* 3rd ed. (Downers Grove: IVP, 2010), 27–28. In the period of prophetic eschatology, the new exodus is associated with spiritual renewal in Israel.

36. The word occurs in Luke 9:31 in the transfiguration narrative where Moses and Elijah were speaking with Jesus about his (Jesus') departure (ἔξοδος).

37. Allison sees Jesus as the new Moses and believes that the birth and infancy narratives are cast in Moses' birth and infancy narrative. See Allison, *The New Moses,* 140. See also Swartley who says that the infancy narrative shows, "liberational exodus motif" (Swartley, *Israel's Scripture Traditions,* 62). For more on this exodus motif, see Elaine M. Wainwright, *Shall We Look for Another? A Feminist Rereading of the Matthean Jesus* (New York: Orbis

exodus include Herod's killing of the male babies (Matt 2:16–18) that correspond to Pharaoh's edict to kill all Hebrew boys in Egypt (Exod 1:15–16) and how both Jesus and Moses had to flee from Herod's and Pharaoh's wrath respectively (Exod 2:15; cf. Matt 2:13–15).

There are evidences that Second Temple Judaism had expectations of a new exodus. 2 Baruch 4:36–37 says, "Look toward the east, O Jerusalem, and see the joy that is coming to you from God! Behold, your sons are coming, whom you sent away; they are coming, gathered from east and west, at the word of the Holy One, rejoicing in the glory of God." Similarly, 2 Maccabees 1:27, 29 reads: "Gather together our scattered people, set free those who are slaves among the gentiles. . . . Plant your people in your holy place, as Moses promised."[38] This new exodus is a messianic task (*Pss. of Sol.* 8:28).[39] Matthew seems to take a cue from these widespread expectations. Matthew is therefore presenting Jesus as the typological "recapitulation of Israel."[40]

But the key issue here is Matthew's citation of Hosea 11:1 as prophecy fulfilled. Does the context of Hosea 11:1 suggest that prediction is in view? It is debated whether or not the evangelist took the text of Hosea in its original context and sense and used it as a genuine prophecy concerning Jesus.[41] The immediate context is about Israel's rebellion, a theme that is traced to the beginning of the book and exemplified by Hosea's wife, Gomer. Therefore, Hosea 11:1–7 is like a lament song for a rebellious Israel. But God recalls the past exodus in which he delivered Israel whom he loved. Yet Hosea anticipates a "new exodus" (11:8–11). This new exodus is "the historic sign of the covenant" which is also "the past exodus with which Jesus is identified."[42] Therefore, the most important theological and

---

Books, 1998), 60; Neusner, *Recovering Judaism*, 62–63. For detailed implicit citation of Exod 4:19–20 in Matt 2:19–21 see Allison, *The New Moses*, 142–146.

38. Evans, "Jesus and the Continuing Exile of Israel," 88.

39. Ibid.

40. Carson, "Matthew," 14.

41. See S. V. McCasland, "Matthew Twists the Scriptures," in *The Right Doctrine from the Wrong Texts? Essays on the Use of the Old Testament in the New*, ed. G. K. Beale (Grand Rapids: Baker Academic, 1994), 146–163.

42. Keener, *A Commentary on the Gospel of Matthew*, 108. Matthew refers back to the exodus because it is crucial in Israel's history. In the exodus God called Israel to be his *people* (Exod

missional import of 2:13–15 for Matthew is that God's salvation for his people has begun in Jesus.[43]

Similarly, scholars differ on the emphasis of this pericope, especially on whether it expresses exodus motif or Jesus' divine sonship. Two approaches to the question dominate scholarly discussion. First, there are scholars who think that Matthew sees Hosea 11:1 as a prediction about Jesus' sojourn in and departure from Egypt. Those who follow this approach either discredit Matthew's hermeneutic or "attribute to Matthew revelatory insight into the *sensus plenior* of Hosea."[44] Second, there are scholars who believe that Matthew has not distorted Hosea 11:1 by his application of the text to Jesus. This position holds that the text of Hosea 11:1 is not a prediction in its original context but a reminiscence of the exodus. Davies and Allison believe that Matthew's citation of Hosea 11:1 is an allusion to Numbers 24:8.[45] In this position, a theological motif is alluded to by Matthew,

---

6:7). This calling is the starting point of the concept of election. See Willem VanGemeren, *The Progress of Redemption: The Story of Redemption from Creation to the New Jerusalem* (Grand Rapids: Baker Academie, 1988), who says, "The word 'people' gradually acquired the significance of an elect nation, to whom the Lord gave the privilege of being his own kingdom, characterized by royalty and holiness" (169). See Exod 19:5–6). Israel became his theocratic kingdom and those mighty acts performed on behalf of Israel became "the backbone of faith for the future (Charles L. Holman, *Till Jesus Comes: Origins of Christian Apocalyptic Expectations* [Peabody: Hendrickson Publishers, 1996], 10). In this calling God also delivered his people from the hands of Pharaoh, and the significance of this salvific act is demonstrated by the annual Passover that Moses to be instituted as a constant reminder that he had rescued them from Egypt with a powerful hand (Exod 12; Deut 16:1–8; Josh 5:10). The prophets and the Psalms also aided to keep the memory of the exodus alive (see 1 Sam 2:27; 10:18; 12:6–8; 1 Kgs 8:9, 16; 2 Kgs 17:7; Hos 11:1; Isa 11:16; Jer 2:6; 11:7; Ps 78:9–20, 42–53; 105:26–45; 106:6–33; 114:1). This redemptive work of God remained a historic event in the life of the people of Israel because it "was the foundation of Israel's national birth, which in turn formed the basis for covenant relation with its God" (Holman, *Till Jesus Comes*, 10). Moses relates this Sinaitic covenant to the saving act from Egypt (Exod 19:4; 20:1ff; 24:1–8). In addition to the covenant (בְּרִית) that is "descriptive of Israel's relation to Yahweh," the themes of election and promise-fulfillment are also rooted in the exodus, for it is a fulfillment of the promise made to the patriarchs (Holman, *Till Jesus Comes*, 11–12).

43. Keener, *A Commentary on the Gospel of Matthew*, 108. According to Carson, Matthew (and other NT writers) is not reading back into the OT something that is not already there germinally. In the context, God is looking forward "to a saving visitation" and "son language is part of this messianic matrix" that points to Jesus the Messiah (Carson, "Matthew," 14).

44. Turner, *Matthew*, 90. See Gordon Fee and Douglas Stuart, *How to Read the Bible for All Its Worth*, 2nd ed. (Grand Rapids: Zondervan, 1993), 185. The concept of *sensus plenior* is discussed further in the section of prophecy.

45. Davies and Allison, *A Critical and Exegetical Commentary*, 1.262–263.

namely, the divine sonship in relation to the exodus. The exodus shows that Israel is God's son. As Israel is God's son, this is "more profoundly true of Jesus the Messiah."[46] Just as Hosea 11:1 "provides a historical pattern" of how God preserved his son Israel from Pharaoh's wrath, this event is recapitulated, from a Christian perspective, "by God's loving preservation of his Son, Jesus, from Herod's wrath."[47] Under this interpretative approach, Nolland also suggests that Matthew's quotation of Hosea 11:1 in 2:15 "establishes an Israel typology"[48] and Wright sees the text as a legitimate antitype.[49]

But some scholars argue that the emphasis of the pericope is not on the exodus motif. Gundry argues instead that the "emphasis falls on Jesus' divine sonship, not on the geography of Jesus' travels," because the quotation comes before the return from Egypt and as such does not highlight Jesus' departure from it.[50] Similarly, Kaiser says that the emphasis of the text is "the preserving love of God for his seed, Israel," because Matthew introduces the quote at 2:15 and not after 2:20 or even 2:22 to make it clear that it is not the exodus or the departure from there that is the concern

---

46. Turner, *Matthew*, 90. Matthew 2:13, 20 is also understood by Gundry as "the Moses-Jesus typology" as this "plays on the experiences of Moses in Exod 2 and 4" (Robert H. Gundry, *The Use of the Old Testament in St. Matthew's Gospel with Special Reference to the Messianic Hope* [Leiden: E. J. Brill, 1967], 206). Brevard S. Childs also sees Moses typology in Matt 2, see Brevard S. Childs, *The Book of Exodus* (Philadelphia: Westminster, 1974), 21. But Childs thinks that Matthew uses Moses' story from Hellenistic influence rather than in its OT form (21).

47. Turner, *Matthew*, 90–91. According to Turner, it is in Jesus "whose individual life is an antitypical microcosm of macrocosmic typological Israel" that the themes of God's love and covenant for his people Israel and their kings are consummated (91).

48. Nolland, *The Gospel of Matthew*, 123. Other scholars who lean toward the typological interpretation include: Keener, *A Commentary on the Gospel of Matthew*, 109. He adds that the passage (2:13–14) also foreshadows Jesus' rejection as an adult in addition to the typology of a new exodus; France, *The Gospel of Matthew*, 80. He argues here that the essence of typology is dependence on transferable models from the OT and not on predictions (80); Hendriksen, *Matthew*, 178. He says that Matthew's application of Hos 11:1 "is evident that he regards Israel as a type of the Messiah" (178); Blomberg sees the passage as "a classic example of pure typology" (see Bomberg, "Matthew," in *Commentary on the New Testament use of the Old Testament*, 8); Darrell L. Bock, "Scripture Citing Scripture: Use of the Old Testament in the New," in *Interpreting the New Testament Text*, 273. According to Bock, exodus is a pattern image for salvation and that Jesus recapitulates Israel's history (273).

49. C. H. Wright, *Knowing Jesus through the Old Testament* (Downers Grove: IVP, 1992), 55.

50. Gundry, *Matthew*, 34.

of Matthew.⁵¹ For Gundry, Matthew's fulfillment-quotations usually refer backward to events that had already taken place in the narrative, but this "quotation comes before the return from Egypt to Palestine."⁵² But Hagner argues that Gundry's hypothesis is "strained in view of the actual content of the quotation."⁵³ Hagner reasons that the fulfillment quotation, although it belongs properly at the end of 2:21, anticipates the narrative of Herod's death and Joseph's return to the land of Israel,⁵⁴ a view also shared by Davies and Allison.⁵⁵

Differing from Gundry and Kaiser, this researcher believes that geography is crucial for Matthew in chapter 2 and the rest of the book. In this chapter Matthew mentions seven geographical locations, namely, Jerusalem, Bethlehem, Egypt, Rama, Nazareth, Judea, and Galilee. Apart from Jerusalem and Judea, the rest fulfill Scripture. Therefore, one suggests rather that emphasis falls on geographical locations, albeit the sonship of Jesus is equally important. The emphasis on Egypt as a geographical location is suggested by the flight into Egypt and return from it. The exodus typology appears complete in the life of Jesus just as Israel also had to "flee" into Egypt because of famine in Canaan. Having been preserved for about four hundred years, she comes out of it by God's powerful hand into the land of Canaan again.⁵⁶ Therefore, "in Jesus the exodus from Egypt is

---

51. Kaiser, *The Uses of the Old Testament in the New*, 51.
52. Gundry, *Matthew*, 34.
53. Hagner, *Matthew 1–13*, 36. See also Nolland, *The Gospel of Matthew*, 122.
54. Hagner, *Matthew 1–13*, 36.
55. Davies and Allison, *A Critical and Exegetical Commentary*, 1.261.
56. Those who follow this typological approach and believe that Matthew cannot be charged "with an inept hermeneutical method" nor as "naively oblivious" of the meaning of the the text but follows a common practice of ancient Jewish sources concerned with eschatological matters for which the redemption from Egypt is a type for the messianic redemption and the prospect of a new exodus, indicating that before the consummation there will be another exodus followed by another return include Allison, *The New Moses*, 141, and France, *Matthew*, 86. According to France, "Hosea's words are not a prediction, but an account of Israel's origin. Matthew's quotation thus depends for its validity on the recognition of Jesus as the true Israel, a typological theme found elsewhere in the New Testament, and most obviously paralleled in Matthew by Jesus' use of Israel-texts in the wilderness [in chapter 4], there too it is as God's son that Jesus is equated with Israel (86).

repeated and completed."[57] But Jesus delivers his people from the bondage of sin (1:21).

From exodus motif we will explore the significance of the Torah in Matthew's concept of mission.

3.2.2 The *Torah*

The issues surrounding the Torah were highlighted in chapter 2, precisely as relating to the mission of Jesus and the identity of Israel as a nation. We noted that the Gospel of Matthew is replete with references to the Torah (11:3, 9; 12:1–8; 19:1–9; 22:34–40). But this study is limited to 5:17–20 as a representative of Jesus' attitude toward the Torah.[58] Jesus' teaching on the Torah is set on a mountain[59] (5:1–2; cf. Mark 3:13; Luke 6:17a). Luke puts the setting "on a level place," having prayed all night on a mountain before calling his disciples in the morning. Matthew's mountain corresponds with Mark's mountain (Mark 3:13), except that Mark's mountain is the mountain on which Jesus called the twelve apostles, not a mountain of Beatitudes. Matthew adds "and seeing the crowds" (Ἰδὼν δὲ τοὺς ὄχλους) to give room for the application of Jesus' teaching on the law to the universal church.[60]

---

57. Ulrich Luz, *Matthew 1–7: A Commentary*, trans. W. Linss (Edinburgh: T & T Clark, 1990), 146. By extension, Matt 2:15 draws a parallel between the events in chapter 2 and what "unfolded long ago in Egypt" (Allison, *The New Moses*, 141). Since Matthew focuses so much on redemptive history, the typological approach to the text of 2:15 appears more logical as Jesus fulfills "biblical-historical patterns and prophetic predictions with their ultimate significance" (Turner, *Matthew*, 91).

58. Jesus' attitude toward the Torah is "another focal point of current scholarship" because it speaks about Matthew's relationship to Judaism (Senior, *What are they saying about Matthew?* 62)

59. The writer examines the mountain motif in the section of typology in this chapter and the next. Allison sees Jesus on the mountain as the new Moses who "gives commentary on the decaloque, the Law of the Covenant, thus giving it its definitive and fullest meaning" (see Allison, *The New Moses*, 172). Similarly, Michael P. Knowles draws interesting parallels between the Beatitudes of Matt 5 and Isa 61 (LXX) and concludes that Jesus fashions his ministry according to prophetic expectations, see Michael P. Knowles, "Scripture, History, Messiah: Scriptural Fulfillment and the Fullness of Time in Matthew's Gospel," in *Hearing the Old Testament in the New Testament*, ed. Stanley E. Porter (Grand Rapids: Eerdmans, 2006): 67–68.

60. Gundry, *Matthew*, 65. A typological parallel is drawn between Jesus and Moses (Gundry, *Matthew*, 65 and Nolland, *The Gospel of Matthew*, 192). It is believed to be both an allusion of giving the law at Mount Sinai and "the Zion eschatology where the people of Israel

It is argued here that Matthew 5:17–20 (cf. Luke 16:16–17) is a key[61] to Jesus' relation to the law.[62] In its literary context, Jesus begins his ministry in Galilee as fulfillment of prophecy (4:12–17). He preached, he called out his first disciples, he taught, he healed, and he drove out demons (4:17–24). A large crowd from Galilee, the Decapolis, Jerusalem, Judea, and the region across the Jordan came to him. Seeing the crowd, he went up on a mountain and sat down. Then his disciples came to him, and he began to teach them. The context shows a wider audience is in view here (5:1; 7:28–29). After he spoke the words of the Beatitudes and declared that his followers are the salt and the light of the world, Jesus makes his "thesis statement"[63] in 5:17–20 for what follows. In 5:17 Jesus states: "Do not (Μὴ νομίσητε) that I came to abolish the law or the prophets; I did not come to abolish but to fulfill (πληρῶσαι) [them]" (translation mine). In this "thesis statement" he declares his mission as one who did not come to abolish the law, but to fulfill it.[64] He regarded himself as one who had come

---

will gather at the mountain of Yahweh to be reconstituted afresh as the people of God" (Nolland, *The Gospel of Matthew*, 192–193). This typological mountain motif is taken up in the last subheading of this chapter and in chapter 4.

61. Élian Cuvillier says the passage is central, "not only with the Sermon on the Mount, but more widely in the Gospel as a whole. It is, indeed, Jesus' very first declaration about the meaning of his coming (v.17: ἦλθον)". See Élian Cuvillier, "Torah Observance and Radicalization in the First Gospel; Matthew and the First-Century Judaism: A Contribution to the Debate," *NTS* (2009): 148.

62. Many regard the passage as representing the debate between factions in the church; namely, between those who uphold the law and those who think that the law has been abolished. See J. Zumstein, *La Condition du Croyant dans l'Evangile selon Matthieu* (Fribourg: Editions Universitaires/Göttingen: Vandenhoeck & Ruprecht, 1977), 171–200; Klyne Snodgrass, "Matthew and the Law," in *Treasures New and Old*, 101–02. Snodgrass also says that the text is the most important and the most difficult to treat because of the issues it raises. These issues include an understanding of the views of the law in Judaism and the diversity of its application; the question of whether it is permissible to treat Matthew in light of what is known about other discussions of law in the NT; a determination of what one may conclude from silence; the character of Matthew's community; interpreting what Matthew means by "law and prophets"; the question of whether Matthew presents Jesus as abrogating the law; the issue of antithesis; the role of the love command; understanding 23:2–3, 23 and 24:20 and the detailed observation of the law; and the kind of author/theologian Matthew was: one who carefully crafted his document or sloppy and inconsistent writer? (101–105).

63. Keener, *A Commentary on the Gospel of Matthew*, 175.

64. For Jesus' expression of positive relationship between him and Moses, see Celia M. Deutsch, *Lady Wisdom, Jesus, and the Sages: Metaphor and Social Context in Matthew's Gospel* (Harrisburg: Trinity Press International, 1996), 96; Davies and Allison, *Matthew*, 72.

to fulfill (πληρῶσαι) the law. For Matthew both the prophets and the law promised what was to come. Therefore Jesus fulfills the hopes of prophets and the Scriptures.[65] But how does Jesus fulfill the law and the prophets? This has generated heated scholarly discussion, especially in light of what some scholars consider the antithesis in 5:21–48.[66] This writer believes that the correct understanding of Matthew 5:21–48 as either antithesis or not, lies in 5:17–20. Jesus knew that some of his hearers would construe his teaching as one that opposes the Torah. He anticipates such objections and responds to them by his "thesis statement" that he had not come to abolish but to fulfill the Torah. The issue here is the meaning of πληρῶσαι and how this connects with the redemptive mission of Jesus. What Jesus says might be interpreted to mean that he had come to carry out the law's demands and as such to complete it.[67] It may also mean that he had come to give a fuller and true meaning of the law. In this sense, the perceived antithesis may be said to have been properly directed against the rabbinic interpretation, and not against the Mosaic Law.[68] And if "all the Prophets and the Law prophesied until John" (11:13), this may be interpreted to mean that all the components of the law prefigure Christ.[69] It is in this sense that the

---

According to Davies and Allison, "Jesus may well have wished to defend his loyalty to the *Torah* against those who made him out to be an antinomian" (Davies and Allison, *A Critical and Exegetical Commentary*, 1.482).

65. For the theme of fulfillment in Matthew with emphasis on πληρῶσαι and formulae quotations, see H. Frankemölle, *Jahweh-Bund und Kirche: Studien zur Form- und Traditionsgeschichte des "Evangeliums" nach Mattäus* (Münster: Aschendorff, 1984), 388; W. Rothfuchs, *Die Erfüllungszitate des Mattäus-Evangeliums* (Stuttgart: Kohlhammer, 1969). See also Senior and Stuhlmueller, *The Biblical Foundations for Mission*, 241.

66. Meier, *Law and History in Matthew's Gospel*, 1; Richard S. McConnel, "Law and Prophecy in Matthew's Gospel: The Authority and Use of the Old Testament in the Gospel of St. Matthew," (a doctoral dissertation submitted to the University of Basel, Basel: Friedrich Reinhart Kommissionsverlag, 1969), 41. Levine, however, thinks that the recurrent phrase "but I say to you" is not to be regarded as antithesis but "intensification" because calling these passages antitheses implies that Jesus opposes the law, "and, because congregants will associate Mosaic Law with 'the Jews'" (Levine, "Matthew and Anti-Judaism," 410).

67. France, *The Gospel of Matthew*, 183.

68. See McConnel, "Law and Prophecy in Matthew's Gospel," 44.

69. See Poythress, *The Shadow of Christ in the Law of Moses*. He follows a christocentric interpretation of the OT Law and the entire OT. He sees the OT as "a witness, foreshadowing, anticipation, and promise of salvation as it has now been accomplished by the work of the triune God in Jesus Christ Incarnate" (285).

Torah is "provisional" and not God's final word to his people, for it looked forward to a time of full realization through the coming of the Messiah.[70]

Therefore, Jesus shows that his ministry is not in collision with the OT as some of his opponents might have begun reasoning out.[71] The Torah regulated Jewish life and practice, and was therefore central. Its several functions include a constant reminder of the work of God as Creator in Genesis; a reminder about the holiness of God as stated explicitly in Leviticus 19:2 and implied through the various ceremonial laws; a constant pointer back to the redemptive work of God in the land of Egypt;[72] and, finally, it looked forward to the fulfillment in Christ Jesus.[73] Therefore, instead of setting aside the law and the prophets, Jesus brings it to fulfillment. Jesus did not come to abolish the Torah because it stands forever (Matt 5:18). The ἕως ἂν παρέλθῃ ὁ οὐρανὸς καὶ ἡ γῆ, expresses the enduring nature of the Torah.[74] This enduring nature of the Torah is underscored by Jesus' use of the clause ἀμὴν γὰρ λέγω ὑμῖν occurring several times in the gospel. To stress that the law must be accomplished and no aspect of it may pass away (ἰῶτα ἓν ἢ μία κεραία οὐ μὴ παρέλθῃ ἀπὸ τοῦ νόμου), "emphasis

---

70. France, *The Gospel of Matthew*, 181. Similarly, Davies and Allison believe that among the various meanings of "fulfill" (such as adding to the laws of the OT, to obey, bringing the law to perfection with a new law of his own, Jesus enabling others to keep the law, Jesus reducing the law to love), the fulfillment Jesus speaks about is eschatological: "Jesus does not abolish the Torah but, on the contrary, fulfill its prophecies" (Davies and Allison, *Matthew*, 72).

71. Wallace points out that Matt 5:17 is a summary of the views of Jesus' opponents (Wallace, *Greek Grammar Beyond the Basics*, 457). See Hendriksen, *Matthew*, 288; France, *The Gospel of Matthew*, 181. Although to this point in the gospel no such opposition is mentioned. Instead the gap is filled by those who postulate competing groups in early Christianity like the conservative (Palestinian) communities and the antinomian (Hellenistic) Christians (see Nolland, *The Gospel of Matthew*, 217 and Meier, *Law and History in Matthew's Gospel*, 55). The assumption is that at the time Matthew was writing, these antinomian Christian leaders were giving the impression that the law was abolished by Christ. This is suggested by the use of καταλῦσαι which implies a systematic destruction or dismantling of a building or institution (France, *The Gospel of Matthew*, 182).

72. This salvific work is a recurring theme in the Torah, the Prophets and the Psalms. Israel is reminded that God wrought deliverance for it and set it apart for himself.

73. See Poythress, *The Shadow of Christ*, 98.

74. 2 Bar 4:1–4 expresses the enduring nature of the law and the blessedness of those who live by it. Pss 93:5; 119:144, 160 also affirm that the law endures forever. For clauses introduced by ἕως depending on verb of future time, see Burton, *Syntax of the Moods and Tenses in New Testament Greek*, 127.

falls on the authority of Scripture down to the details of its wording."[75] For the ἰῶτα and the κεραία are regarded, in Jesus' usage, as metaphors for inconsequential parts of the law.[76] Matthew suggests that his hearers cannot choose for themselves which laws they wish to obey as of greater significance, and that the entire law has eternal significance.

This, then, is followed by the caveat and encouragement in Matthew 5:19. Matthew warns that punishment awaits every teacher of the law who undermines any aspect of the law. He will be called least (ἐλάχιστος) in the kingdom of heaven. The Qumran community has similar teaching. In its community rule, "anyone of them who breaks one word of the Law of Moses impertinently or through carelessness will be vanished from the community council and shall not go back again; none of the men of holiness should associate with his goods or his advice on any matter" (IQS VIII 21).[77] The difference is that Jesus speaks about the kingdom of heaven, while the Qumran community emphasizes immediate excommunication from the community. The one who upholds the importance of every part of the law is rewarded with greatness, for he will be great (μέγας) in the kingdom of heaven.

In 5:20, Jesus demands greater righteousness (δικαιοσύνη)[78] from his followers. The Torah forbids murder, but Jesus forbids anger. Jesus seems to be teaching that the act of murder is preceded by anger (5:21–26). And while the Torah forbids adultery, Jesus condemns adulterous thought, to show that adultery begins in the heart (5:27–30). In the Torah Moses permitted divorce, but Jesus restricts this permission (5:31–32). The love for

---

75. Gundry, *Matthew*, 80.

76. Meier, *Law and History in Matthew's Gospel*, 51.

77. Martínez, *The Dead Sea Scrolls Translated*, 13. Similarly, the Qumran community have Beatitudes on those who obey the law (4Q525 [4QBéat]). It says in part, "Blessed are those who adhere to his laws, and do not adhere to perverted paths" (Martínez, *The Dead Sea Scrolls Translated*, 395).

78. Matthew's use of the term (7 times: Matt 3:15; 5:6, 10, 20; 6:1, 33; 21:32 as against Mark who does not use it and Luke's 1 time [Luke 1:75]) shows Matthew's emphasis of the theme of righteousness. See Michael H. Burer, "Narrative Genre: Studying the Story," in *Interpreting the New Testament Text*, 213. But Burer does not include the adjective form δίκαιος in Matt 1:19 which brings the count to 8 times.

neighbor is realized fully by requirement of love for enemy (5:38–48). The full intent of the Torah is therefore realized in the teaching of Jesus.[79]

The theological and missional significance of the text is that discipleship demands total obedience and commitment to Jesus and his teaching through heart transformation. Matthew also teaches that without a transformed heart no one will be saved (Matt 5:8). For "despite their commitment to Scripture, religious people without transformed hearts will have no place in the kingdom."[80] He equally teaches that righteousness that leads to salvation must surpass that of the Pharisees and teachers of the law.

What the Torah means for Matthew's universal church is taken up in the next chapter. Meanwhile, the next discussion centers on the significance given to the Davidic king in the Gospel of Matthew. The discussion focuses on how Jesus fulfills the Davidic covenant in the OT.

3.2.3 The Davidic Shepherd-King

The theme of the Davidic shepherd king was briefly discussed in chapter 2, especially in the light of first-century restoration hopes of the Jews. It is noteworthy that prominence is given to "son of David" in the Gospel of Matthew than the other gospels.[81] But how does Jesus fulfill the Davidic covenant in this gospel? Not only does the genealogy link Jesus with David, but also there are significant passages that explicitly teach that Jesus is the expected Davidic shepherd-king from the OT perspective. These include Matthew 2:1–12; 21:1–11; 26:31 (cf. Luke 1:32; John 1:49[82]). Matthew 26:31 appears as an inclusio on the shepherd motif. Jesus is born as shepherd king (Matt 2:6). He sees the people of Israel as sheep without a shepherd (Matt 9:36). Now he lays down his life for the sheep (cf. John 10:10). This too happens in fulfillment of the prophecy of Zechariah 13:7.[83]

---

79. According to Gundry, Jesus carries out the tendencies of the law to their radical end. He does not deny the law, but perfect it (Gundry, *Matthew*, 7).

80. Keener, *A Commentary on the Gospel of Matthew*, 176.

81. D. R. Bauer, "Son of David," in *Dictionary of Jesus and the Gospels*, 768. The meaning of this title has been treated in chapter 2 and needs no further comments here.

82. From the angelic announcement to the confession of Nathanael, Jesus is the king of Israel.

83. That God's action lies at the base of Jesus' passion, see Gundry, *Matthew, 530,* citing W. G. Kümmel, *Promise and Fulfillment*, 2nd ed.; SBT 1/23 (London: SCM, 1961), 77–79.

Throughout his narrative, as we established in this discourse, "Matthew records history so as to bring out its theological significance to Scripture as prophecy-fulfillment."[84] This means that in Matthew's interpretive framework, history is divinely orchestrated and finds fullness of expression in the coming of the long-awaited Davidic shepherd-king and savior from sins. The writer limits the treatment to Matthew 2:1–12 as representative text for the concept of the Davidic shepherd-king. Matthew 21:1–11 is treated in the section dealing with Zion as geographical location in relation to Jesus as king. But we will first highlight Matthew's emphasis by looking at the OT text he cites in the following table.

Table 3: *The Shepherd-king Born in Bethlehem*

MT	LXX	NT
Mic 5:1 וְאַתָּה בֵּית־לֶחֶם אֶפְרָתָה צָעִיר לִהְיוֹת בְּאַלְפֵי יְהוּדָה מִמְּךָ לִי יֵצֵא לִהְיוֹת מוֹשֵׁל בְּיִשְׂרָאֵל וּמוֹצָאֹתָיו מִקֶּדֶם מִימֵי עוֹלָם׃	Mic 5:1 καὶ σὺ Βηθλεεμ οἶκος τοῦ Εφραθα ὀλιγοστὸς εἶ τοῦ εἶναι ἐν χιλιάσιν Ιουδα ἐκ σοῦ μοι ἐξελεύσεται τοῦ εἶναι εἰς ἄρχοντα ἐν τῷ Ισραηλ καὶ αἱ ἔξοδοι αὐτοῦ ἀπ' ἀρχῆς ἐξ ἡμερῶν αἰῶνος	Matt 2:6 Καὶ σὺ Βηθλέεμ, γῆ Ἰούδα, οὐδαμῶς ἐλαχίστη εἶ ἐν τοῖς ἡγεμόσιν Ἰούδα· ἐκ σοῦ γὰρ ἐξελεύσεται ἡγούμενος, ὅστις ποιμανεῖ τὸν λαόν μου τὸν Ἰσραήλ.
"But you, Bethlehem Ephrathah, though you are small among the clans of Judah, out of you will come for me one who will be ruler over Israel, whose origins are from of old, from ancient times."	**"But you, Bethlehem Ephrathah, though you are small among the clans of Judah,** out of you will come for me one who will be ruler over Israel, whose origins are from of old, from ancient times."	**"'But you, Bethlehem, in the land of Judah, are by no means least among the rulers of Judah**; for out of you will come a ruler who will be the shepherd of my people Israel.'"

In treating Matthew 2:1–12, the exegetical analysis is limited to verses 5–6 while the rest of the verses serves as background of the discussion.

---

84. Carson, "Matthew," 11.

Unlike Luke (2:1–7), Matthew omits some of the details concerning the birth of Jesus. Yet Matthew 2:1 connects well with the last pericope that ends with Jesus who had been born in fulfillment of prophecy. He is born in Bethlehem in Judea, the city of David. He is of the royal blood, for the angel had earlier called Joseph the son of David (2:20). This comes as fulfillment of Micah's prophecy.[85] Matthew departs from both the MT and the LXX in his citation as highlighted above. "Bethlehem Ephrathah" is changed to "Bethlehem, land of Judah."[86] Davies and Allison think that Matthew is interpreting Micah rather than quoting him. As they suggest, "The text has been altered by Matthew in order to make it serve his ends."[87] Gleason L. Archer and Gregory Chirichigno suggest that the mention of γῆ Ἰούδα by Matthew is to clarify which of the two Bethlehems is intended.[88] The second alteration of the original rendering of the text is Matthew's οὐδαμῶς ἐλαχίστη εἶ instead of the LXX's ὀλιγοστὸς εἶ τοῦ εἶναι. Matthew suggests that this town is of great significance regardless of its size.[89] Finally, Matthew changes the MT's בְּאַלְפֵי ("among thousand") and the LXX's χιλιάσιν to ἡγούμενος. He changes the "thousands" of the MT and LXX to provide the best possible meaning that fits his own context.[90]

A few points are significant in Matthew 2:5–6. First, Matthew alludes to both Micah 5:2 and 2 Samuel 5:2 in order to portray Jesus as leader and shepherd of his people like his father David. As we noted in chapter

---

85. Some manuscripts add "Isaiah" to διὰ τοῦ προφήτου·to read "through Isaiah the prophet." Bruce M. Metzger explains: "Not content with merely the mention of τοῦ προφήτου several witnesses (4 syr^hmg (ms) cop^boms) add Μιχαίου, and it^a reads *per Esiam prophetam dicentem* ("through Isaiah the prophet saying")" See Bruce M. Metzger, *A Textual Commentary on the Greek New Testament*, 2nd ed. (Stuttgart: Deutsche Bibelgesellschaft/German Bible Society, 1994), 8.

86. According to R. T. France, the mention of Judah in the text (2x) reinforces the fact that Jesus is from the royal tribe (see R. T. France, "The Formula-Quotations of Matthew 2 and the Problem of Communication," in *The Right Doctrine from the Wrong Texts? Essays on the Use of the Old Testament in the New*, ed. G. K. Beale (Grand Rapids: Baker Academic, 1994), 124.

87. Davies and Allison, *A Critical and Exegetical Commentary*, 1.242.

88. Gleason L. Archer and Gregory Chirichigno, *Old Testament Quotations in the New Testament* (Chicago: Moody Press, 1983), 157.

89. Blomberg, *Matthew*, 64.

90. Archer and Chirichigno, *Old Testament Quotations in the New*, 157; see also Blomberg, "Matthew," in *Commentary on the New Testament Use of the Old Testament*, 6.

2, Israel is like a sheep without a shepherd (Matt 9:36). Jesus is born to fill the role of a shepherd-king. Second, Matthew shows that the birth of Jesus in Bethlehem is a fulfillment of prophecy. Matthew indicates that the chief priests and teachers of the law are aware of the prophecy concerning the birthplace of this new born king of the Jews. The reason is that their response, "in Bethlehem in Judea," is immediately followed by οὕτως γὰρ γέγραπται διὰ τοῦ προφήτου and the quotation of the prophecy of Micah 5:2. Matthew's theological viewpoint is that this geographical location, Bethlehem, fulfills God's plan concerning the Davidic shepherd-king. He begins by elucidating Matthew 1:1, giving the meaning of "Jesus Christ the son of David." Like his father David, Jesus assumes the role of a shepherd of τὸν λαόν μου τὸν Ἰσραήλ. He saves them from their sins in 1:21. He now shepherds them. This Davidic shepherd-king motif runs throughout the narrative.

Third, when Matthew 2:6 is treated along with other passages such as 12:22–23; 21:4–9, Matthew gives the impression that there was widespread expectation of the coming of a Davidic king. This hope is expressed in the *Pss. of Sol.* 17:4, 21, 26–28. Written about the first century BCE, the writer of that psalm expresses this hope thus:

> Lord, you chose David to be king over Israel, and swore to him about his descendants forever, that his kingdom should not fail before you . . . See, Lord, and raise up for them their king, the Son of David, to rule over your servant Israel in the time known to you, O God. . . . He will gather a holy people whom he will lead in righteousness. . . . He will distribute them upon the land according to their tribes.[91]

Similarly, the Qumran community interprets Genesis 49:10 in the *Pesher* on Genesis (4Q252 5:1–7) as the promise of God to the community concerning the Davidic Messiah.[92] We will explore this further here and in

---

91. Evans, "Jesus and the Continuing Exile of Israel, 88. See also *Pss. of Sol.* 17:44 on the blessedness of those who are born in the time of the expected Davidic king.
92. Their interpretation is as follows: "(1 Gen 4:9:10) A sovereign shall [not] be removed from the tribe of Judah. While Israel has dominion, (2) there will [not] lack someone who

the section of exile and restoration. For Matthew, then, the numerous OT promises of an heir who would sit on the throne of his father David and the expectation of the Jews concerning this figure, find fulfillment in Jesus (cf. Luke 1:32).

Fourth, Matthew places considerable significance on Bethlehem as noted above. The response of the chief priests and the teachers of the law to Herod on the question of the birthplace of ὁ τεχθεὶς βασιλεὺς τῶν Ἰουδαίων is "in Bethlehem in Judea" (2:4–5). The emphasis on Bethlehem is treated in 2:6 in the textual analysis. Matthew reconstructs the text of Micah 5:2. He renders the LXX's ὀλιγοστὸς εἶ τοῦ εἶναι ἐν χιλιάσιν Ιουδα ("*though you are small* among the clans of Judah") as οὐδαμῶς ἐλαχίστη εἶ ἐν τοῖς ἡγεμόσιν Ἰούδα ("*you are by no means least* among the rulers of Judah"). Matthew de-emphasizes the geographical size of Bethlehem and magnifies its importance for what Bethlehem accomplishes in Judah. It is from Bethlehem that a ruler, the shepherd of Israel, would come.

But what was Micah's context? From Micah 4:1–13 the prophet presents several related themes. These include Zion's future glory when the mountain of the Lord's temple will become prominent among all mountains;[93] many nations that will come to Israel and learn the word of the Lord from Jerusalem (4:1–5); Yahweh's restoration of the exiled remnant and his reign on Mount Zion (4:6–8); and the distress caused by Babylonian invasion and the eventual deliverance of the nation Israel (4:9–13). The Lord plans salvation for his people, yet they do not know his thoughts or plans. Although Micah 5:1 presents Jerusalem as a city that the enemy has laid waste and Israel's ruler struck by the enemy, Micah 5:2 goes back to the thoughts and plans of the Lord. God's plan is to raise a ruler for Israel who "will stand and shepherd his flock in the strength of the Lord, in the majesty of the name of the Lord" (5:4). It is in his shepherding care that

---

sits on the throne of David. For the 'staff' is the covenant of royalty, (3) [the thou]sands of Israel are 'the feet.' Until the messiah of justice comes, the branch (4) of David. For to him and his discendants has been given the covenant of royalty over his people for all everlasting generations, which (5) he has observed . . . the Law with the men of the Community, for (6) . . . it is the assembly of the men of . . . . See C. Marvin Pate, *Communities of the Last Days: The Dead Sea Scrolls, the New Testament and the Story of Israel* (Downers Grove: IVP, 2000). 110.

93. Cf. *Pss. of Sol.* 11:1–4

Israel will live securely. But the greatness of this king reaches to the ends of the earth and he becomes their peace.

We will now examine the connection between Jesus and the Davidic king. For one of the historical events in the life of Israel that is interpreted along God's redemptive acts is the institution of the Davidic kingdom.[94] David became God's anointed servant and son (1 Sam 16:12–13; 2 Sam 2:4, 7; 3:39; 5:3, 17; 12:7; 1 Kgs 1:34, 39, 45; 5:1; Ps 89:20, 38, 51; 130:10, 17). This son is eventually associated with the "One whom the God of heaven would install as his righteous king in Zion as ruler over all the earth and nations (Ps 2:7), the Son of the Holy One and whose name is unknown."[95] Matthew (1:1) links this messianic promise with the coming of Jesus. He emphasizes this royal Davidic messiahship more than all the NT writers.[96] Jesus is of the lineage of David (1:1–17) as an adopted son of Joseph.[97] And Jesus is "the Anointed One, Israel's long-awaited king."[98]

---

94. A kingdom is a domain, a physical territory, a realm in which a king exercises his dominion over a particular group of people who share a certain kind of identity. The Davidic kingdom was marked by geographical boundaries and with the people of Israel as the subjects of that kingdom. But as this study unfolds, the promised kingdom to the house of David is interpreted in Matthew as *reign* in which God rules in the lives of those who come to Jesus by faith, and unlike the Davidic kingdom, is not characterized by geographical or racial boundaries. There is therefore a transformation from the physical realm to a spiritual kingdom.

95. Kaiser, *The Use of the Old Testament in the New*, 49. The designation "my son" soon became a technical term applied either collectively to the nation Israel "as the object of God's love and election or specifically to that final representative person who was to come in Christ" (49).

96. Verseput, "The Davidic Messiah and Matthew's Jewish Christianity," 102. In Luke 1:31–33 the angel of the Lord declares specifically that Jesus would sit on the throne of his father David. He is the son of David and king of the Jews in Matthew. Against the background of those who argue that the royal Davidic messiahship in the Gospel of Matthew is ultimately of Christian derivative as Matthew's version of Mark 10:47–48, Verseput posits that the theme of royal Davidic king in Matthew has Jewish origins and not entirely Christian formulation (103). But U. Luz, "Eine thetische Skizze der matthäischen Christologie," *Anfänge der Christologie: FS für F. Hahn* (ed. C. Breytenbach and H. Paulsen; Göttingen: Vandenhoeck & Ruprecht, 1991), 221–235; I. Broer, "Versuch zur Christologie des ersten Evangeliums," *The Four Gospels 1992: FS F. Neirynck* (ed. F. Van Seybroeck et al.; Leuven: University Press, 1992), 2.125–82 believe that the concept is of Christian derivative.

97. This *Son of David* is the key christological category in the Gospel of Matthew (Bauer, "Son of David," in *Dictionary of Jesus and the Gospels*, 811).

98. Jack Dean Kingsbury, *Gospel Interpretation: Narrative-Critical & Social-Scientific Approaches*, ed. Jack Dean Kingsbury (Harrisburg: Trinity International Press, 1997), 16. According to D. E. Aune, T. J. Geddert, and C. A. Evans, messianism in the Second Temple period could be classified into two main categories: the restorative and utopian messianism.

As *the* Son of David he qualifies as the Messiah king whom God sent to the house of Israel to bring salvation and healing from all their diseases. He is referred to as the Son of David by those who needed healing from him (9:27; 15:22; 20:31). When he healed the demon possessed, the people wondered if he was the Son of David (12:23).[99] Similarly, when he rode on a donkey on his way to Jerusalem (and in the temple) the people called him Son of David (21:9; 15). And "the innocent Jesus dies as true king and son of God (Matt 26:57–27:54)."[100]

Theologically, as noted above, Matthew portrays the birth of Jesus as fulfilling the OT expectation of a shepherd-king who rules Israel in righteousness and justice. And this is supported by the geographical location of Bethlehem. On the missional import of the text, the pericope is centered on "the worship of Jesus by a vanguard of gentiles."[101] The shepherd-king comes for the salvation of the people of Israel, but the nations, represented by the magi, put their hope in him and come as the first to worship him.

Second Temple Jews who longed for restorative messianism were looking for the restoration of the Davidic monarchy which would bring about improvement and perfection of the world through development that could be attained naturally (*Pss. of Sol.* 17). On the other hand, the utopian messianism "anticipated a future era which would surpass everything previously known." Both groups, however, believe in a single Messiah king who would be sent by God in order to restore the fortunes of Israel. See D. E. Aune, T. J. Geddert, and C. A. Evans, "Apocalypticism," in *Dictionary of New Testament Background*, ed. Craig Evans and Stanley Porter (Downers Grove: IVP, 2000), 49.

99. C. H. Dodd says that the miracle stories of Jesus in Matt 11:5 correspond to "symbols which the prophets had used to depict the supernatural character of the Age to Come," (see Dodd, *Apostolic Preaching and Its Developments* [New York: Harper and Brothers Publishers, 1962], 86). See also Wayne Baxter, "Healing and the 'Son of David': Matthew's Warrant," *NovT* 48.1 (Leiden: Brill, 2006), 36–50; C. Burger, *Jesus als Davidssohn* (Göttingen: Vandenhoeck & Ruprecht, 1970).

100. John Paul Heil, *The Death and Resurrection of Jesus: A Narrative-Critical Reading of Matthew 26–28* (Minneapolis: Fortress Press, 1991), 57. He was crucified because the world could not comprehend a servant kingship that he manifested (Swartley, *Israel's Scripture Traditions*, 255).

101. Gundry, *Matthew*, 26. This is "to hint at the fact that gentiles would be drawn into his reign" (Carson, "Matthew," 11). They come from the east, mysteriously led by a star, to worship the newborn king of the Jews. Jesus is here portrayed as the born king of the Jews, perhaps to contrast him with Herod (Blomberg, "Matthew," in *Commentary on the New Testament Use of the Old Testament*, 7) who is of Idumean origin. The magi's inquiry about Jesus' birth challenges Herod's right to the throne. Similarly, "Matthew challenges prejudice that unjustly accommodates political power" (Keener, *A Commentary on the Gospel of Matthew*, 100) and that "God's redemptive purposes extend beyond the nation of Israel" (Turner, *Matthew*, 76).

We will return to the Magi from the East in chapter 4. Next in this discussion is the significance of the temple, also related to the kingship.

3.2.4 The Temple[102]

The issue of the cleansing of the temple as a sign of restoration has been referred to in chapter 2. We noted that Matthew cites OT passages in connection with the temple and in support of Jesus' action. As we examine further, Matthew's gospel is replete with references to the temple (4:5; 12:6; 17:24–26; 21:12–13; 23:16, 21, 35; 24:1; 26:61; 27:5, 40, 51). The text chosen for discussion here (as well as in chapter 4) is 21:12–13 because of its relevance as fulfillment of prophecy. The OT text Matthew cites needs closer examination from its textual background as follows:

Table 4: *The Temple as House of Prayer*

MT	LXX	NT
Isa 56:7 כִּי בֵיתִי בֵּית־תְּפִלָּה יִקָּרֵא לְכָל־הָעַמִּים׃	Isa 56:7 ὁ γὰρ οἶκός μου οἶκος προσευχῆς κληθήσεται πᾶσιν τοῖς ἔθνεσιν	Matt 21:13 καὶ λέγει αὐτοῖς, Γέγραπται, Ὁ οἶκός μου οἶκος προσευχῆς κληθήσεται, ὑμεῖς δὲ αὐτὸν ποιεῖτε σπήλαιον λῃστῶν.
"for my house will be called **a house of prayer for all nations** [to all the people]."	"for my house will be called **a house of prayer for all nations**."	"It is written," he said to them, "'My house will be called **a house of prayer**,' but you are making it a 'den of robbers.'"

---

102. For a comprehensive work on temple, see G. K. Beale's *The Temple and the Church's Mission: A biblical theology of the dwelling place of God,* ed. D. A. Carson, NSBT 17 (Downers Grove: IVP, 2004). Beale insightfully traces the temple motif in the Bible. He looks at the cosmic symbolism of temples in the OT and its purpose, its end-time purpose, the "already and not yet" fulfillment of the end-time temple in Christ in the Gospels, the inauguration of a new temple in Acts, the epistles of Paul, and the world-encompassing temple in Revelation.

In the quoted text Matthew follows the MT and the LXX. But unlike Mark 11:17, Matthew does not include the final phrase πᾶσιν τοῖς ἔθνεσιν. This omission follows Luke 19:46. Matthew, however, differs from Luke by using κληθήσεται ("shall be called") instead of Luke's ἔσται ("shall be"). The use of καλέω is almost exclusively Matthean. It is noteworthy that the LXX changes the MT's לְכָל־הָעַמִּים ("to all the people") to πᾶσιν τοῖς ἔθνεσιν ("for all the nations"). The LXX rendering is understood from the context of the entire chapter of Isaiah in which salvation is extended to foreigners who join themselves to the Lord, for they will not be excluded from God's people (Isa 56:3, 6). Why does Matthew omit לְכָל־הָעַמִּים (MT) and πᾶσιν τοῖς ἔθνεσιν (LXX)? According to Gundry, "Matthew may omit the gentiles because they are to become disciples and live as church members outside Palestine, not make pilgrimages to Jerusalem in order to pray in the temple."[103] Gundry's important observation will be discussed in chapter 4.

To understand Matthew 21:12–13, the significance of the temple needs to be stressed here. The temple is a symbolic representation of God's dwelling with his people.[104] Solomon's temple is called בֵּית יְהוָה (Ps 122:1; 116:19, MT) or הֵיכַל יְהוָה (2 Chr 8:1; Jer 7:4, MT).[105] It is essentially a place of prayer (2 Chr 6:14–40). According to Isaiah, the temple is a house

---

103. Gundry, *Matthew*, 413.

104. At the time of Jesus the temple in Jerusalem "was a significant element in the religious, social and political setting of Jesus' life and ministry" (M. O. Wise, "Temple," in *Dictionary of Jesus and the Gospels*, 769) and a focal point in Jewish national life (Wright, *The New Testament and the People of God*, 224). It was a symbol of holiness and purity within Judaism (Achtemeier, Green, and Thompson, *Introducing the New Testament,* 44). The temple was also closely associated with kingship in Israel (Swartley, *Israel's Scripture Traditions*, 154). Jon D. Levenson rightly observes that the three religious institutions of Israel—the Torah, the temple, and the kingship—are related (see Levenson, *Sinai and Zion: An Entry into the Jewish Bible* [New York: Harper Collins, 1985], 97–8). In 2 Sam 7:2–16 the dynasty and the temple are inextricably interwoven such that the temple is a royal sanctuary. And for the king to rule righteously, he must be guided by the Torah.

105. In Solomon's dedicatory speech, the temple was now seen as a place where God would dwell with his people forever (2 Chr 6:1–2). The promise to the house of David, cited as "a free composition integrating the choice of Judah and Jerusalem," also forms part of this dedicatory speech (6:4–6). See Raymond B. Dillard, *2 Chronicles,* Word Biblical Commentary, (Nashville: Nelson Reference and Electronic, 1987), 15.47. He says further, "For the Chronicler completing the temple does not exhaust the promises of God, but represents an incipient stage; Solomon praises God for fulfilling what he had spoken to David (6:14–15), and yet prays that God would keep his promise for the future (6:16–17). Cf. 6:7–11. A passage of this type makes it difficult to eliminate royalist/messianic hopes from the Chronicler's theology" (Dillard, *2 Chronicles,* 15.48).

of prayer for all nations, that is, the foreigners who bind themselves to the Lord to serve him (56:6 cf. 2 Chr 6:32, 33). These foreigners are brought to God's holy mountain and are given joy in the house of prayer. Matthew (21:13) says that Isaiah 56:3–7 is fulfilled; for Isaiah looked forward to the gathering of Israel[106] along with the nations to God's holy mountain. God will give them joy in his house of prayer.

What, then, does the cleansing of the temple by Jesus mean? The two major positions are that the cleansing is either a symbol of purification and restoration or judgment of the temple establishment. Keener thinks that Jesus' action could be a prophetic sign, "stressing the judgment against the temple establishment" as in Jeremiah 7, especially with Matthew writing probably after AD 70.[107] Sanders also reads Jesus' action as prophetic condemnation of the temple but stresses that, "destruction, in turn, looks toward restoration."[108] This "restoration" agrees with Jesus' positive attitude toward the temple. In this text Jesus not only drives out the traders from the temple, but he also teaches in it everyday (21:23; cf. Luke 19:47). He also pays the temple tax (17:24–27).[109] Jesus' attitude in cleansing the temple is rather similar to what is found in Luke 2:49 when he refers to the temple as his father's house. As suggested in chapter 2 of this work, this writer argues that Jesus' action is seen partly as a restoration of the purity of the temple. In 2 Maccabees 2:17, the time for the restoration of the kingdom and priesthood is envisaged. "God, who saved his entire

---

106. On this gathering of Israel, see *Pss. of Sol.* 11:1–4. The children of Israel come together from the east and the west and assemble together by the Lord.

107. See Keener, *A Commentary on the Gospel of Matthew*, 501.

108. Sanders, *Jesus and Judaism*, 71. For more discussion on this, see Craig A. Evans, "Jesus' Action in the Temple: Cleansing or Portent of Destruction?" *CBQ* 51 (1989): 237–270; idem., "From 'House of Prayer' to 'Cave of Robbers': Jesus' Prophetic Criticism of the Temple Establishment," in *The Quest for Content and Meaning: Studies in Biblical Intertextuality in Honor of James A. Sanders*, Biblical Interpretation Series 28, ed. C. A. Evans and S. Salmon (Leiden: Brill, 1997); J. Neusner, "Money-Changers in the Temple: The Mishnah's Explanation," *NTS* 35 (1989): 287–290.

109. Whether or not Jesus' action shows respect for the temple as an acknowledgment that it was a provisional place of atonement, given the creative way he paid the tax, see France, *The Gospel of Matthew*, 665–671; Nolland, *The Gospel of Matthew*, 721–729; Blomberg, *Matthew*, 269–271. Theologically, Jesus and his disciples' relationship to God as King are never dependent on the temple. It is in this regard that Jesus' entire public ministry is believed to be actual fulfillment of what the temple symbolized. See David E. Holwerda, *Jesus and Israel: One Covenant or Two?* (Grand Rapids: Eerdmans, 1995), 69.

people and restored the heritage to us all, will also restore the kingdom and priesthood and the sanctification." The restoration of the priesthood and sanctification are directly related to the temple cultus. Therefore, Jesus' action in the temple (Matt 21:12–23) symbolizes this restoration. Its cleansing shows that the οἶκος προσευχῆς has been corrupted[110] and has lost its essence in the life of the people.[111] Matthew seems to suggest that some kind of exploitation was taking place in the temple by his use of σπήλαιον λῃστῶν. According to Blomberg, σπήλαιον λῃστῶν "does not necessarily mean that all the merchants sold their goods at inflated prices, but it does suggest at least that Jesus considered many of them generally corrupt."[112] This exploitation and wickedness is denounced in Jeremiah 7:9–11. The one who comes to restore the kingdom of David also restores the temple to its rightful use. Matthew's citation of both Isaiah and Jeremiah is in order. Jesus' cleansing of the temple stands both as judgment against the corrupt practices that was taking place in it and the restoration of it to its original purpose—house of prayer. While Sanders' and Keener's views of judgment on temple establishment are convincing, the writer adds that Jesus seems to condemn the leaders and their unlawful practices rather than the temple itself as an institution.[113] Although the temple establishment is judged, the temple remains the house of prayer in Jesus' own words. Theologically,

---

110. B. Chilton, P. W. Comfort, and M. O. Wise believe that the cleansing of the temple indicates that "its present cultus is corrupt" (B. Chilton, P. W. Comfort, and M. O. Wise, "Temple, Jewish," in *Dictionary of New Testament Background*, ed. Craig A. Evans and Stanley E. Porter [Downers Grove: IVP, 1992], 1176).

111. It is believed that the cleansing occurred in the Court of the Gentiles, a place not considered holy by the Jews, signifying that in the eschatological era all the nations are gathered together in the worship of the one God. Holwerda, *Jesus and Israel*, 70. The problem with this, following Gundry's observation above, is that the nations need not come to Jerusalem to worship.

112. Blomberg, *Matthew*, 314. Or as Blomberg says, "if 'robbers' (*lēstai*) is given the meaning it most probably has in 26:55 and 27:38, 44 (*insurrectionist*), then Jesus may be accusing the leaders of having converted the temple into a 'nationalist stronghold'" (314–315). But beyond the given options, Jesus might have in mind "God's imminent judgment on the temple and the nation" (315).

113. Sanders' and Keener's position is probably based on the negative sayings attributed to Jesus concerning the destruction and rebuilding of the temple (Matt 26:61; 27:40; cf. Mark 14:57–58; John 2:18–22) and related texts (Matt 24:1–2, 15; Mark 13:2–3). But it seems that the cleansing of the temple displays Jesus' positive attitude toward it. Therefore, the judgment on the temple is for purification (Blomberg, *Matthew*, 314). Yet Chilton, Comfort, and Wise say, the negative pericopes about the temple "are all problematic, and

therefore, Jesus teaches that there is both continuity and discontinuity in the temple as an institution itself.

We will discuss further in chapter 4 the importance of the temple for the gentile mission. Now, the eschatological import of the temple leads to the discussion of the exile and restoration in the Gospel of Matthew.

3.2.5 The Exile and Restoration

The researcher briefly referred to the significance of the exile and restoration as a focal point in Israel's prophetic ministry in chapter 2. It was noted that the restoration is linked with the coming messiah.[114] The interest at this point is the frequent mention of τῆς μετοικεσίας Βαβυλῶνος in the genealogy as a chronological marker in the Gospel of Matthew 1:11, 12, 17. This mention of the μετοικεσία suggests to the reader that the exile is a significant event in the life of Israel and that it shaped Matthew's theology of the Messiah.[115] Matthew mentions the exile to Babylon but does not speak about a return. In 1:17 Matthew divides the generations into three periods that climax with the coming of Christ. By this Matthew suggests that "Jesus, as the 'Messiah' brings the return from captivity to its culmination and so restores Israel."[116]

It is argued, therefore, that exile and restoration are important in the section of Matthew 1:1–17.[117] Matthew connects Jesus Christ to David

---

their interpretation is often a function of a particular scholar's model for understanding the historical Jesus" (Chilton, Comfort, Wise, "Temple, Jewish," 1176).

114. The theme of exile and restoration needs to be understood in the light of all that has been discussed already about the new exodus, the fulfillment of the Torah by Jesus, the restoration of the temple, the role of Jesus as the Davidic king, and the fulfillment of all prophecies concerning Jesus (Matt 11:13). These themes taken together provide a solid ground for understanding the concept of restoration in Matthew.

115. Verseput, "The Davidic Messiah and Matthew's Jewish Christianity," 104. He says, "The taproot of Israel's future hope lay in the painful incongruity between belief and historical reality" (104).

116. Rollin G. Grams, "Some Geographical and Intertextual Dimensions Matthew's Mission Theology," ed. Rollin G. Gram et al., *Bible and Mission: A Conversation Between Biblical Studies and Missiology* (Germany: Neufeld Verrlag, 2008), 43.

117. According to Wright, Jesus's ministry is set according to deuteronomic framework. The genealogic record, and especially the unexpected focal point—the exile—is said to be special for Matthew because "most Jews of the second-temple period regarded themselves as still in exile, still suffering the results of Israel's age-old sin. Until the great day of redemption dawned, Israel was still 'in her sins,' still in need of rescue. The genealogy then says to

(1:1, 17) to demonstrate that the final restoration has now come through Jesus Christ the son of David. Moreover, the mention of the deportation to Babylon recollects Israel's period of national hopelessness and yearning for restoration through the coming of the Messiah.[118] For disobedience and rebellion, Israel had to endure the painful reality of suffering under the yoke of captivity instead of glory, prosperity, and peace exemplified by the Davidic kingdom. The prophets of Israel dwelled on the problem of sin, the exile, and eventual return.[119] But even after the return, "the continued dispersion of the Jews and the failure of history to bring about the vindication of Israel's divine election led to the conclusion that, at least in some sense, the affliction of the exile had not yet reached a proper end."[120] Hope for the final gathering of the exiles is expressed in *Targum of Isaiah*, which is traced to the first century. (See *Targum of Isaiah* 6:13; 8:18; 27:6; 28:2, 6, 13,19, 25; 35:6, 10; 42:7; 43:6, 14; 46:11; 51:11; 54:7, 15; 66:9;

Matthew's careful reader that the long story of Abraham's people will come to its fulfillment, its seventh seven, with a new David, who will rescue his people from their exile, that is 'save his people from their sins'" (Wright, *The New Testament and the People of God*, 386). As Wright points out, what follows in 1:18–21 is to be understood against this background.

118. According to Alfred Edersheim, the coming of of the Messiah "undoubtedly implied the restoration of Israel's kingdom, and, as a first part in it, the return of the dispersed", see Alfred Edersheim, *The Life and Times of Jesus the Messiah* (Peabody: Hendrickson Publishers, 1993), 53. Edersheim's perspective is shared by Verseput whose point is worth quoting at length: "The genealogy with which Matthew begins his work is certainly more than a pedantic effort to establish the royal legitimacy of the narrative's protagonist. The carefully ordered scheme of the generational sequence, which is reiterated by the concluding comment of 1:17, deliberately confronts the reader with the interruption of the Davidic dynasty caused by the Babylonian exile. The heirs of David, 'the king' (1:6) no longer sat on their ancestral throne due to the tragedy of 587/6 BCE which, according to Jewish consensus opinion, was brought by Israel's apostasy and sin. As Matthew represents the story, the people of Israel remained without a divinely appointed shepherd from the exile onward until the appearance of 'Jesus', who is the Christ'" (Verseput, "The Davidic Messiah and Matthew's Jewish Christianity," 108).

119. In *Targum of Isaiah* 53:8 the chastisement of exile and eventual restoration is captured thus: "From chastisements and punishment he will bring our exiles near" (Evans, "Jesus and the Continuing Exile of Israel, 89). This return is celebrated as God's new saving event. See Gerhard von Rad, *Old Testament Theology*, vol. 2, *The Theology of Israel's Prophetic Traditions*, trans. D. G. M. Stalker (London: SCM Press, 1965), 243. See also Robertson, *The Christ of the Prophets*, 453. According to Robertson, "exile and restoration provided the focal moment in history for Israel's prophetic ministry."

120. Verseput, "The Davidic Messiah and Matthew's Jewish Christianity," 104; VanGemeren, *The Progress of Redemption*, 284.

cf. *Targum of Jeremiah* 30:18; *Targum of Hosea* 2:2; 148; *Targum of Micah* 5:3).[121] This may also be found in in 2 Maccabees 2:17–18:

> It is God who saved his people, and has returned the inheritance to all, and the kingship and the priesthood and the consecration, as he promised through the law. We hope in God that he will soon have mercy on us and will gather us from everywhere under heaven into his holy place, for he has rescued us from great evils and has purified the place.[122]

According to 2 Maccabees 2:17–18, the work of restoration began through the Maccabean revolt which gave hope for a full return in the future. As such, several groups in Second Temple Judaism were persuaded that Israel did not fully recover from the exile "in the ways which God had promised."[123] Some of the Jewish sects interpreted this final restoration as applying only to the community of the devout as the defiled Abraham's descendants would suffer the wrath of God.[124] Yet "the basic contours of the messianic hope do not change much" in the Gospel of Matthew because "the First Evangelist appears to portray Jesus as the Davidic Messiah who, although unique in his filial submission to the cross, nevertheless

---

121. Evans, "Jesus and the Continuing Exile of Israel", 89. "The exile of Israel will come to an end when the Messiah appears, judges truly, enjoys victory in battle and returns the Jews in peace to their house" (89).

122. See also 2 Macc 1:27, 29; *Pss. of Sol.* 11:1–4.

123. Verseput, "The Davidic Messiah and Matthew's Jewish Christianity," 105. Cf. CD 1:3–7; 1 Enoch 85–90; 93:1–10; 91:11–17.

124. For instance, 4Q521 *Frag.* 2 *col.* II 1–14 says, 1"[for the heav]ens and the earth will listen to his Messiah, 2 [and all] that is in them will not turn away from the holy precepts. 3 Be encouraged, you who are seeking the Lord in his service! 4 Will you not, perhaps, encounter the Lord in it, all those who hope in their heart? 5 For the Lord will observe the devout and call the just by name, 6 and upon the poor he will place his spirit, and the faithful he will renew with his strength. 7 For he will honor the devout upon the throne of eternal royalty, 8 freeing prisoners, giving sight to the blind, straightening out the twisted. 9 Ever I shall cling to those who hope. In his mercy he will jud[ge], 10 and from no one shall the fruit of good [deeds] be delayed, 11 and the Lord will perform marvelous acts such as have not existed, just as he sa[id] 12 for he will heal the badly wounded and will make the dead live, he will proclaim good news to the meek 13 give lavishly [to the needy], lead the exiled and enrich the hungry. 14 [. . .] and all [. . .]." (The English translation is taken from Martínez, *The Dead Sea Scrolls Translated*, 394).

awakens traditional expectations of a divine visitation upon the oppressed and downtrodden laboring under the curses of the covenant."[125]

Theologically, the theme of restoration linked with the coming Messiah offered a "valid hermeneutical prism" for interpreting the Gospel of Matthew.[126] Therefore, "Jesus is a new David, the culmination of Israel's history, who will bring about an end to the exile."[127] It was Israel's sins that caused God to turn away from his chosen people, and now the Messiah would deliver them from their sins.[128]

The discussion of the theme of exile and restoration leads to prophetic ministry as one of the key OT perspectives that shaped Matthew's mission theology. This is discussed under prophetic ministry before John the Baptist and the ministry of John the Baptist.

3.3 Prophetic Ministry and Mission[129]

Matthew presents a period of prophetic preparation for the coming of the Messiah. To demonstrate the significance of this period of prophetic

---

125. Verseput, "The Davidic Messiah and Matthew's Jewish Christianity," 107. This hope is linked with the concept of a "new age" of salvation in a coming kingdom portrayed in the pre-exilic, the exilic, and the post-exilic prophets. Isaiah speaks frequently about the salvation of the people of God after judgment as in 1:24–26. Similarly, this kingdom was a common hope in Amos' day with popular expectation of success, blessing, prosperity, and victory over Israel's enemies as sign of a restored Davidic kingdom (Ladd, *The Presence of the Future*, 57). In Ezekiel (37:15–22; 48:30–34; cf. 36:10), Israel and Judah are united in a restored land with the reinstitution of the Davidic monarchy.

126. The majority of the Second Temple Jews "saw themselves as still in exile, at least in theological and spiritual terms" (Eloff, "From the Exile to the Christ," iii).

127. Stephen G. Dempster, *Dominion and Dynasty: A Theology of the Hebrew Bible,* ed. D. A. Carson, NSBT 15 (Downers Grove: IVP, 2003), 232.

128. This is the consensus understanding of the messianic role in which forgiveness of sins is part of the salvific purposes of God. Luke 1:76–79 is an allusion to Isa 9:1–2 just as in Matt 4:16. Restoration then means, generally speaking, that Israel would return to its land and would once more enjoy the promised blessings of peace, prosperity and justice under the leadership of a Davidic king—a Messiah king. For Matthew, this general notion has the added perception that the Messiah would not only save his people from their sins, but that he would also heal the sick, cast out evil spirits, raise the dead, and proclaim the good news of the kingdom to the poor.

129. For a general and good treatment of the origin and development of prophetism in Israel, see Robertson, *The Christ of the Prophets;* Walter Eichrodt; *Theology of the Old Testament,* vol. 1, trans. J. A. Baker (London: SCM Press, 1961); von Rad, *Old Testament*

preparation he says, "For all the Prophets and the Law prophesied until John" (11:13; cf. Luke 16:16).[130] A brief discussion of Matthew 11:12–13 is probably in order since it connects John and Jesus and the kingdom of God in the prophetic scheme. Verse 12 shows that "John is a transitional figure" and "stands shoulder to shoulder with Jesus in working for God in bringing in the coming of the kingdom."[131] Matthew (11:10; cf. Luke 7:27) supports the crucial role of John as a bridge by citing Malachi 3:1. And in Matthew 11:14 John is the Elijah of Malachi 4:5.[132] According to Matthew 17:11, the work of Elijah is restoration.[133] Matthew 11:13 links John with the prophets and the law and that prophetic activity points to a time of fulfillment which Matthew "is eager to identify as taking place in and through Jesus."[134] The pericope, then, shows the pivotal role of John who serves as Elijah (Mal 4:5–6) and at the same time "belongs to the period of fulfillment."[135] The aim of this section, therefore, is to provide an overview of how Jesus' life, death, and resurrection are presented as fulfillment of OT promise in the Gospel of Matthew. In this section the central

---

Theology; D. Aune, *Prophecy in Early Christianity and the Ancient Mediterranean World* (Grand Rapids: Eerdmans, 1983); J. Blenkinsopp, *A History Prophecy in Israel: From the Settlement in the Land to the Hellenistic Period* (Philadelphia: Westminster, 1983).

130. Here the days of John the Baptist are located in the past but is connected with the time when Jesus spoke.

131. Nolland, *The Gospel of Matthew*, 457. "The Law and the Prophets are until John; after John comes the time of the messianic salvation" (Ladd, *A Theology of the New Testament*, 123). But the kingdom is marked by both growth and opposition (Turner, *Matthew*, 294; Nolland, *The Gospel of Matthew*, 458; R. Steven Notley, "The Kingdom of Heaven Forcefully Advances," in *The Interpretation of Scripture in Early Judaism and Christianity: Studies in Language and Tradition*, ed. Craig A. Evans [London: T & T International, 2004], 279–311).

132. In John 1:21, 23 John the Baptist denies that he is Elijah. According to Luke (1:17), John the Baptist came in the spirit and power of Elijah. Walter C. Kaiser, Jr., explains, "even when it is clear that John only denied being Elijah in the popular misconceptions entertained by the people of John's day, John could be identified as Elijah only because the same Spirit and power that had energized Elijah had now fallen on him". See Walter C. Kaiser, Jr., *The Uses of the Old Testament in the New* (Chicago: Moody Press, 1985), 86.

133. Kaiser, Jr., says that this restoration includes restoration of Israel to their own land and "moral restoration of their inner man" (Kaiser, Jr., *The Uses of the Old Testament in the New*, 87).

134. Nolland, *The Gospel of Matthew*, 459.

135. Ibid.

issue of the relationship between the OT and the NT is treated in the light of Matthew's use of the OT, using Isaiah 7:14 as an example.

In Matthew's portrait, the prophets "pointed forward to the promised Deliverer."[136] Matthew picks up this understanding of what God had been doing in history through the prophets. Matthew uses the word προφητης more than any of the gospels.[137] He believes that Jesus' coming into the world, all the events of his life, his deeds and words, and his betrayal and death were the fulfillment of prophecy.[138] The ministry of the prophets is discussed broadly under the period of prophetic ministry before John the Baptist and the ministry of John the Baptist because Matthew suggests that these are the two periods that define prophet ministry regarding the life of Jesus (Matt 11:13).

3.3.1 Prophetic Ministry before John the Baptist

3.3.1.1 A Panoramic View of Promise-Fulfillment in Matthew

Before examining prophetic ministry prior to John the Baptist, it is important to tabulate some of Matthew's formal quotations concerning Jesus' mission in order to give a panoramic view of the subject.[139] But the purpose of this section is not to examine the individual passages here because most of them have been treated in the course of the study in the relevant sections; rather, the section provides a graphic view of Matthew's dependence on the OT prophetic ministry for his understanding of the mission of God. This underscores Matthew's view of prophetic ministry as a vehicle through which God spoke to his people and revealed his salvific scheme for

---

136. Hendriksen, *Matthew*, 120.
137. Harvey, "Mission in Matthew," 123. See 1:22; 2:15, 17, 23:4:14; 8:17; 13:35; 21:4; 26:56; 27:9. Matthew focuses on the OT prophets, mentioning some by name and quoting others without identifying their names (123).
138. It is noteworthy that Matthew mentions even the author of Ps 78 as a prophet in 13:35. Josephus also mentions that the events in Christ's life were "as the divine prophets had foretold concerning him," (*Antiquities,* XVIII, iii, 3).
139. For a comprehensive table of prophecy and fulfillment in the Gospel of Matthew that includes recitation, recontextualization, general reference, and echoes, see DeSilva, *An Introduction to the New Testament,* 247; Carson, "Matthew," 134–135.

mankind. The writer highlighted this vital area of mission for the Gospel of Matthew in chapter 2.

Table 5: *God sends the prophets regarding Jesus' mission*

TEXT	THEME	OT (Eng. Vers.)
1:22–23	The Birth of Jesus	Isa 7:14
2:6	The Birth of Jesus in Bethlehem	Mic 5:2
2:15	The Escape to Egypt	Hos 11:1
2:18	Slaughter of Infants	Jer 31:15
2:23	Jesus in Nazareth	Unidentified
3:3	John the Baptist's Ministry	Isa 40:3
4:15–16	Ministry in Galilee	Isa 9:1–2
8:17	Jesus' Healing Ministry	Isa 53:4
9:13	Jesus Calling Sinners	Hos 6:6
10:35	Hostility against the Disciples	Mic 7:6
11:10	John the Baptist Prepares Way	Mal 3:1
12:18–21	God's Anointed Servant	Isa 42:1–4
13:14–15, 35	Jesus' use of Parables	Isa 6:9
21:4, 5	Jesus Rides on a Donkey	Zech 9:9
21:42	The Rejected Cornerstone	Psa 118:22, 23
22:44	Jesus is Lord over David	Psa 110:10
26:24, 54	Jesus' Arrest and Death	Unspecified
26:31	The Shepherd Struck	Zech 13:7
27:9–10	Judas' Wages and Purchase of a Field	Zech 11:12–13

What the table demonstrates is that Jesus fulfills all the OT expectations of redemption as announced beforehand by the prophets. For although the OT prophets were God's spokespersons concerning issues of their time, they were also sent on mission as God's special messengers in the foretelling of his scheme of salvation as they were led by the Spirit of God.[140] Jesus states this both explicitly and implicitly. In Matthew 23:37 Jerusalem is described as "the one that kills the prophets and stones those sent to her."[141]

---

140. Cf. 2 Pet 1:20–21.
141. See also the parables of the vineyard (21:34–37) and the marriage feast (22:2–14).

Because the prophets were messengers of God, the one who receives them in the name of a prophet receives the prophet's reward (Matt 10:41). But "more prominent, however, is the eschatological component of the prophets' mission."[142] This prominence is illustrated by the number of times Matthew introduces quotations with fulfillment formulae (11 times),[143] many without any parallel in either Mark or Luke. Matthew also identifies both Jonah and Daniel as prophets (12:39; 24:15), a record that is absent in both Mark and Luke. "This special attention to the way in which Jesus' life and teaching relate to the OT suggests that Matthew saw the prophets' primary mission as one of proclaiming the promised Messiah."[144] As noted in chapter 2, not only did God send the prophets with the message of judgment, he also sent them with "the message of salvation and hope leading to repentance and fellowship." This salvation and hope would include the entire earth, as "people from far nations will worship Israel's God."[145]

3.3.1.2 The Use of the OT in the NT: Direct Prediction, Typology or Christological Readings

But the key issue is Matthew's interpretative method of applying the prophetic message to the life and ministry of Jesus. The central matter is "the relationship between the OT and the NT authors' intended meanings."[146] Five "orbiting questions" that surround the discussion include the following: the appropriateness of using *sensus plenior* in explaining the NT's use of the OT; the understanding of typology; the NT writers and the context of the OT passages cited; if the NT writers' use of the Jewish exegetical method explains the NT's use of the OT; and, finally, if we could "replicate the exegetical and hermeneutical approaches to the OT that we find in the

---

142. Harvey, "Mission in Matthew," 123.
143. These include 1:22; 2:5, 15, 17, 23; 4:14; 8:17; 12:17; 13:35; 21:4; 27:9.
144. Harvey, "Mission in Matthew," 124.
145. McDaniel, "Mission in the Old Testament," in *Mission in the New Testament,* 11. See Isa 66:19; 19:18–25.
146. Jonathan Lunde, "An Introduction to Central Questions in the New Testament use of the Old Testament," *Three Views on the New Testament use of the Old Testament,* eds. Stanley N. Gundry, Kenneth Berding, and Jonathan Lunde (Grand Rapids: Zondervan, 2008), 12.

writings of the NT."[147] Relevant to our discussion are the issues of *sensus plenior*, direct prediction, typology (treated further in a separate section), christological readings, and the context of the OT passages cited or alluded to by the NT writers. The writer limits himself to three views, although these are by no means the only ones. But, first, we will investigate the concept of *sensus plenior* because it is relevant to the discussion as we will see in Kaiser's viewpoint, although none of the authors surveyed here accepts it as valid way of explaining the NT's use of the OT.

The concept of *sensus plenior* ("the fuller sense") has its genesis and development in Roman Catholic scholarship. One of its prominent promoters, Raymond Brown, defined the concept thus: "The *sensus plenior* is that additional, deeper meaning, intended by God but not clearly intended by the human author, which is seen to exist in the words of the biblical text (or group of texts, or even a whole book) when they are studied in the light of further revelation or development in the understanding of revelation."[148]

This definition shows that there are two levels of meaning, the literal sense communicated by the human author and the *sensus plenior* intended by God and discerned by the NT author. The "deeper meaning," existing in the biblical text, was "not clearly intended by the human author." This intended meaning is understood only when studied in the light of God's further revelation. The difference between the literal and the *sensus plenior* is that "the literal sense answers the question of what this text meant according to its author's intention as that author was inspired to compose it in his particular stage in the history of God's plan of salvation," while *sensus plenior* "answers the question of what the text means in the whole context of God's plan, a meaning which God, who knew the whole plan from the start, intended from the moment he inspired the composition of the

---

147. Lunde, "Introduction," 12. N. Longenecker responds to the questions: "Is there a *sensus plenior* in the New Testament's use of the Old Testament?" or "Can we reproduce the exegesis of the New Testament?" (Longenecker, *Biblical Exegesis in the Apostolic Period*, xxxi–xxxix; see also D. J. Moo, "The Problem of *Sensus Plenior*," in *Hermeneutics, Authority and Canon*, ed. D. A. Carson and J. D. Woodbridge [Grand Rapids: Zondervan, 1986], 179–211).

148. Raymond Brown, *The Sensus Plenior of Sacred Scripture* (Baltimore: St. Mary's University Press, 1955), 92, as cited Gundry, Berding, and Lunde, *Three Views*, 14.

text."[149] Therefore, the issue in promise-fulfillment is in what was meant in the original author's context and what it means in the NT's context, both within God's salvific plan. Because "God inspired the scriptural writers, the meanings and referents he intended in the biblical text may often exceed the limited vision and understanding of the human authors, even though this divine intention retains 'homogeneous' connection to what the human author intended."[150] It is the "inspired NT authors" who are able to decipher the fuller meaning "as it pertains to Jesus and their own day."[151]

There are three[152] schools of thought on the issue of the use of the OT in the NT, especially within scholars outside of the Catholic circle. First, some scholars deny any distinction between the intention of the OT and that of the NT. In other words, what the OT author intended is what the NT author communicated. This direct prediction viewpoint is often referred to as "single meaning, unified referents,"[153] or "the full human intent school," based on the premise that "if hermeneutics is to have validity then all that is asserted in the Old Testament passages must have been part of the *human author's intention and meaning*"[154] (emphasis added). It means that the text of Scripture communicates a single meaning including the referents of the text, such that the people and events that OT writer had in mind are the same people and events to which the NT authors refer. In this case, the OT prophets had "a fairly comprehensive understanding of what it is they are declaring about the ultimate consummation of God's promise."[155] This position is a rejection of the dual sense or double fulfillment or meaning. Walter C. Kaiser, who is prominent among the defendants of a single meaning, argues against double fulfillment because he sees the concept as taking away meaning "out of the hands of the human authors who stood in the counsel of God" and therefore no "final court of appeal" left "for discover-

---

149. Raymond Brown, "The *Sensus Plenior* in the Last Ten Years," *CBQ* 25 (1963), 278, as cited by Gundry, Berding, and Lunde, *Three Views,* 15.
150. Lunde, "Introduction," 15.
151. Ibid.
152. Gundry, Berding, and Lunde, *Three Views.* See also Darrell L. Bock, "Evangelicals and the Use of the Old Testament in the New," *BSac* (July 85): 210–224.
153. Gundry, Berding, and Lunde, *Three Views,* 40.
154. Bock, "Evangelicals and the Use of the Old Testament in the New," 210.
155. Ibid., 210–211.

ing the authoritative meaning of a biblical text."[156] Kaiser believes that a canonical reading of Scripture does not allow for *sensus plenior* and that the NT authors respected the context of the OT writers in their approach to promise-fulfillment. What is perhaps less convincing with Kaiser's position is the exceptional clause in the time frame as he accepts that the human author had the whole picture of God's intention except the time frame.[157] If there was one thing the human author was not fully aware of, then, there could be more than just one.

A second approach to NT use of the OT is that which sees single meaning but multiple contexts and referents. This view is closely related to Kaiser's on the issue of singular meaning intended by the OT as cited by the NT. It is believed that the meaning of the NT is related to that of OT, and that the NT's exegesis is not to be regarded as arbitrary. The point of departure from Kaiser, however, is that in this school of thought "the words of the OT authors frequently take on new dimensions of significance and are found to apply appropriately to new referents and new situations as God's purposes unfold in the larger canonical contexts—referents that were not in the minds of the OT authors when they penned their texts."[158] This viewpoint allows for typological reading of Scripture. Bock defends this view by arguing that "the use of the OT in the NT involves two sets of contexts: that of the OT passage, sometimes in a canonical versus a merely exegetical context, and that of the NT passage."[159] Bock's premise is that "God works both in his words *and* in revelatory events that also help to elaborate his message."[160] Therefore, *text* and *revelation* must be taken together as they "often combine, in prediction and pattern, to show what God is doing in history through word and deed."[161] This view is that revelation is progressive and the text has multiple contexts and referents within

---

156. Kaiser, Jr., "Single Meaning, Unified Referents," 48. He says that the Roman Catholic Church may appeal to tradition for meaning, but that the Protestant church has no such ground for meaning outside the Scripture (48). See also Kaiser, Jr., *The Uses of the Old Testament in the New*, 88.
157. Bock, "Evangelicals and the Use of the Old Testament in the New," 212.
158. Lunde, "Introduction," 40.
159. Bock, "Single Meaning, Multiple Contexts and Referents," 106.
160. Ibid., 107.
161. Ibid.

this progressive revelation. This appeal to historical progress of revelation is shared by Earle E. Ellis, Richard Longenecker, and Walter Dunnett.[162]

Finally, some suggest that "the NT writers often perceive new meanings in OT texts that are not necessarily closely related to the meaning intended by the original authors."[163] However, the NT authors legitimize the new meanings by their "single-minded conviction that the Scriptures point to and are fulfilled in Christ."[164] This is, broadly speaking, christological reading of Scripture. The OT is studied in its grammatical-historical context and its authors are understood "on their own terms." However, "since the NT writers assume that Jesus is the *goal* to which the OT story is moving, they perceive this meaning in OT texts, even when the OT authors did not have that meaning in mind when they wrote."[165] The meaning that the NT writers give to OT texts, according to this view, is based on the NT writers' assumption "that Jesus is the goal to which OT story is moving" and the meaning given to the OT text by the NT authors may not have been the meaning intended by the OT writers.[166]

But Peter Enns argues that in spite of this overarching purpose, there is usually a considerable distance between the OT's context and the NT's use. "Although there are certainly differences in degree throughout the NT, the distinction between what the OT passage meant originally and how it is used in the NT is not a matter of isolated incident or two, but a phenomenon that readers confront with some frequency."[167] To return to the overarching purpose, therefore, fulfillment is more than an OT text corresponding to NT text. Instead, "the utter hermeneutical centrality of Christ's person and work shows us how a 'full' understanding of God's ultimate program for the world awaits the climax of the story."[168] In this sense the NT writers provide "hermeneutical template" for the interpretation of promise-fulfillment.

---

162. Bock, "Evangelicals and the Use of the Old Testament in the New," 216.
163. Lunde, "Introduction," 40.
164. Ibid., 41.
165. Ibid.
166. Enns, "Fuller Meaning, Single Goal," 167.
167. Ibid.,168.
168. Ibid., 214–215.

Although the uniting factor in these three views is the fact that all the authors believe that the NT authors demonstrate, by their citation of the OT, that "the person and work of Christ are a continuation, fulfillment, and climax of the Father's redemptive work that began in the early chapters of Genesis,"[169] Enns' position shifts attention from God's intention to the NT writers' perception as against Kaiser's and Bock's positions. For while Kaiser emphasizes "single meaning" of the text, Bock sees God at work "both in his words and in revelatory events that also help to elaborate his message."[170] On the one hand, Enns sees the OT permeating the NT "because the NT describes how Christ's life and his work are the realization of God's purposes throughout Israel's history as recorded in the OT."[171] On the other hand, when Enns says that the NT authors "assume that Jesus is the goal to which the OT story is moving," he suggests that the context of the OT author is ignored,[172] and that the theological concerns of the NT writers shaped their interpretation rather than God's original purposes. Yet, for Enns, God "was pleased to allow interpretive methods and traditions, so different from what we consider normative today, to be the matrix within which Israel's Scripture was interpreted—in the most pressing moment in human history, the incarnation of the Son of God."[173]

How would the three views summarized above apply to Matthew 1:23 as fulfillment of Isaiah 7:14? In other words, is it direct prediction, typology, or christological reading? The text of Isaiah 7:14 that Matthew cites is first explored in its textual and literary context. First, the text is given in the following table:

---

169. Ibid., 167.
170. Bock, "Single Meaning, Multiple Contexts and Referents," 107.
171. Enns, "Fuller Meaning, Single Goal," 179.
172. Ibid., 168–169.
173. Ibid., 203.

Table 6: *Matthew's Immanuel*

MT	LXX	NT
Isa 7:14 לָכֵן יִתֵּן אֲדֹנָי הוּא לָכֶם אוֹת הִנֵּה הָעַלְמָה הָרָה וְיֹלֶדֶת בֵּן וְקָרָאת שְׁמוֹ עִמָּנוּ אֵל׃	Isa 7:14 διὰ τοῦτο δώσει κύριος αὐτὸς ὑμῖν σημεῖον ἰδοὺ ἡ παρθένος ἐν γαστρὶ ἕξει καὶ τέξεται υἱόν καὶ καλέσεις τὸ ὄνομα αὐτοῦ Εμμανουηλ	Matt 1:23 Ἰδοὺ ἡ παρθένος ἐν γαστρὶ ἕξει καὶ τέξεται υἱόν, καὶ καλέσουσιν τὸ ὄνομα αὐτοῦ Ἐμμανουήλ, ὅ ἐστιν μεθερμηνευόμενον Μεθ' ἡμῶν ὁ θεός.
"Therefore the Lord Himself will give you a sign: Behold, **a virgin** will be with child and bear a son, **and she will call** His name Immanuel" (NAS)	"Therefore the Lord Himself will give you a sign: Behold, **a [the] virgin** will be with a child [conceive] and bear a son, **and she [you] will call** His name Immanuel" (NAS)	"Behold, **the virgin** shall be with child, and shall bear a Son, **and they shall call** His name Immanuel," which translated means, "God with us" (NAS)

The text of LXX is like the MT's. Although Matthew follows both the MT and the LXX closely in wording, he changes the וְקָרָאת (third person feminine singular and "she shall call") or the καλέσεις ("you shall call") to καλέσουσιν ("they shall call"). This is thought to be Matthew's alteration of the text rather than a variant.[174] The sign of עִמָּנוּ אֵל ("God with us") in Isaiah is in the context of the conflict between king Ahaz of Judah and the allied forces of Rezin king of Aram and Pekah king of Israel. This alliance against king Ahaz brought great panic to the southern kingdom (Isa 7:2). Seeing the distress of Ahaz and his people the Lord sends the prophet Isaiah to Ahaz for a sign that would assure him that God was going to keep his promise and that the two allied forces would not defeat him. But Ahaz refuses to ask for a sign.[175] God, however, decides to give a sign to Ahaz that would come through the virgin (LXX's ἡ παρθένος) or the young woman

---

174. Hagner, *Matthew 1–13*, 20.
175. Probably for a wrong reason as Isaiah seems to indicate. See Blomberg, "Matthew," in *Commentary on the New Testament use of the Old Testament*, 4.

(הָעַלְמָה) whose child would be named Immanuel. Before this child knows what is right and wrong the lands of Rezin and Pekah would be destroyed and would be replaced by Assyria.

Matthew summarizes the second pericope of his narrative (1:18–25) with a fulfillment quotation, citing Isaiah 7:14. All that took place happened in order that what was spoken by God through the prophet might be fulfilled. With ὑπὸ κυρίου διὰ τοῦ προφήτου Matthew demonstrates, as he does throughout the narrative, that God is the ultimate agent in communicating his word while the prophet is the immediate agent.[176] Moreover, Matthew follows the translation of the LXX in rendering the MT's הָעַלְמָה as ἡ παρθένος because it best suits his theological view point, namely, that the birth of Jesus is the work of God.

But the issue in the text is whether or not Isaiah 7:14 is a direct predictive messianic prophecy. Although the exact identity of the "son" is disputed by scholars—as some argue for Isaiah's own son while others believe he may be Ahaz' royal son—a common understanding among most scholars is that the prophecy finds "at least a provisional fulfillment in Isaiah's day."[177] Scholars who do not believe in *sensus plenior* would suggest that the single meaning and unified referents of the text must have been apparent for God and Isaiah, and Matthew captures this same meaning and unified referents, since he would not have found a meaning beyond what God and Isaiah saw. However, those who argue for multiple contexts and referents would suggest that the single meaning of the text of Isaiah is to be maintained while multiple contexts and referents may be allowed according to the progress of revelation. In this sense, Matthew could apply the text of Isaiah 7:14 in his own context since "God works both in his words *and* in revelatory events that also help to elaborate his message."[178] The advocates of new meaning of text by NT authors would suggest a reading of Isaiah on its own terms and say that the "fuller meaning" and the "single goal" that Matthew brings into the text is allowed by Matthew's theological concerns which God permitted.

---

176. See Wallace, *Greek Grammar Beyond the Basics*, 434.
177. See Blomberg, "Matthew," in *Commentary on the New Testament use of the Old Testament*, 4.
178. Bock, "Single Meaning, Multiple Contexts and Referents," 107.

In summary, the complexity of the concept of the NT's use of the OT requires that each position be given special attention according to its strengths and weaknesses. Although some see a single meaning and unified referents (so Kaiser), the idea that God alone controls the time frame of prophetic utterances weakens the position. This position makes it hard to maintain that the human author was fully aware of God's purposes. While the position of Enns' also recognizes a fuller meaning and a unified goal of prophecy, when this fuller meaning and unified goal are dictated by the NT writer and only permitted by God, the overarching purpose of God's salvific purpose from the OT seems to be ignored. It seems that God simply approves what he did not have in mind. This position is therefore less convincing. It is for this reason that Bock's position seems a more appealing option in understanding promise-fulfillment, for "God works both in his words *and* in revelatory events that also help to elaborate his message."

From this general view of prophetic ministry and the NT's use of the OT as applicable to the Gospel of Matthew, the ministry of John the Baptist as the forerunner of Jesus is examined. More attention is given to the OT passages Matthew cites as fulfillment of prophecy concerning John's mission.

3.3.2 Prophetic Ministry of John the Baptist

Jesus calls John the Baptist the greatest of the prophets (Matt 11:11).[179] The Synoptics draw parallel accounts of John the Baptist with the status of a forerunner of Christ (Matt 3:3; 11:10; cf. Mark 1:2–3; Luke 3:4–6; 7:27). Matthew quotes Isaiah and Malachi and explains that Elijah who was to come had now appeared in the person of John the Baptist (11:14; 17:13).[180] But the key text for discussion here is Matthew 3:1–3. Matthew shows that

---

179. See Nolland, *The Gospel of Matthew*, 456–457; Turner, *Matthew*, 293–294; Ladd, *A Theology of the New Testament*, 31–33; J. P. Meier, "John the Baptist in Matthew's Gospel," *JBL* 99 (1980): 383–405. John's greatness is suggestive of his pivotal role in the prophetic ministry (see treatment of this at the beginning of this section on Matt 11:12–13 and below).

180. It is said, "Every statement about John the Baptist in the Gospel of Matthew is related to his function in redemptive history. Matthew develops John's role in terms of his relation to the Kingdom of Heaven and his identity as Elijah". See Morris M. Faierstein, "Why Do the Scribes Say that Elijah Must Come First," *JBL* 100.1 (1981): 75, citing W. Wink, in *John the Baptist in the Gospel Tradition* (Cambridge: Cambridge University Press, 1968), 28.

John the Baptist fulfills Isaiah 40:3. The textual and literary background of Isaiah 40:3 is considered from the text as follows:

Table 7: *A Voice Crying in the Wilderness*

MT	LXX	NT
Isa 40:3 קוֹל קוֹרֵא בַּמִּדְבָּר פַּנּוּ דֶּרֶךְ יְהוָה יַשְּׁרוּ בָּעֲרָבָה מְסִלָּה לֵאלֹהֵינוּ׃	Isa 40:3 φωνὴ βοῶντος ἐν τῇ ἐρήμῳ ἑτοιμάσατε τὴν ὁδὸν κυρίου εὐθείας ποιεῖτε τὰς τρίβους τοῦ θεοῦ ἡμῶν	Matt 3:3 οὗτος γάρ ἐστιν ὁ ῥηθεὶς διὰ Ἠσαΐου τοῦ προφήτου λέγοντος, Φωνὴ βοῶντος ἐν τῇ ἐρήμῳ· Ἑτοιμάσατε τὴν ὁδὸν κυρίου, εὐθείας ποιεῖτε τὰς τρίβους αὐτοῦ.
A voice of one calling: "In the desert prepare the way for the Lord; **make straight in the wilderness a highway for our God.**"	**A voice of one calling:** "In the desert prepare the way for the Lord; **make straight in the wilderness a highway for our God.**"	This is he who was spoken of through the prophet Isaiah: **"A voice of one calling in the desert,** 'Prepare the way for the Lord, **make straight paths for him.'"**

The first issue in the text is that while the MT has "a voice of one calling" this voice is personalized[181] in the LXX (and translated by the KJV as "The voice of him that crieth"). The second issue in the text is the difference between the MT and the LXX on how "in the wilderness" is to be understood.[182] Is the prepositional phrase "in the wilderness" to be understood as the KJV has it, "The voice of him that crieth in the wilderness" (that is, the one speaking is in the wilderness) or the NAS "A voice is calling, 'Clear the way for the Lord in the wilderness'" (that is, a way is to be cleared in

---

181. France, *The Gospel of Matthew*, 105.
182. The different understanding of the sense of the phrase is demonstrated by various translations such as KJV: "The voice of him that crieth in the wilderness" NAS: "A voice is calling, 'Clear the way for the Lord in the wilderness'"; NIV: "A voice of one calling in the desert, 'Prepare a way for the Lord.'"

the wilderness)? The basic question is whether בַּמִּדְבָּר is construed with קוֹל קוֹרֵא or with פַּנּוּ.[183] The LXX sees "in the wilderness" as giving location of the speaker and is followed by Matthew. Moreover, the LXX's omission of בָּעֲרָבָה in the second line appears to be a deliberate way of strengthening the idea that "in the wilderness" speaks about the location of the speaker rather than the command to prepare a way in the desert. Finally, in the second part of the verse, the LXX translates the MT's מְסִלָּה ("highway") as τρίβους ("pathway") but omits the MT's second "in the desert" (בָּעֲרָבָה). According to France, the syntax of the LXX makes it easier for Matthew to find scriptural justification "for John's personal role and for his location "in the wilderness" (v. 1), and the words of the "voice" in its LXX original form avoid locating God's predicted coming directly "in the wilderness," thus leaving open the question of when and where John's preparatory proclamation was to find its fulfillment."[184] But Gundry thinks that there is the possibility that the MT is wrong while the LXX may be correct because the Targum, the OT Peshitta, Vulgate, and rabbinical expositors also construe בַּמִּדְבָּר with קוֹל קוֹרֵא (that is, "a voice crying in the wilderness") instead of the MT's construing בַּמִּדְבָּר with פַּנּוּ (that is, "prepare in the wilderness" after "a voice crying").[185] For Davies and Allison, the agreement of the other witness "lessens the geographical impact of the passage."[186] A final note on the text is that the MT's לֵאלֹהֵינוּ ("for our God") followed by LXX is translated by Matthew as τρίβους αὐτοῦ ("his paths").[187] This is generally a characteristic way of Matthew who abbreviates, paraphrases, omits, or follows one or the other of the two original texts. The actual text form, which Matthew cites for his formula quotations, is a subject of interest among scholars.[188] Gundry believes that Matthew "was his own targumist

---

183. Gundry, *The Use of the Old Testament in St. Matthew's Gospel*, 172.
184. France, *The Gospel of Matthew*, 105.
185. Gundry, *The Use of the Old Testament in St. Matthew's Gospel*, 172.
186. Davies and Allison, *A Critical and Exegetical Commentary*, 1.293.
187. Archer and Chirichigno failed to see that it is Matthew who shortened the MT and the LXX here. They think that it is the LXX that abbreviated the MT. However, this is against the evidence of the text. (See Archer and Chirichigno, *Old Testament Quotations in the New Testament*, 111).
188. France, *The Gospel of Matthew*, 13.

and drew on a knowledge of the Hebrew, Aramaic, and Greek textual traditions of the OT."[189] It is necessary to examine this text further.

The three Synoptic Gospels begin their account of the ministry of Jesus by first describing the ministry of John.[190] The thrust of the discussion is on John as "a voice crying in the desert" of Judea (3:1, 3). Matthew connects John the Baptist with "a voice crying in the wilderness" of Isaiah 40:3. What is the significance[191] of this "voice in the wilderness"?[192] How does the ministry of John the Baptist relate to the prophecy of Isaiah 40:3?[193] And does this "voice" fulfill the "voice in the wilderness" in Isaiah and the "messenger" in Malachi 3:1 (Matt 11:10)? Why would John the Baptist be accepted by the people as the Elijah who was to come? According to Hagner, "The importance of the quotation is especially apparent in the words ἐν τῇ ἐρήμῳ 'in the wilderness,' of 3:1 and the theological connection between the exhortation 'to prepare the way of the Lord' and that of John 'to repent' (v 2)."[194] In Matthew's view, "repentance" is the way Israel was to prepare the way of the Lord. In Isaiah 40:3, the immediate context is that of the envoys from Babylon to king Hezekiah and the prophet Isaiah's warning

---

189. Gundry, *The Use of the Old Testament in St. Matthew's Gospel*, 172.

190. Parallels include 11:1–19; Mark 1:1–8; Luke 1:76; 3:1–9; 7:18–35. Not only do the Synoptic Gospels begin by describing the work of John the Baptist, the Gospel of John does so as well, although in this work attention is given primarily to the Synoptics (see John 1:6–27). The Gospel of Matthew presents John the Baptist as a unique person who was spoken of from the OT by the prophets Isaiah and Malachi. According to David Hill, "of the Synoptics, Matthew seems the most concerned to give John his proper place in the plan of God". See David Hill, *The Gospel of Matthew*, The New Century Bible Commentary, ed. Matthew Black (Grand Rapids: Eerdmans, 1972), 88–9.

191. Hendriksen says, "John is immensely important historical figure, especially because he is the link between God's saving activity in the Old Testament and his saving activity in the ministry of Jesus," cf. Matt 11:11, (see Hendriksen, *Exposition of the Gospel According to Matthew*, 130.

192. Craig S. Keener, *Matthew, The IVP New Testament Commentary Series*, ed. Grant R. Osborne (Downers Grove: IVP, 1997), 76. It appears that the Jews acknowledged that the wilderness is the right place for prophets and the awaited messiah(s) (Matt 24:26; Acts 21:38; Jos. *Ant.* 20:189; *War* 2:259, 261–62). See Qumran Community's interpretation of Matthew 3:3, appropriating Isa 40:3 in The Rule of the Community 8:12–16 (Pate, *Communities of the Last Days*, 94).

193. Hill says that the text is also used by the Qumran Community in their eschatological expectations, especially the phrase "in the wilderness" which appeals to their own setting, (Hill, *The Gospel of Matthew*, 91).

194. Hagner, *Matthew 1–13*, 45.

that Israel would soon go into captivity. It appears therefore that the words of comfort in chapter 40:1–2 relate directly to the exile. The return from the exile seems to have been envisaged by the prophet and preparation for return through the desert of the captives who would be delivered by their God.[195] They would return to Israel and to Yahweh their God.[196]

According to Garland, John "seems to have interpreted his baptism as a preparation for the new exodus to be led by the messiah (3:5–12)."[197] In Matthew, therefore, John appears in the spirit and power of Elijah in the wilderness. But in treating this issue trace must be made to the grand messianic hope of the Jews. This messianic expectation has been highlighted from Jewish sources in the section of redemptive events and institutions. C. H. Dodd comments that Isaiah 40:1–11 is "a *locus classicus* of the hope of redemption."[198] Therefore, "In Matthew 11:10, Jesus employs a combined citation of Exodus 23:30 and Malachi 3:1 (//Mark 1:2) to identify John the Baptist as Elijah *redivivus,* the prophet whose appearance was widely thought in Judaism to herald the messianic age."[199] This hope is rooted in the intertestamental writings and carried to the Gospels.[200] As

---

195. See also France, *The Gospel of Matthew,* 105. He says that the wider setting of Isa 40:3 refers to the new exodus when God takes his people from Babylon back to Palestine.

196. Keener, *Matthew,* 76. On the importance of the wilderness Keener says, "Although true prophets could function within society (as in 2 Sam 12:1–25; 24:11–12), in evil times it was mainly corrupt prophets who remained in royal courts (1 Kgs 22:6–28; compare Matt 11:8) as God's true messengers were forced into exile (1 Kgs 17:3; 18:13). Most Jewish people in the first century practiced their religion seriously; but the religious establishment could not accommodate a prophet like John whose lifestyle dramatically challenged the status quo" (77).

197. Garland, *Reading Matthew,* 34. He says that is why John retreated in the desert, believing that the new exodus would begin here. He adds, "John's baptism symbolically implied 'a new passage through the Red Sea, whereby Israel is again cleansed from its heathen ways of life and from its sins, and its people become true sons of Abraham, worthy of receiving the Messiah on his arrival,'" 34, citing Harald Sahlin, "The New Exodus of Salvation According to St. Paul," in *The Root of the Vine,* ed. A. Fridrichsen (London: Dare, 1953), 88–89.

198. C. H. Dodd, *According to the Scriptures,* 84. The word *testimony* is used in a special way by Dodd to refer to all the references alluded to in the OT as witnesses to the facts that gospel writers proclaimed. It is the passage from the OT that supports a particular theology, theme or fulfillment.

199. Knowles, "Scripture, History, Messiah" 62–63.

200. Sir 48:10; 4 Ezra 6:26; Tob 13:5, 13; 14:5; 2 Macc 1:27, 29; 2:17; 2 Bar 4:36–37; *Pss. of Sol.* 8:28; 2 Bar 78:7.

Robert H. Mounce writes, "For four hundred years Israel had been without a prophetic voice. Now there appears on the scene the promised 'Elijah,' (Mal 4:5; Sir 48:10; cf. Matt 17:10–13)."[201]

Theologically, therefore, John the Baptist had a special mission of preparing the way of the Lord. "He both proclaimed the promise of Messiah and functioned as part of the fulfillment of that promise."[202] He was the forerunner of Jesus and as the Elijah who was to come. Matthew reasons from the OT that the prophets played a decisive role in the coming of the Messiah and that John the Baptist comes as a fulfillment of OT promises to prepare his way. The missional importance of the text is the call for repentance through the voice in the desert. The issue of Matthew's geography and mission is discussed in the next section.

3.4 Geography and Mission

Geography is an important element in Matthew's understanding of mission[203] because "the promises and actions of God in the Old Testament are

---

201. Robert H. Mounce, *Matthew*, New International Biblical Commentary (Peabody: Hendrickson Publishers, 1991), 22. Mounce, *Matthew*, 22. He compares the garments and the lifestyle in general with that of Elijah.

202. Harvey, "Mission in Matthew," 124.

203. Some of the significant works in recent times in this direction include Holwerda, *Jesus and Israel*. In the question of identity between Jesus and Israel, Holwerda provides, among others, a geographical answer and suggests that "Old Testament stories associated with Egypt shape Matthew's presentation of the story of Jesus" (37). Similarly, the identity between Jesus and Israel is found in the wilderness motif in the Gospel of Matthew with regard to the temptation story. Another work is R. Riesner's "Archaeology and Geography," in *Dictionary of Jesus and the Gospels*, ed. J. Green, S. McKnight, I. H. Marshall (Downers Grove: IVP, 1992), 33–46. Riesner examined the geographical data in all the gospels. His particular attention is on the question of whether the results of archeological investigation can shed light on the documents of the NT and early church traditions relating to details of locality (33). His investigation includes geographical areas that pertain to the infancy narratives, John the Baptist's ministry, the public ministry of Jesus in Galilee, withdrawal areas and Galilee, the journey to Jerusalem, and Jerusalem itself. On the historical and theological significance of all these for Matthew he says, "Corresponding to the scribal and characteristics that the first gospel bears, one encounters geographical information most of all in connection with the fulfillment of OT promises" (45). Grams' "Some Geographical and Intertextual Dimensions of Matthew's Mission Theology" examines how geography features prominently in Matthew's narrative and the theological significance of these geographical locations. Sean Freyne's "Galilee and Judea: The Social World of Jesus," in *The Face of New*

closely associated with nations, certain geographical areas" that "become prophetically significant."[204] This features prominently in the Gospel of Matthew where many of the fulfillment quotations focus on geographical locations such as Bethlehem, Egypt, Ramah, Nazareth, Capernaum, and Zion.[205] One of the significant works done in this direction in recent times is that of Rollin Grams. His thesis is that geographical locations in Matthew often bring OT texts to remembrance, and that this contributes "to the notion in Matthew that Jesus is restoring a remnant of Israel in order also to offer salvation to the gentiles."[206] The primary objective of this section is to focus on some of these geographical locations that relate to God's salvific purposes. These geographical areas include:

3.4.1 Bethlehem and Ramah

As noted earlier in this chapter, Bethlehem in Matthew 2:5–6 calls attention to the prophecy of Micah 5:2 regarding the birthplace of the ruler of Israel.[207] The textual background and context of Micah 5:2 have been treated and will not be repeated here. Both Luke (2:4) and Matthew (2:5–6) draw attention to Bethlehem as the city of David. Matthew does not record the circumstances that led Joseph and his wife Mary to go to Bethlehem. Luke does so by saying that Joseph and Mary went there in response to a decree by Caesar Augustus for a census of the entire Roman world. So between the angelic announcement to Mary and Joseph and the actual

---

Testament Studies: A Survey of Recent Research, ed. Scot McKnight and Grant R. Osborne (Grand Rapids: Baker Academic, 2004) looks into the history of Galilee, the identity of the Galileans, social stratifications, economic systems, and Galilee and Jerusalem.

204. Holwerda, *Jesus and Israel*, 36.

205. Riesner, "Archaeology and Geography," 33–46.

206. Grams, "Some Geographical and Intertextual Dimensions of Matthew's Mission Theology," 42. For him, Matthew does not advocate a "replacement theology", that is, "the gentile church replaces recalcitrant Israel" (42). He cites Joachim Jeremias' *Jesus' Promise to the Nations,* trans. S. H. Hooke (London: SCM Press, 1958), 19–39 who believes that the gentiles would replace Israel. Against this view, Grams believes that Jesus' mission to the nations as formalized in the Great Commission is realized "through a restoration of a remnant of Israel in Jesus' disciples and followers" (43). It is for this reason that "salvation remains open to the Jews as well as to the gentiles, but it comes only through Jesus." And the phrase "for many" is also echoed in 26:28 "where the redemptive aspect of his mission is also made explicit" (43).

207. Grams, "Some Geographical and Intertextual Dimensions of Matthew's Mission Theology," 43. He notes how geography features in the infancy narrative of Matthew.

birth of Jesus, Luke filled in the *lacuna* concerning what happened. France refers to Matthew's citation here as "geographical apologetic."[208] Matthew achieves this "geographical apologetic" of the birthplace of the Messiah by combining Micah 5:2 and 2 Samuel 5:2 in which David is to be the shepherd of God's people. For Matthew, "if Bethlehem is the house of David, a 'son of David' born there is to be 'King of the Jews.'"[209] Since Micah's context is the ruler to be born who would restore the rest of Israel from captivity, subdue the nations, and return Israel to right worship, Matthew finds a remarkable correspondence as the magi, being gentiles, bow down and worship Jesus (2:11), and by offering him gifts signify that they were paying him the tribute of *subdued* nations.[210] In this case, however, "their submission to Jesus' rule means their inclusion in His salvation; by bringing frankincense they offer him the symbol of worship."[211]

In addition to the significance of Bethlehem as the birthplace of the expected Messiah, some other parallels are drawn between the two important figures, namely, Jesus and David. This geographical location was David's home, and it was here that he was anointed king. The circumstances of David's anointing are believed to be similar to Jesus' anointing as king. Incidentally, both Samuel, whom God sent to anoint David, and the magi, were fearful of the reigning ruler (1 Sam 16:2). And just as the magi were told to go another way to avoid the wrath of the king, so Samuel was also shown a safe way to go to Bethlehem to avoid Saul's suspicion.[212]

Moreover, Bethlehem is associated with Rachel's burial place, which is in Ramah (Gen 35:19 and 48:7), approximately two miles from Bethlehem on the way to Jerusalem. This geographical location is said to be the point of departure into exile for the Jews (Jer 40:1). Matthew (2:18) quotes Jeremiah (31:15) in reference to King Herod's purge of boys under two years of age in Bethlehem. In Jeremiah 31:16, the mourning for Rachel's

---

208. France, *The Gospel of Matthew*, 61.
209. Ibid.
210. Grams, "Geographical and Intertextual Dimensions," 44. On Bethlehem, Gundry also says, "Jesus fills the role of the royal Messiah supernaturally born (1:23) in Bethlehem (2:6), growing up in obscurity like a branch out of the cut-off stump of David (2:23) . . ."(Gundry, *The Old Testament in St. Matthew's Gospel*, 208).
211. Grams, "Geographical and Intertextual Dimensions," 44.
212. Ibid.

children of 31:15 turns now into a message of future hope for Israel because "they will return from the land of the enemy," that is, from their exile.[213] For Matthew, then, the "formula-quotation (2:17–18) interprets the events at Bethlehem in the light of Jeremiah's words about the 'loss' of Rachel's children in the exile to Babylon (Jer 31:15), as a passage which sees that loss as a prelude to a joyful return and restoration of the people of God, just as Jesus is now to be restored from his exile in Egypt."[214] Therefore, theologically Jesus is son of David and Messiah king who restores Israel.

3.4.2 Egypt

In Matthew 2:13–15 Jesus' time in Egypt is explained as fulfillment of Hosea 11:1. We have discussed the typological import of the text in the exodus section. It will be reiterated that Matthew shows that Egypt fulfills a significant role in God's salvific scheme for Israel. Israel lived in slavery in the land of Egypt. But God preserved his people from extinction for a purpose. He delivered the nation Israel and set it apart for himself. This work of salvation is recorded for posterity as noted earlier on in this chapter. Yet this deliverance finds completion in the work of Jesus as the representative Son of God. Jesus goes into Egypt and God preserves his life there (Matt 2:13–15). He later comes out of Egypt as divinely planned (Matt 2:19–21). In essence, Jesus' ministry completes the prophetic word concerning Israel's deliverance from Egyptian bondage. In quoting Hosea 11:1 Matthew is not only concerned about Jesus' going into Egypt as a mark of identity with Israel but also with the promised return of Israel from exile.[215] Theologically, therefore, Egypt is significant for Matthew because of its unique place in the history of Israel, namely, bondage and deliverance. But Matthew stresses deliverance from the bondage of sin (Matt 1:21).

3.4.3 Nazareth

Joseph's return to Nazareth after the death of Herod is important for Matthew. In Matthew 2:19, 20 Joseph received instruction from the angel

---

213. Ibid. Cf. Fred Strickert, "Rachel on the Way: A Model of Faith in Times of Transition," *CurTM* 34.6 (December 2007), 444–452; Holwerda, *Jesus and Israel,* 42.
214. See France, *Matthew: Evangelist and Teacher,* 208.
215. Grams, "Geographical and Intertextual Dimensions," 44–5.

of the Lord to return to the land of Israel because the one who was seeking to kill Jesus was now dead.[216] Joseph obeyed the angel of the Lord as he did before. But when he came to Galilee he found out that Archelaus was ruling in place of his father Herod. He feared to go to the preferred region of Judea because he was probably aware that his family was unsafe with Archelaus as ruler. After he received warning in a dream he went to settle in a "despised place"—Nazareth.[217] But how does this despised place fit into the messianic script of Matthew 2:23? The reference to Jesus' life in Nazareth is rather complicated because it finds no scriptural basis in the OT or known apocryphal or pseudepigraphal text.[218] Matthew mentions prophets (plural). And it is probably for this reason that Matthew does not indicate a specific source for this prophecy. France sees the text as indicating a theme of prophecy, supported by the name Nazorean that is not found in the OT or other contemporary literature.[219] Grams argues that since there is no text that explicitly says he will be called a Nazarene, Matthew probably has in mind the fact that the Messiah would come from David's line based on the Hebrew word for 'branch.'[220] For him, the best way for identifying Jesus' dwelling in Nazareth with a specific OT text is the understanding of the play on words in Isaiah 11:1. In this case, the stump (גֶּזַע) and the shoot (נֵצֶר) in the verse is what Grams sees as Matthew's attempt to bring out an analogy. "A shoot will come from the stump (גֶּזַע) of Jesse,

---

216. Some scholars compare this with Exod 4:19–20 (see Keener, *A Commentary on the Gospel of Matthew*, 112).

217. Carson, "Matthew," 16; cf. John 7:42, 52. Nazareth appears as an unlikely city to produce Israel's prophet, probably due to its insignificance compared to other cities in Israel (John 1:46). According to Carson, "when Christians were referred to in Acts as the 'Nazarene sect' (24:5), the expression was meant to hurt" (Carson, "Matthew," 16). In his article, "Mit der Herkunft Jesu aus Nazaret gegen die Geltung des Gezetzes? *ZNW* 92 (2001): 273–282, Volker Wagner looks at passages like Matt 2:23; 21:11; Mark 1:9; 14:67 and John 1:46 and examines if the humble beginning of Jesus as prophet coming from Nazareth goes against the law. He concludes that the popular opinion that a prophet would not come from Nazareth had no basis in the law.

218. Blomberg, "Matthew," in *Commentary on the New Testament Use of the Old Testament*, 11. See also Carson, "Matthew," 16.

219. France, *The Gospel of Matthew*, 92.

220. Grams, "Geographical and Intertextual," 44–5. For this word play, see also France, *The Gospel of Matthew*, 92; Hagner, *Matthew 1–13*, 39–40.

and a shoot (נֵצֶר) from his root will bear fruit."[221] While Moyise admits that most scholars interpret the passage based on word play, he thinks that the link with Nazareth is superfluous.[222] But as Grams says, in Isaiah 10 a remnant of Israel is restored from its captivity in Assyria. Chapter 11 speaks of the same restoration based on a shoot from a stump of Jesse on whom the Spirit of the Lord rests, and who brings justice to the needy and punishes the wicked of the earth.[223] Therefore, for Matthew Bethlehem, Egypt, and Nazareth speak of Israel's restoration from captivity through the Davidic Messiah based on OT promises.[224] Consequently, the mention of Jesus' presence in Bethlehem, Egypt and Nazareth are far more than mere proof texts but suggestive of the time of restoration from captivity. However, this return from captivity, unlike the previous ones, would extend God's rule to the nations.[225] Carson also notes the numerous suggestions concerning this verse. He points out that the best of these suggestions is one that "sees Matthew using 'Nazarene' as an adjectival form meaning 'from Nazareth,' even though the Greek spelling is unusual."[226] According to Carson, Matthew does not mention Nazareth to show that a particular OT prophet foretold that the Messiah would live in Nazareth. Rather, what Matthew means by the quotation is that the Messiah would be despised (e.g. Ps 22:6–8, 13; 69:8, 20–21; Isa 11:1; 49:7; 53:2–3, 8; Dan 9:23). Carson sees Matthew picking up this theme of Jesus as despised in 8:20; 11:16–18; 15:7–8.[227] At any rate Matthew shows, theologically, that

---

221. Grams, "Geographical and Intertextual Dimensions," 44–5. See also Nolland, *The Gospel of Matthew*, 34.

222. Moyise, *The Old Testament in the New*, 43. He asks, "What is it that is being fulfilled by Jesus settling in Nazareth? Surely no more than the fact that the letters can be rearranged to correspond to known messianic title?"

223. Grams, "Geographical and Intertextual Dimensions," 45–6. Cf. Isa 4:2; Jer 23:5; 33:15; Zech 3:8; 6:12.

224. Ibid., 46. He says, "As Matthew has already made plain in his genealogy, the New Exodus is a key to interpreting Jesus' identity and role (Matt 1:11, 12, 17)."

225. Ibid.

226. Carson, "Matthew," 16.

227. Ibid. According to Carson, Nazareth was a despised place (John 7:42, 52), even to other Galileans (cf. John 1:46)." Therefore, the reference to Christians as the Nazarene sect (Acts 24:5) was meant to hurt.

geographical location such as Nazareth also serves God's salvific purpose for the despised Messiah.

Next in this discussion, the researcher examines Galilee and how this region fulfills prophecy in the Gospel of Matthew.

3.4.4 Galilee[228]

From Matthew 2:21–23 Joseph goes to live in Galilee instead of Judea because Archelaus was reigning in Judea in place of Herod his father. This also fulfills prophecy. We will begin with the textual evidence as follows:

---

228. The discussion on Galilee by Freyne (Freyne, "Galilee and Judea," 21–35) and other scholars is treated in chapter 4 in relation to gentile mission.

Table 8: *Galilee of the Gentiles*

MT	LXX	NT
Isa 8:23 - 9:1 ²כִּי לֹא מוּעָף לַאֲשֶׁר מוּצָק לָהּ כָּעֵת הָרִאשׁוֹן הֵקַל אַרְצָה זְבֻלוּן וְאַרְצָה נַפְתָּלִי וְהָאַחֲרוֹן הִכְבִּיד דֶּרֶךְ הַיָּם עֵבֶר הַיַּרְדֵּן גְּלִיל הַגּוֹיִם: 9:1 הָעָם הַהֹלְכִים בַּחֹשֶׁךְ רָאוּ אוֹר גָּדוֹל יֹשְׁבֵי בְּאֶרֶץ צַלְמָוֶת אוֹר נָגַהּ עֲלֵיהֶם:	Isa 8:23 - 9:1 καὶ οὐκ ἀπορηθήσεται ὁ ἐν στενοχωρίᾳ ὢν ἕως καιροῦ τοῦτο πρῶτον ποίει ταχὺ ποίει χώρα Ζαβουλων ἡ γῆ Νεφθαλιμ ὁδὸν θαλάσσης καὶ οἱ λοιποὶ οἱ τὴν παραλίαν κατοικοῦντες καὶ πέραν τοῦ Ιορδάνου Γαλιλαία τῶν ἐθνῶν τὰ μέρη τῆς Ιουδαίας 9:1 ὁ λαὸς ὁ πορευόμενος ἐν σκότει ἴδετε φῶς μέγα οἱ κατοικοῦντες ἐν χώρᾳ καὶ σκιᾷ θανάτου φῶς λάμψει ἐφ᾿ ὑμᾶς	Matt 4:15-16 Γῆ Ζαβουλὼν καὶ γῆ Νεφθαλίμ, ὁδὸν θαλάσσης, πέραν τοῦ Ἰορδάνου, Γαλιλαία τῶν ἐθνῶν, ¹⁶ ὁ λαὸς ὁ καθήμενος ἐν σκότει φῶς εἶδεν μέγα, καὶ τοῖς καθημένοις ἐν χώρᾳ καὶ σκιᾷ θανάτου φῶς ἀνέτειλεν αὐτοῖς.
8:23 "But there will be no *more* gloom for her who was in anguish; in earlier times He treated **the land of Zebulun** and the land of Naphtali with contempt, but later on He shall make *it* glorious, by the way of the sea, on the other side of Jordan, Galilee of the Gentiles. **9:1 The people walking in** darkness have seen a great light; on those living in the land of the shadow of death a light has dawned."	8:23 "But there will be no *more* gloom for her who was in anguish; in earlier times He treated the land of Zebulun and the land of Naphtali with contempt, but later on He shall make *it* glorious, by the way of the sea, on the other side of Jordan, Galilee of the Gentiles. **9:1 The people walking** in darkness have seen a great light; on those living in the land of the shadow of death a light has dawned."	"**Land of Zebulun** and land of Naphtali, the way to the sea, along the Jordan, Galilee of the Gentiles — ¹⁶ **the people living** in darkness have seen a great light; on those living in the land of the shadow of death a light has dawned."

The Galilean ministry occupies the most important place in the earthly ministry of Jesus, beginning from 4:12–16:20. This Galilean ministry is recorded by all the Synoptics (Mark 1:14–15; Luke 4:14–15). According to Matthew (4:12–13), Jesus returned to Galilee because he heard that John the Baptist was put in prison. But he went to live specifically in Capernaum in the area of Zebulun and Naphtali, a Galilean region, in fulfillment of prophecy of Isaiah 9:1–2. There are no major differences between the MT, LXX or Matthew, except that Matthew seems to have abbreviated both.[229] Matthew 4:15–16 is derived from the MT's and LXX's Isaiah 8:23–9:1 (9:1–2). Some of the differences include the LXX's translation of the MT's אַרְצָה ("toward land") as χώρα ("country") which Matthew renders γῇ, that is, Γῆ Ζαβουλὼν ("land of Zebulun"), and Matthew has γῇ before Zebulun and Naphtali while LXX has γῇ before Napthali. The γῇ here logically and symbolically means "people" since the next verse speaks about people walking in darkness. Furthermore, the MT's הָעָם הַהֹלְכִים ("the people walking") in 9:1 is rightly and literally translated by the LXX's ὁ λαὸς ὁ πορευόμενος, while Matthew has τοῖς καθημένοις ("to those sitting")[230] where Matthew seems to have taken liberty in his rendering of the MT and the LXX.[231] The MT has רָאוּ אוֹר גָּדוֹל in Isaiah 9:1. The LXX has ἴδετε φῶς μέγα. The LXX changes the MT's third person plural רָאוּ ("they see") into second person plural, aorist active imperative ("see"). Matthew follows the MT closely by translating φῶς εἶδεν μέγα. But he uses the third person singular (εἶδεν).[232] What Matthew does is an abbreviation of the text of Isaiah.[233]

Matthew raises some significant exegetical points in 4:12–16. First, Jesus comes to live in Capernaum in fulfillment of Scripture. Matthew considers every event in the life of Jesus, including his movement to settle in a particular region, as fulfillment, using his frequent phrase ἵνα

---

229. Nolland suggests that the LXX of the text of Isa 9:1–2 (8:23–9:1) might have been based on a Hebrew version that lost a phrase and therefore restructured. Matthew follows the LXX but differs in many of the wordings (see Nolland, *The Gospel of Matthew*, 172). See also France, *The Gospel of Matthew*, 141.
230. Blomberg thinks that Matthew is probably echoing Ps 107:10 or Isa 42:7 (Blomberg, "Matthew," in *Commentary on the New Testament use of the Old Testament*, 19).
231. Archer and Chirichigno, *Old Testament Quotations in the New*, 99.
232. Ibid.
233. France, *The Gospel of Matthew*, 141.

πληρωθῇ τὸ ῥηθὲν. This fulfillment motif justifies the ministry of Jesus in this "despised"[234] area. With ἵνα πληρωθῇ Matthew suggests that nothing is happening by chance in the life of Jesus. Everything is divinely orchestrated. Second, the land Jesus settles in for ministry is described as Γαλιλαία τῶν ἐθνῶν. The land of Zebulun and land of Naphtali is "Galilee of the Gentiles," meaning that the gentiles own this region or occupy it. The mention of ἔθνη in connection with the ministry of Jesus who saves τὸν λαὸν αὐτοῦ ἀπὸ τῶν ἁμαρτιῶν αὐτῶν would probably raise some questions in the minds of Matthew's readers about Jesus and his mission. Would Jesus' ministry involve the nations as well? Therefore, Matthew seems to have deliberately put Γαλιλαία τῶν ἐθνῶν at the beginning of Jesus' ministry in order to pursue the theme of gentile mission which he begins from the genealogy and the magi episode. Third, Matthew points to the condition of the people in this region. They are people living in darkness and in the land of the shadow of death. What is חֹשֶׁךְ and צַלְמָוֶת for Isaiah and how does Matthew understand this σκότος and σκιᾷ θανάτου? We will take this shortly. Fourth, Matthew says that upon these people φῶς ἀνέτειλεν ("light rises") according to prophecy. What is this light?

Meanwhile, the immediate literary context of Isaiah (8:11–22) focuses on the believing remnant who are "the people of hope."[235] These remnants wait for the Lord and for his plans for Zion to come to fulfillment. Even in the prevailing darkness there is hope, because they wait for what God is about to do. The imagery of darkness and hopelessness, based on the context, is due to the invasion of the Assyrian army. The darkness (חֹשֶׁךְ) here is socio-political in nature. But God prophetically turns their darkness into light. The text is therefore a prelude to the child that is born, on whose shoulders the government will be, ruling on David's throne (Isa 9:6, 7). This king establishes and upholds justice and righteousness in the land.

The land that experiences this hope is the territory of Zebulun and Naphtali. It is "Galilee of the Gentiles, by the way of the sea, along the Jordan." Matthew equates Isaiah's "the way of the sea" with the Lake of

---

234. Carson describes the region as "despised Galilee" (Carson, "Matthew," 15).
235. J. Alec Motyer, *The Prophecy of Isaiah: An Introduction and Commentary* (Downers Grove: IVP, 1993), 98.

Galilee.[236] On the one hand, "Galilee of the nations" may reflect "the region's greater openness to surrounding gentile populations, and perhaps especially Isaiah's Judean awareness of the deportation of the Israelites from Galilee by the Assyrians both before (2 Kgs 15:29) and after the Assyrian conquest (2 Kgs 17:24–34), to be replaced by foreign populations."[237] Therefore, this place became "despised Galilee, the place where people live in darkness without the religious and cultic advantages of Jerusalem and Judea, where the darkness is most dense, here the light has dawned."[238] On the other hand, darkness (σκότος) in Matthew may represent "a symbol of moral and spiritual darkness in the writings of the NT."[239] It is due to this moral and spiritual darkness that both John the Baptist and Jesus call for repentance from sins (Matt 3:1–2; 4:17). It is not hard to make the connection between the darkness caused by invasion and the moral darkness of this region because it was the moral condition of Israel, from the prophets' perspective, that caused the invasion. In Matthew's theological hermeneutic a fulfillment has taken place because there is a comparable situation of turning darkness into light. Theologically and missionally, Matthew interprets the *light* that dawned in Galilee of the Gentiles as the kingdom of heaven that has come near (5:17). This kingdom is characterized by preaching, teaching, healing, exorcism, and, ultimately, salvation from sin (1:21; 4:23). On the whole, then, the citation of Isaiah's prophecy authenticates Jesus' ministry in this region and counters regional prejudice.[240] Whatever the prejudice against Galilee Matthew portrays this region in a positive light in the entire gospel. Not only does Jesus begin his ministry in this region, Jesus is called a Galilean (Matt 26:69).

In spite of this disadvantaged geographical location, Jesus began his ministry in Galilee. In his ministry in Galilee Jesus offers to the sick both healing and salvation (Matt 9:12–13; Mark 2:17; Luke 5:31–32). For

---

236. See France, *The Gospel of Matthew*, 142 for the more likely description of this region by Isaiah as against Matthew's understanding.

237. France, *The Gospel of Matthew*, 142–43. Even by NT times the southern Jews suspected Galilee's mixed population (143). See also 1 Macc 5:14–23 for the evacuation of the Jewish population here because the region had become paganized (143).

238. Carson, "Matthew," 20.

239. Davies and Allison, *A Critical and Exegetical Commentary*, 1.385.

240. Keener, *A Commentary on the Gospel of Matthew*, 146.

Schnabel, Jesus' offer of salvation for sinners is best demonstrated as he dines with tax collectors and sinners (Matt 9:10; Mark 2:15; Luke 5:29). These "sinners" could be properly understood as the lost sheep of Israel.[241] Therefore "when the Pharisees and scribes criticize Jesus' table fellowship with tax collectors and sinners, Jesus responds by emphasizing his divine commission to save the lost sinners and to heal the sick (Matt 9:13; Mark 2:17)." This focus on Galilee, according to Schnabel, is a symbolic messianic action, a fulfillment of Jesus' mission to Israel.[242] Schnabel and Grams differ on this. While Schnabel looks at the region on the basis of Jesus' mission to Israel, Grams examines Galilee in the context of gentile mission. Yet Schnabel also notes the citation of Isaiah 9:1–2 by Matthew. Based on the weight of the text such as Jesus' ministry to people coming from all over the places including people from the Decapolis and the region across the Jordan (Matt 4:25) and Jesus' positive response to the needs of the gentiles like the centurion (8:5–13) Matthew most likely cites Isaiah 9:1–2 with the gentiles in view.[243] Apart from Galilee Jesus also conducts his ministry in the regions of Batanea and Gaulanitis, Judea, and in Samaria.[244] Schnabel treats all of these regions under Jesus' ministry to the house of Israel. But it is understood that Jesus seeks "the lost sheep of the house of Israel" from some of the predominantly gentile regions, and in the process the kingdom of heaven advances even to the gentiles who come to him by *faith*. Faith in Matthew is the prerequisite for all to enter the kingdom heaven.

3.4.5 Mount Zion/Jerusalem[245]

The researcher has examined Matthew 2:5, 6 in relation to Jesus' kingship. The second passage of equal significance about Jesus as heir of the Davidic kingdom is Matthew 21:1–11. Since the cleansing of the temple has been treated earlier in this chapter and in chapter 4, it does not form part of the discussion here. The focus now is on Jesus's symbolic act of riding on

---

241. Schnabel, *Jesus and the Twelve*, 214.
242. Ibid., 247.
243. This matter is examined in detail in chapter 4.
244. Schnabel, *Jesus and the Twelve*, 250–262.
245. See Sanders, *Jesus and Judaism,* 78, for how Zion is used interchangeably for Jerusalem and the temple in the OT.

a donkey. In its larger literary context (Matt 16:21–22) Jesus explains that he must go to Jerusalem and suffer in the hands of the elders, chief priests and teachers of the law. He must be killed, and on the third day be raised to life. He then goes up to Jerusalem (20:17). And as he approaches the city he sends two of his disciples for a donkey. He rides on it as a fulfillment of Zechariah 9:9[246] (cf. Isa 62:11).[247] The text reads as follows:

Table 9: *Israel's King enters Zion*

MT	LXX	NT
Zech 9:9 גִּילִי מְאֹד בַּת־צִיּוֹן הָרִיעִי בַּת יְרוּשָׁלַ͏ִם הִנֵּה מַלְכֵּךְ יָבוֹא לָךְ צַדִּיק וְנוֹשָׁע הוּא עָנִי וְרֹכֵב עַל־חֲמוֹר וְעַל־עַיִר בֶּן־אֲתֹנוֹת׃	Zech 9:9 χαῖρε σφόδρα θύγατερ Σιων κήρυσσε θύγατερ Ιερουσαλημ ἰδοὺ ὁ βασιλεύς σου ἔρχεταί σοι δίκαιος καὶ σῴζων αὐτός πραῢς καὶ ἐπιβεβηκὼς ἐπὶ ὑποζύγιον καὶ πῶλον νέον	Matt 21:4-5 Τοῦτο δὲ γέγονεν ἵνα πληρωθῇ τὸ ῥηθὲν διὰ τοῦ προφήτου λέγοντος, ⁵ Εἴπατε τῇ θυγατρὶ Σιών, Ἰδοὺ ὁ βασιλεύς σου ἔρχεταί σοι πραῢς καὶ ἐπιβεβηκὼς ἐπὶ ὄνον καὶ ἐπὶ πῶλον υἱὸν ὑποζυγίου.
"Rejoice greatly, O Daughter of Zion! Shout, Daughter of Jerusalem! See, your king comes to you, **righteous and having salvation**, gentle and riding on a donkey, on a colt, the foal of a donkey."	**"Rejoice greatly, O Daughter of Zion!** Shout, Daughter of Jerusalem! See, your king comes to you, **righteous and having salvation**, gentle and riding on a donkey, on a colt, the foal of a donkey."	This took place to fulfill what was spoken through the prophet: ⁵ **"Say to the Daughter of Zion,** 'See, your king comes to you, **gentle and riding** on a donkey, on a colt, the foal of a donkey.'"

---

246. The textual variation here is explained by Metzger as follows: "Several witnesses (M^mg 42 it^(a, c, h) cop^boms Hilary) add Ζαχαρίου before or after προφήτου; other witnesses (vg⁴ mss cop^boms eth) prefix 'Isaiah'" (see Metzger, *A Textual Commentary on the New Testament,* 44).

247. According to Carson, this ride on a donkey, "because it was planned by Jesus, could only be an acted parable, a deliberate act of self disclosure for those with eyes to see" (Carson, "Matthew," 93).

In this citation Matthew agrees with both the MT and the LXX text forms except that Matthew omits the MT's צַדִּיק וְנוֹשָׁע and the LXX's δίκαιος καὶ σῴζων. Why did Matthew omit the aspect of "justice" and "having salvation"? It is not quite clear. But this aspect of salvation and justice/righteousness are probably taken for granted in the light of what the expected Messiah-king would do as in 1:21 and 12:18–21. In this text, "Jerusalem's king enters her gates."[248] The crowds receive Jesus as Son of David who comes in the name of the Lord (21:9). This too fulfills Psalm 118:26. Matthew presents the crowds as people who have keenly followed the unfolding plan of God. But just as in Matthew 2:3 when the news of his birth disturbed Herod and all Jerusalem with him, even now the whole city is stirred (21:10). The only difference is that the crowds that followed him hail him as king and prophet. The crowd is portrayed as בַּת־צִיּוֹן that is urged to rejoice greatly (גִּילִי מְאֹד) in Zechariah 9:9. But the response of the chief priests and the teachers of the law are indignation and hostility as in Matthew 2:3. Of primary importance in this discussion is Matthew's citation of Zechariah 9:9 and its context. The king who appears as Zion's king is at the same time one who proclaims peace to the nations and whose rule extends to the ends of the earth (9:10). That Israel recognized Jesus as king who comes in fulfillment of Scripture is seen in the shouts of "Hosanna to the Son of David! Blessed is he who comes in the name of the Lord" (21:9).

The people saw Jesus as a prophet in Galilee. But they now see him as the Messiah king of Israel in Jerusalem. But his peaceful disposition,[249] demonstrated by the riding on a donkey, shows that he is much more than a national Messiah who fulfills OT Scripture but shows "the kind of peace-loving approach he was now making to the city."[250] And another significance of riding a donkey into Jerusalem is that he claims "to be the one to restore Israel *and* to be the coming universal ruler" (see Zech 8).[251]

The theological and missional significance of geography for Matthew's mission to the house of Israel may be summarized in the words of Holwerda

---

248. Keener, *A Commentary on the Gospel of Matthew*, 489.
249. Carson says that rulers sometimes rode on donkeys in times of peace (e.g. Judg 5:10; 1 Kgs 1:33; see Carson, "Matthew," 93).
250. Carson, "Matthew," 93.
251. Grams "Geographical and Intertextual Dimensions," 62, 3.

that those "places that were important in the redemptive history of the past become important again in the redemptive history of the present because what happened in the past *provides types* of the person and life of Jesus"[252] (emphasis added). This leads to the final subheading of intertextual typology.

3.5 Intertextual Typology[253] and Mission

Baker traces the revival of typological interpretation in the 1950s.[254] He focuses on the works of key scholars in this period such as Arnold A. van Ruler whose thesis is "defining the place of Jesus Christ in God's plan and the authenticity of the Old Testament as the canonical Word of God"[255] and of Gerhad von Rad who treats the subject from "salvation history."[256] One of the challenges facing the use of typology as a hermeneutical approach is its close link with allegorical interpretation in which the relationship is "sometimes little more than a rhetorical trick."[257] Baker also notes this challenge but says that the concept originates from the Bible itself "and should not be dropped simply because it has been misunderstood in some periods of history."[258] Another reason against it is that it does not reflect a true historical understanding of the OT "but only a 'reading back' of the

---

252. Holwerda, *Jesus and Israel*, 37.
253. Intertextuality is a broad concept. Bruce K. Waltke classifies the uses of the term into seven categories, namely: citation, key words and motifs, allusion, salvation history, prophecy, typology, and conceptualization. See Bruce K. Waltke, *An Old Testament Theology* (Grand Rapids: Zondervan, 2007), 125–142. Since the whole work is intertextual in nature as it deals with the importance of the OT in Matthew's mission, this section narrows the search to a few typological elements in the gospel, hence the rubric intertextual typology.
254. Baker, *Two Testaments, One Bible*, 115–117.
255. Ibid. Cf. Arnold A. van Ruler, *The Christian Church and the Old Testament*, (Grand Rapids: Eerdmans, 1971, trans. from German 1955).
256. Baker, *Two Testaments, One Bible*, 169; Gerhard von Rad, "Typological Interpretation of the Old Testament," *Int* 15 (1961): 174–192.
257. George Wesley Buchanan. *Typology and the Gospel*, (Lanham: University Press of America, 1987), 3.
258. Baker, *Two Testaments, One Bible*, 170.

interest of the NT writers."²⁵⁹ This argument is rooted in the eighteenth and nineteenth centuries when the objectivity of history was asserted such that the "historically conditioned deafness to oblique allusions in the Bible" led many to doubt typological interpretation.²⁶⁰ But "typological exegesis assumes a divine sovereignty over history," an assumption objected to by some.²⁶¹ Yet it is on this assumption that the NT establishes similarities and correspondences of persons, institutions, offices, events, actions, and objects between the OT and the NT that may be rightly regarded as types and antitypes. For Baker, typology is historical—events, people, institutions— and implies real correspondences.²⁶²

Before looking at typology in Matthew there is need to examine briefly the meaning and nature of typology since no separate literature review has been provided to this effect.²⁶³ A type, from the Greek τύπος, means "model" or "pattern." Biblical type is defined as "pattern of dealings of God with men that is followed in the antitype."²⁶⁴ Those dealings of God are said to be repeated with fullness and finality at the coming of Christ. In this understanding, all the types point to Christ or are in some way related to

---

259. Leonhard Goppelt, *Typos: Typological Interpretation of the Old Testament in the New*, trans. Donald H. Madvig (Grand Rapids: Eerdmans, 1982), xiv.

260. Allison, *The New Moses,* 18. Allison developed clear criteria for identifying typological allusions which include explicit statements, inexplicit statements, similar circumstances, key words or phrases, similar narrative structure, and word order, syllabic sequence, poetic resonance (19–20). The whole book provides a complete survey of how Moses has been used as a typological figure from ancient texts and how Matthew depicts Jesus as the antitype of Moses.

261. Goppelt, *Typos,* xv.

262. Baker, *Two Testaments, One Bible*, 179–180.

263. David L. Baker, "Typlogy and the Christian Use of the Old Testament," in *The Right Doctrine from the Wrong Texts? Essays on the Use of the Old Testament in the New Testament*, ed. G. K. Beale (Grand Rapids: Baker Academic, 1994), 313–330; G. P. Hugenberger, "Introductory Notes on Typology," in *The Right Doctrine from the Wrong Texts?* 331–341. Francis Foulkes, "The Acts of God: A Study of the Basis of Typology in the Old Testament," in *The Right Doctrine from the Wrong Texts?* 342–371.

264. R. T. France, *Jesus and the Old Testament: His Application of Old Testament Passages to Himself and His Mission* (London: The Tyndale Press, 1971), 38. The word is well analyzed in its various nuances by D. L. Baker, *Two Testaments, One Bible: A study of some modern solutions to the theological problem of the relationship between the Old and the New Testaments* (Downers Grove: IVP, 1976), 251–253. See also A. B. Mickelsen, *Interpreting the Bible* (Grand Rapids: Eerdmans, 1963), 237. He sees correspondences as present because God controls history.

him as the antitype.[265] France explains that a type is not a prediction in the manner of prophecies. It is simply a person or event which is pure historical fact without intrinsic reference to the future.[266] In the same manner, the antitype is not a fulfillment of prediction but rather a re-embodiment of a principle which has been previously exemplified in the type.[267] The question that one may raise concerning France's point is whether or not there was anything intrinsic in the type since God was in each type working out his overall salvific purposes.

Next in this discussion is the concept of intertextuality. Waltke defines it as "the phenomenon whereby one passage of Scripture refers to another."[268] Intertextuality, therefore, has the idea of interaction of texts in which a "prior body of discourse" provides meaning to subsequent text(s) so that the subsequent text "implicitly or explicitly takes up, prolongs, cites, refutes, transposes" the prior text.[269] In other words, texts serve "as generative matrices of further meaning projected by other texts through a textual network or textual grid," such that they are "framed or re-contextualized in different ways within different biblical texts."[270] Within the OT, "innerbiblical exegesis" takes place as prior biblical texts are used by later writers "to re-use, re-contextualize, extend, reformulate, re-interpret, or transform" the former text(s).[271] In this work, intertextual typology refers to Matthew's typological use of the OT in the light of his recontextualization, re-in-

---

265. E. Earle Ellis looks at typology broadly as prophetic representation of NT realities. See Ellis, *The Old Testament in Early Christianity: Canon and Interpretation in the Light of Early Christianity* (Grand Rapids: Baker Book House, 1991), 106.

266. France, *Jesus and the Old Testament*, 39–40.

267. Ibid., 40. According to Ellis, typology became, in early Christianity, "a basic key by which the Scriptures were understood" (Ellis, *The Old Testament in Early Christianity*, 105). See also John E. Alsup for origins of Patristic development of typology. John E. Alsup, "Typology," in *ABD*, ed. David Noel Freedman, et al (New York: Double Day, 1992), 6.684–685.

268. Waltke, *An Old Testament Theology*, 125.

269. Anthony C. Thiselton, *New Horizons in Hermeneutics* (Grand Rapids: Zondervan, 1992), 38. See also Paul R. House, "Biblical Theology and the Wholeness of Scripture: Steps Toward a Program for the Future," in *Biblicla Theology: Retrospect and Prospect*, ed. Scott J. Hafemann (Downers Grove: IVP, 2002), 268–270.

270. Thiselton, *New Horizons in Hermeneutics*, 39.

271. Ibid., citing Michael Fishbane, *Biblical Interpretation in Ancient Israel* (Oxford: Clarendon Press, 1985), 1, 140, 410, 414, 440, 473. The example is given in the Chronicler's use of the Books of Kings.

terpretation, reformulation, and transformation[272] of the materials at his disposal. Although there are many antitypes in Matthew, the ones treated here are chosen for their theological and missional relevance for this work. These include the wilderness, the mountain, the sign of Jonah, and the stone. Israel and Moses typology are not treated separately under this section because they are treated within the exodus, the wilderness, and the mountain motifs.

3.5.1 The Wilderness

The writer referred to the wilderness motif in chapter 2 with regards to Jesus' temptation and in this chapter concerning John the Baptist's ministry. This motif is prominent in Matthew, all appearing in connection with the salvific purpose of God (3:1–3; 4:1–11; cf. Mark 1:1–4; Luke 3:4–6; 4:1–12). Matthew 3:1–3 and 4:1–11 are chosen as representative texts on the wilderness motif. Matthew cites from Isaiah to show that John's ministry in the wilderness of Judea is a fulfillment of God's promise and that Jesus' temptation in the wilderness alludes to the wilderness experience of the Israelites.[273]

---

272. For Waltke there is only transformative versus nontransformative intertextuality. The former refers to the use of earlier text(s) by way of interpretation in order "to meet new historical situations and so advance our understanding," while the latter occurs when a writer uses earlier text(s) merely "to fortify or explain their message and/or to embellish their rhetoric" without advancing or deepening theology (Waltke, *An Old Testament Theology*, 126). Walte cites "a possible nontransformative" use of Zephaniah (3:3) by Ezekiel (22:27), but he does not include any scholar supporting this idea.

273. The wilderness theme is prominent in Exodus–Numbers, although it is found also in both the prophets and the Psalms. It evokes the memory of testing and God's miraculous intervention, for when the Israelites left Egypt God led them "around by *the desert* road toward the Red Sea" (Exod 13:18). The wilderness motif has both positive and negative connotations. On the one hand, God provided for his people in the wilderness and guided them by pillar of cloud and fire (Exod 13:21–22). The wilderness was also a place of revelation and where the good news is proclaimed (Isa 40:3). On the other hand, the wilderness resonates with the attitude of unbelief and rebellion, deprivation, attack, testing, disobedience, and punishment (see G. I. Davies, "Wilderness," in *ABD*, 6.914). But one "fascinating aspect of the prophetic treatment of the wilderness tradition is its development of the expectation of a new wilderness experience," see O. Palmer Robertson, *The Israel of God: Yesterday, Today, and Tomorrow* (Philipsburg: P&R Publishing, 2000), 92. The Lord is depicted as one who prepares a way for his people through the wilderness and leads them to their new Zion (Isa 40:3–5; 42:16; 43:19).

It is in the wilderness of Judea that John the Baptist performs his ministry in keeping with prophecy (3:1–3).[274] The major point about the geography of John's baptism for Matthew is the fact that this event took place in the wilderness around the Jordan. The "wilderness" is depicted in 1 Maccabees 2:29, 31; 2 Maccabees 5:27 and Josephus, *Ant.* 12:336; 13:8; 20:167, 188; *Jewish Wars* 2:259 as a place where Jewish zealots such as Mattathias and Judas Maccabeus, among others, found refuge and also planned their attacks on Syria or Rome.[275] In *Ant. 13:8, 13* Jonathan and his brother Simon fled to the wilderness where Jonathan "pitched his camp among the lakes of the Jordan." But John and Jesus did not go to the wilderness for the same purpose as those mentioned above. John chose the wilderness so that he could be set apart from the world as the wilderness represented a place set apart from sinful Israel, "a place to depend on and draw close to God, and so also a fitting place to call people to repentance."[276]

The wilderness typology is also significant for Jesus' ministry.[277] The wilderness temptation of Jesus (Matt 4:1–11) follows the exodus motif in Matthew 2:13–15. This motif is brought out more clearly by the repeated

---

[274]. The wilderness in relation to John's ministry has been discussed earlier in the section on John the Baptist's ministry. In John's gospel John baptized in Bethany, east of the bank of Jordan, opposite the wilderness of Judea.

[275]. Grams, "Geographical and Intertextual Dimensions," 47.

[276]. Ibid. John's choice of wilderness is usually compared with the Qumran community which lived about eight miles away from the area of his ministry. But Grams observed that although some parallels could be drawn between John and the Qumran community, they are not strong enough to identify John with that community. Instead, those parallels "help us to understand the theo-political significance of John (47). Theologically, John the Baptist's location of his ministry in the wilderness, like the Qumran community, is interpreted as a reconstitution of Israel for the return from exile as in Josh 3 or Isa 40. See L. F. Badia, *The Qumran Baptism and John the Baptist*' (The Qumran Community interprets Matt 3:3 as fulfillment of Isa 40:3 in The Rule of the Community 8:12–16 [Pate, *Communities of the Last Days*, 94]. As noted earlier in this chapter regarding the ministry of John the Baptist, Isa 40:3 is used by the Qumran Community in their eschatological expectations [Hill, *The Gospel of Matthew*, 91]). Further parallel is seen in Jesus who, like Joshua, "chose 12 men to symbolize this return from exile and restoration of God's rule over Israel in the land (Grams, "Geographical and Intertextual Dimensions," 47; see also Keener, *Matthew*, 76). The restoration in Isa 40:15–17 would also include God dealing in justice for the nations (Grams, 50–51). But since John preaches repentance, Israel's restoration would include salvation from sins (Matt 1:21).

[277]. See note 522 for the theme of the wilderness in Matthew against its OT background.

"If you are the son of God" in the context of privation in the wilderness.[278] As God's son, Israel was tested before entering the Promised Land. In the same manner Jesus, the Son of God, was tested before beginning his mission.[279] Similarly, parallels are drawn from such things as the "wilderness," the testing, the period of forty, Jesus' identity as "son," and Jesus' three responses from Deuteronomy that "all serve to identify Jesus with Israel, except in the fact that, where Israel failed, Jesus succeeded."[280] Next, we will discuss the mountain motif.

3.5.2 The Mountain

The mountain motif[281] has been referred to in chapter 2 with regard to the transfiguration and the Triune God's involvement in the mission of Jesus. The mountains in Matthew include the mountain of temptation (4:8–11); the Mount of Beatitudes or teaching on God's kingdom (5–7); the mountain of prayer (14:23); the mountain of ministry (15:29–38); the mountain of transfiguration (17:1–8); the mountain of private instruction regarding the end (24:3–25); and the mountain of commission (28:16–20).[282] Each of the mountains plays a significant role in the life and ministry of Jesus. According to Köstenberger and O'Brien, "the Matthean mountain motif highlights, among other things, the correspondence between Jesus' temptation to pursue his calling as the Son of God in worldly terms and his com-

---

278. According to France, "this is put beyond doubt by the three-fold quotation of texts from Deuteronomy 6–8, a passage which focuses throughout on that episode and the lessons it contained for Israel's filial obedience" (France, *Matthew: Evangelist and Teacher*, 208).

279. Holwerda, *Jesus and Israel*, 44.

280. Grams, "Geographical and Intertextual Dimensions," 51.

281. Mountains may be literal landscapes and therefore merely physical features. But in the poetical books the mountains generally signify God's strength and power (e.g. Gen 22:14; Ps 125:1–2). Most important designation of mountains in the Bible is their depiction as sacred sites (Gen 22:1–14; Exod 24:18; Ezek 2813–15; Matt 17:1–8) and their eschatological significance (Isa 5:25; 40:4; Ezek 38:20. While others see the mountain motif in Matthew in light of Jesus as the new Moses such that in the Sermon on the Mount Jesus sits and "gives a commentary on the decalogue" (see, for example, Allison, *The New Moses*, 172), Terence L. Donaldson sees the motif primarily in terms of christological themes, depicting Jesus as the Son of God gathering Israel and the nations in the eschatological age (see Terence L. Donaldson in his *Jesus on the Mountain: A Study in Matthean Theology*, JSNTSS 8 [Sheffield: JSOT Press, 1985]: 101ff).

282. See Andreas J. Köstenberger and Peter T. O'Brien, *Salvation to the Ends of the Earth: A Biblical Theology of Mission*, NSBT 2 (Downers Grove: IVP, 2001), 97–98.

Mission to Israel: Foundations and Framework 133

prehensive authority subsequent to his vindication and exaltation as the risen Son who issues the 'Great Commission.'"[283] Relevant mountain motif for this work is the Mount of Beatitudes that was treated in connection with the Torah. We will treat briefly the temptation mountain of Matthew 4:8–10 and reserve the mountain of commission for chapter 4.

In Matthew 4:8–11 the devil took Jesus to a very high mountain.[284] What is the significance of this mountain in the narrative? Although most scholars argue for Moses typology, Nolland does not think that the episode echoes "Moses' viewing of the land from Mount Pisgah" because Moses was not allowed to enter the land while Satan promises it to Jesus.[285] But Allison argues that the event is "probably related to Matthew's new Moses theme," arguing from the analogy that God showed Moses all the land from Mount Pisgah (Deut 3:27; 34:1–4).[286] It is believed by some scholars like Donaldson and Grams that Matthew structures the three temptations in the order of wilderness-temple-mountain that is likened to Jesus' baptism in the wilderness, to his temple ministry, and finally to the Great Commission on the Galilean mountain. Whether this ordering is intentional or not, "both the third temptation and the Great Commission share an emphasis on sovereignty over the world and on who should be worshiped."[287] Grams proposes that Psalm 2 is in view in the baptism and temptation stories in which "Jesus is declared God's 'Son' and tested three times in relation to this."[288] Grams observed correctly that the mountain in Psalm 2 is Mount Zion and not a mountain from which the nations of the earth are surveyed as in Matthew 4:11. Grams connects this mountain motif with the Great Commission and says that when Jesus assumed the

---

283. Ibid., 98.
284. The description of the mountain as ὄρος ὑψηλὸν λίαν in 4:8 corresponds to Matt 17:1 except that Matthew does not use λίαν in 17:1
285. Nolland, *The Gospel of Matthew*, 166.
286. Allison, *The New Moses*, 170–171; see also Hagner, *Matthew 1–13*, 68; Turner, *Matthew* 129.
287. Grams, "Geographical and Intertextual Dimensions," 51; Donaldson, *Jesus on the Mountain*, 101ff. Similarly, Turner believes that the temptation "recalls Israel's idolatrous worship in the desert (Exod 32)" (Turner, *Matthew*, 130).
288. Grams, "Geographical and Intertextual Dimensions," 51–52.

position of the royal "Son" of Psalm 2 he picks up the task of a universal eschatological reign.[289]

But it is important to draw some distinctions among the three mountains. The temptation mountain clearly represents Satan's attempt to deflect Jesus from accomplishing his mission, an attempt which Jesus rejected. The mountain of the Great Commission is in Galilee and not Mount Zion. The significant shift Matthew makes from Mount Zion to the mountain in Galilee is discussed in chapter 4. Although one may not press for exact correspondence in typology there is the need to draw parallels only when such is warranted by the text(s) of Scripture. Therefore, the mountain of temptation better expresses the exodus motif of the Gospel of Matthew.

Theologically, Matthew places much significance on the mountain motif (cf. Matt 5:1; Luke 6:17). As Mount Sinai and Mount Zion are sacred in the faith traditions of Israel,[290] the seven mountains in the Gospel of Matthew show that Jesus identified with Moses and Israel. The mountain of temptation brings the typological connection between Jesus and Israel much closer. We will explore the mountain motif further in chapter 4.

3.5.3 The Sign of Jonah

The pericope of Matthew 12:38–45 (16:1–4; Mark 8:11–12; Luke 11:16, 24–26, 29–32) appears in the context of Jesus' confrontation with the Jewish leaders. In Matthew 12:22–24, the Pharisees accuse Jesus of driving out demons by the power of Beelzebub, the prince of demons. But now, along with the teachers of the law, the Pharisees are asking for a miraculous sign (12:38).[291] They wanted Jesus to support his claim that his mission

---

289. Ibid., 52. For Grams, this is never to be seen as a replacement theology but a fulfillment theology. "Jesus as a royal Messiah will fulfill Israel's call to reign over the nations."

290. See Levenson, *Sinai and Zion*, 51–52.

291. There are evidences that at Jesus' time people believed that signs would precede the last days. 1Q27 frag. 1, 1:5–8 reads: "This shall be the sign that this shall come to pass: when the sources of evil are shut up and wickedness is banished in the presence of righteousness, as darkness in the presence of light, or as smoke vanishes and is no more, in the same way wickedness will banish forever and righteousness will be manifest like the sun. The world will be made firm and all the adherents of the secrets of [??] <sins> (MS: wonder) shall be no more. True knowledge shall fill the world and there will never be any more folly. This is all ready to happen, it is a true oracle, and by this it shall be known to you that it cannot be averted" (Evans, "Jesus and the Continuing Exile of Israel," 93). For the importance of

was from God by a sign (σημεῖον). They had already seen many of Jesus' miracles. What they were asking for was not signs, but a sign (σημεῖον), that is, an irrefutable confirmation that all the miraculous works he had been doing had God's approval. Jesus rejects their demand and calls them "a wicked and adulterous generation."[292] Instead of a sign, he shows them the typological significance of Jonah. Matthew does not quote from the OT as fulfillment story but rather draws analogy from the life of Jonah. God called Jonah and sent him on a mission to Nineveh, but he refused to go. Yet he later repented and went to Nineveh after his experience in the belly of a fish for three days and three nights (Jon 1:17). The LXX rendering of the text is like the MT. (See the following table).

Table 10: *The Sign of Jonah and the Son of Man*

MT	LXX	NT
Jonah 2:1 וַיְהִ֤י יוֹנָה֙ בִּמְעֵ֣י הַדָּ֔ג שְׁלֹשָׁ֥ה יָמִ֖ים וּשְׁלֹשָׁ֥ה לֵילֽוֹת׃	Jonah 2:1 καὶ ἦν Ιωνας ἐν τῇ κοιλίᾳ τοῦ κήτους τρεῖς ἡμέρας καὶ τρεῖς νύκτας	Matt 12:40 ὥσπερ γὰρ ἦν Ἰωνᾶς ἐν τῇ κοιλίᾳ τοῦ κήτους τρεῖς ἡμέρας καὶ τρεῖς νύκτας, οὕτως ἔσται ὁ υἱὸς τοῦ ἀνθρώπου ἐν τῇ καρδίᾳ τῆς γῆς τρεῖς ἡμέρας καὶ τρεῖς νύκτας.
". . . and Jonah was inside the fish three days and three nights."	". . . and Jonah was inside the fish three days and three nights."	"For as Jonah was three days and three nights in the belly of a huge fish, so the Son of Man will be three days and three nights in the heart of the earth."

---

signs and wonders, see also *Jewish Wars* 1.1.11.28; *Antiquities of the Jews* 20:8.6.168 (Evans, "Jesus and the Continuing Exile of Israel," 93).

292. On the theme of judgment due to unbelief in Matthew, see D. Marguerat, *Le jugement dans l'Evangile de Matthieu* (Geneva: Labor er Fides, 1981), 266–267, as cited by France, *Matthew: Evangelist and Teacher,* 217.

Matthew follows the LXX in word order. Therefore not much could be said about the text.

The "sign" of Jonah in Matthew is what Jonah himself was, not the sign given to him or that which was represented by him.[293] Jonah served as sign of judgment to the Ninevites, and so does Jesus for a wicked and adulterous generation. Matthew refers to Jonah as a prophet, the only place he is referred to as prophet in the NT.[294] Gundry notes that this insertion of τοῦ προφήτου is "in order to stress Jesus' fulfilling the prophetic typology apparent in Jonah."[295] Therefore, "for Matthew the typological relationship sheds light on the meaning of Jesus' ministry in terms of Jesus' and Jonah's respective identities as prophets, their ministries as preachers of repentance, their personal destinies of suffering and death, and their experience of resurrection."[296] The redemptive nature of the sign of Jonah in Matthew is clearly seen in the differences between Mathew and the other Synoptics.

Although Matthew stresses Jesus' death and resurrection, the other Synoptics do not. In Mark 8:11–12, the Pharisees' demand for a sign is never granted. In Luke 11:29–32, Jonah is a sign to the Ninevites, as the Son of Man is to that generation. But in Matthew the typological relationship between Jonah and Jesus is elaborated so that Jonah's three days in the belly of the fish becomes a type of Jesus' own three days and three nights in the heart of the earth. Jesus' resurrection, then, is a fulfillment of the sign of Jonah. Luke, on the other hand, does not link this sign with Jesus resurrection. Therefore, the theological and missional significance of this typology for Matthew is the redemptive work of Christ through his death and resurrection typified by Jonah's three days and three nights in the belly of a fish.

---

293. Carson, "Matthew," 63.

294. See Jack M. Sasson, *Jonah*, The Anchor Bible with Introduction and Commentary (New York: Doubleday, 1990), 342–343 on why Jonah belongs to the category of prophets.

295. Gundry, *Matthew*, 243. Although the conjunction subordinate "as" or "just as" (ὥσπερ) in Matt 12:40 might lead to the conclusion that this could be treated as a simile, the parallels drawn between this OT figure (Jonah) and the life of Jesus would call for more than a simile. Matthew suggests that Jonah's three days and three nights in the belly of a fish provides a good pattern and model for Jesus' death and resurrection.

296. Michael Knowles, *Jeremiah in Matthew's Gospel: The Rejected-Prophet Motif in Matthean Redaction*, JSNTSup 68 (Sheffield: Sheffield Academic Press, 1993), 242.

3.5.4 The Stone[297]

Klyne R. Snodgrass has categorized the parable of the wicked tenants (21:33–46; cf. Mark 12:1–12; Luke 20:9–19) within the parables that are specifically about Israel.[298] The parable of the wicked tenants provides the immediate context for the quotation in Matthew 21:42. Central figures in this parable are the wicked tenants and the stone imagery. Some of the important issues raised concerning the parable include: the judgment statement and how Psalm 118: 22–23 fits with the parable; the reality of the story; the origin of the story, namely, from Jesus or from the early church; and whether the parable teaches that God has rejected Israel by giving the kingdom to the gentiles.[299] The last issue will be discussed in chapter 4. But we will begin with the text as follows:

---

297. The use of stone in Matt 21:42 is metonymical. The stone imagery in the OT is vast. It may depict lifelessness, hard and unresponsive hearts, enduring quality and strength, object for stumbling, object of judgment, and a foundation stone as in Isa 28:16. It is this last imagery that Matthew and the NT apply to Jesus as the living cornerstone.

298. Klyne R. Snodgrass, *Stories with Intent: A Comprehensive Guide to the Parables of Jesus* (Grand Rapids: Eerdmans, 2008), 255–325.

299. Snodgrass, *Stories with Intent*, 289–296.

Table 11: *"The Stone the Builders Rejected"*

MT	LXX	NT
Ps 118:22-23 ²²אֶבֶן מָאֲסוּ הַבּוֹנִים הָיְתָה לְרֹאשׁ פִּנָּה: ²³מֵאֵת יְהוָה הָיְתָה זֹּאת הִיא נִפְלָאת בְּעֵינֵינוּ:	Ps 117:22-23 ²² λίθον ὃν ἀπεδοκίμασαν οἱ οἰκοδομοῦντες οὗτος ἐγενήθη εἰς κεφαλὴν γωνίας ²³ παρὰ κυρίου ἐγένετο αὕτη καὶ ἔστιν θαυμαστὴ ἐν ὀφθαλμοῖς ἡμῶν	Matt 21:42 λέγει αὐτοῖς ὁ Ἰησοῦς, Οὐδέποτε ἀνέγνωτε ἐν ταῖς γραφαῖς, Λίθον ὃν ἀπεδοκίμασαν οἱ οἰκοδομοῦντες, οὗτος ἐγενήθη εἰς κεφαλὴν γωνίας· παρὰ κυρίου ἐγένετο αὕτη καὶ ἔστιν θαυμαστὴ ἐν ὀφθαλμοῖς ἡμῶν;
"The stone the builders rejected has become the capstone; ²³ the LORD has done this, and it is marvelous in our eyes."	"The stone the builders rejected has become the capstone; ²³ the LORD has done this, and it is marvelous in our eyes."	Jesus said to them, "Have you never read in the Scriptures: 'The stone the builders rejected has become the capstone; the Lord has done this, and it is marvelous in our eyes'"?

In Matthew's citation of Psalm 118:22, 23, the LXX follows the MT, and Matthew agrees with both. No textual issues surface.[300] This text is unique in Matthew since he composes his text "after the pattern of OT passages" in which a kingdom is torn from one person and given to another, or a kingdom is established to replace an existing one (1 Sam 15:28; Dan 2:44; 7:27).[301] The quotation of Psalm 118:22–23 concludes the message of the passage (21:33–41). The traditional interpretation of the parable is based on the vineyard allegory in Isaiah 5:1–7[302] in which the vineyard

---

300. See Blomberg, "Matthew," in *Commentary on the New Testament Use of the Old Testament*, 74. See Hagner, *Matthew 14–28*, 623. France, *The Gospel of Matthew*, 816.
301. Gundry, *Matthew*, 429.
302. Snodgrass, "As a prophet Jesus took a prophetic tool, the parable, and more precisely a specific parable theme, the vineyard of Isa 5:1–7, and recast the story to serve as a juridical

stands for the house of Israel and the people of Judah. The Qumran community's *pesher* on Isaiah 5:1–7 regarded their community as "the divine replacements of unfruitful Israel."[303] The climax of this story sees the sending of the son as a last resort. The landowner assumes that the tenants would respect his son. This son is the one he loved (Mark 12:6). Matthew does not use Mark's "beloved" which would have suggested a clear link with 3:17 and 17:5. But "in the context of the Gospel a reader cannot avoid finding a strong christological statement in the image of the son."[304] But this son also suffers the same fate as the servants. Moreover, the tenants kill the son with the hope that the inheritance would eventually be theirs. When they kill the son, the owner of the vineyard comes himself. Gundry thinks that this is a reference to the *parousia*,[305] but other scholars think that this coming of the owner is merely part of the story and needs no allegorical interpretation (such as the destruction of Jerusalem).[306]

Based on the verdict pronounced on the wicked tenants, Jesus cites Psalm 118:22, 23 as prophecy concerning him. The most important issue for Snodgrass is how Psalm 118: 22–23 fits with the parable.[307] The quotation is believed to have been inserted by the early Christians to support the idea of the resurrection. But Snodgrass notes that the psalm "was important in Judaism as part of the great Hallel and for Jesus as well, as is evident in his use of it in the lament over Jerusalem (Matt 23:39; Luke 13:35)."[308] Snodgrass believes that the quotation is not an early church addition but "is the key to understanding the parable" because the stone quotation makes the impact of the parable clear.[309]

Matthew draws from an OT imagery of a "messianic stone."[310] In Isaiah 8:14–15, God himself is the stone and a rock that causes both houses of

---

parable, a self-indicting mirror, for the religious leaders" (Snodgrass, *Stories with Intent*, 295).
303. See Pate, *Communities of the Last Days*, 97.
304. Nolland, *The Gospel of Matthew*, 873.
305. Gundry, *Matthew*, 428. Gundry's position represents the consensus interpretation.
306. See France, *The Gospel of Matthew*, 814.
307. Snodgrass, *Stories with Intent*, 289.
308. Ibid., 290.
309. Ibid.
310. France, *The Gospel of Matthew*, 817. This messianic stone imagery is also found in Acts 4:11; Rom 9:32–33; 1 Pet 2:4–8. See also Scott S. Cunningham, "Ephesians 2:19–22: The

Israel to stumble. Looking at the quoted verses in their context, Psalm 118 is a psalm of praise. It appears that the king of Israel or the psalmist is speaking here and is giving thanks on behalf of all Israel (118:2, 3) because the Lord delivered him or the nation from enemies (118:7, 10–13). Psalm 118:19–21 portrays someone who is so eager to enter the gates of the Lord's house, the temple, to offer thanksgiving for the victory the Lord won on their behalf. The item of praise in the temple of the Lord is probably "Israel's triumph over the enemies who had despised her."[311] Therefore, the "rejected stone" could probably be the nation Israel that was despised by the enemies but exalted and made prominent by God. And if Jesus is interpreted typologically as the new Israel, then the application of the text to him is not hard to understand. "The quotation says explicitly and dramatically what the parables intends: the religious leaders have rejected the son, the climatic envoy from God, but this rejection will be reversed by God and the leaders will lose their role in God's purposes."[312]

The theological and missional significance of the text is that Jesus is the stone the builders rejected, but has become the cornerstone.[313] The builders are the Jewish religious leaders[314] who reject the prophets, the wise men, and the teachers. They kill and crucify some; others they flog in their synagogue and pursue from town to town (23:34). They also reject Jesus, the

---

Temple Motif," in *Interpreting the New Testament Text*, 294, note 25 on the christological interpretation of the cornerstone imagery. But given that the Targums take Ps 118:22 as messianic, it is possible to regard the psalm as directly predictive prophecy and fulfillment, although typology may not be ruled out.

311. France, *The Gospel of Matthew*, 815.

312. Snodgrass, *Stories with Intent*, 290.

313. France argues, "If it was Jesus himself who linked that quotation with his vineyard story, that would go a long way toward accounting for the rapid development of such new Israel typology among his followers" (France, *The Gospel of Matthew*, 815). The "capstone" may literally mean "head of the corner" "understood as the highest stone in a corner of the wall, which holds the two sides of the building together" such that "it is thus both conspicuous and structurally indispensable." And this link would have been more natural if Jesus spoke in Aramaic due to the play on word of stone (אֶבֶן) and son (בֵּן), an echo that is absent in Greek text (815). For the wordplay, see also Snodgrass, *Stories with Intent*, 290. The imagery of cornerstone (κεφαλὴ γωνίας), literally "corner head," "lies behind the description of Jesus as the *akrogōniaios* [ἀκρογωνιαῖος] 'top cornerstone' of God's building, the church, in Eph 2:20; cf. 1 Pet 2:6 where the same term occurs in the LXX quotation from Isaiah 28:16, also applied to Jesus" (815–816).

314. Nolland, *The Gospel of Matthew*, 878. It is said that the Qumran community also used "builders" negatively for Jewish leaders (878).

Son of God, and crucify him. But he triumphs over death and receives all authority and becomes the cornerstone of the church. The church, made up of Jews and gentiles, produces the fruit of the kingdom.

3.6 Summary and Conclusion

Reading Matthew's fascinating matrix of promise-fulfillment narrative from OT foundations and framework in his mission to Israel presents a number of issues and conclusions for consideration. The first and prominent among these multifaceted issues is Matthew's method of citing the OT. The writer observed that Matthew abbreviates and paraphrases the MT and the LXX most of the time, although he does so much more with the MT but reproduces the LXX largely especially when following Mark. He seems to cite the OT as it best serves his purposes. The assumption is that Matthew follows a theological and missional approach using a vantage point of a "teacher of the law who has been instructed about the kingdom of heaven" and "like the owner of a house who brings out of his storeroom new treasures as well as old" (Matt 13:52). In his OT citations, Matthew is a trained theologian who reads, reflects upon, interprets, and applies the OT as he deems appropriate in the light of Jesus and his mission. Therefore, Matthew has transformed, reinterpreted, and recontextualized many of the OT texts he cited.

The second issue is Matthew's transformation and reinterpretation of OT "faith traditions" based on his theme of promise fulfillment. Matthew demonstrates that mission to Israel is embedded in the OT fabric of redemptive events and institutions, prophetic ministry, geographical locations, and typology, which to him are all interconnected with a single saga of God's salvific purpose. The redemptive events and institutions, which are deemed to have found their full realization in the coming of Jesus, include the exodus, the giving of the Torah, the Davidic kingdom, the temple, and the restoration. Matthew's theological and missional reading has colored all of these historical events. The exodus marks the birth of a nation and Canaan was the Promised Land for the chosen nation. The Jewish Passover that Jesus celebrates with his disciples (Matt 26:17–30) commemorates this important event. For Matthew, Jesus leads Israel in a new exodus, and evidently from the bondage of sin. The bond between God and the nation Israel is sealed through the Sinaitic covenant enshrined in the Torah. Jesus comes to fulfill the Torah. But Israel was also given the kingship idealized in the Davidic kinship (guided by the Torah and marked by justice and righteousness) whose dynasty is to last forever and to be a blessing to the rest of the world. The Davidic kingdom, a model of God's rule for his people, was associated with the temple as a symbol of God's abiding presence in Israel. The temple was a royal sanctuary. Therefore, the three religious institutions of Torah, kingship, and temple are inextricably connected. But due to Israel's unfaithfulness it could not enjoy fully the blessings of the Promised Land, and eventually went into exile. Although restoration took place under Cyrus, Israel seemed to have remained in exile until the final restoration could take place with the coming of the Messiah. Matthew shows that the coming of Christ brought that restoration. His hermeneutical method is vivid in the phrases ἵνα πληρωθῇ or οὕτως γὰρ γέγραπται. But the most remarkable is that the eternal kingdom promised to the house of David appears to have become the kingdom of heaven. The spatial realm has assumed a universal dimension of the reign of God. And one enters this kingdom by repentance (Matt 4:17), and by believing (Matt 8:10–12) and receiving Jesus (Matt 10:40).

The third issue emerging from this chapter is Matthew's interpretation of prophecy. For Matthew, not only did God use redemptive events and institutions as promise of greater things to come in the person of Christ, Israel's long-awaited Messiah, the prophets also play a major role as God used them to announce the coming of Christ. "For all the Prophets and the Law prophesied until John" (Matt 11:13). For Matthew, prophetic ministry is the key to unlocking God's salvific purposes for the world through the Messiah. Prophecy, according to him, covers the significant events of Jesus' life—his birth, his ministry, his passion, and his death. All these events in the life of Jesus were a fulfillment of OT promises. But the issue is usually with the context from which Matthew cites his text and its appropriate application to his situation. A conclusion here is that Matthew interprets the OT from a theological and missional viewpoint.

Similarly, since the land is clearly associated with God's promises to the nation Israel—to Abraham and his descendants—geography plays an important role in the scheme of promise-fulfillment. Geographical locations are all programmatically included in God's salvific purposes. Jesus is born in Bethlehem, a fulfillment of the promise of Micah 5:2. Egypt plays a significant role not only as a place where Jesus is preserved from Herod's wrath but also a fulfillment of the promise of the new exodus of Hosea 11:1. But it is not Israel alone who benefits from promises associated with land or geography. As the next chapter illustrates, although Galilee is a starting point of Jesus' mission to Israel, the gentiles are also included in this promise (Isa 9:1–2).

The final issue presented in this chapter is Matthew's typology. There are people, events, places, and things in the OT that Matthew sees in them a corresponding fulfillment in the life of Jesus. For Matthew, they too fulfill the promises of God in the OT. On the whole, then, redemptive events and institutions, prophecy, geography, and intertextual typology form a coherent web in the mission of God in the Gospel of Matthew. Each is inextricably linked to the other.

But if Matthew's gospel portrays that what Jesus does, and represents and fulfills God's salvific purposes for Israel, how do these salvific purposes apply to the nations? The goal of chapter 4 is therefore to examine how Israel's redemptive events and institutions, prophetic ministry, geography, and intertextual typology, directly or indirectly, apply to the nations.

CHAPTER 4

Mission to the Nations: Foundations and Framework

4.1 Introduction

This chapter probes mission to the nations[1] in the Gospel of Matthew.[2] The researcher argues that in Matthew both Israel and the nations[3] are recipients of God's salvific purposes.[4] The promise-fulfillment framework

---

1. This is the universal dimension of mission, seen alongside the particularistic aspect in chapter 3. As Wright says, this double dimension of the mission of Jesus is found throughout the NT. "It is consistent not only with the Old Testament passages in which the eschatological scenario often included this sequence: Israel would be restored and then the nations would be gathered. Or, as in Zech 2 and Zech 9, the king (i.e. YHWH) would return to Zion (thus restoring the kingdom in their midst), and then the nations would be joined to his people" (Wright, *The Mission of God*, 506).

2. Jeremias points out, "Of the three synoptists, Matthew evinces the strongest indication to ascribe to Jesus a missionary activity among the gentiles" (Jeremias, *Jesus' Promise to the Nations*, 34). Hahn says, "In Matthew each of the two missions, Jewish and gentile, involves the other" (Hahn, *Mission in the New Testament*, 127).

3. Hahn, *Mission in the New Testament*, 127. For scholars like Lloyd Gaston, mission to the nations in Matthew comes as a result of the tragic failure of Jesus' mission to Israel; see Lloyd Gaston, "The Messiah of Israel As Teacher of the Gentiles: The Setting of Matthew's Christology," *Int* 29 (1975): 24.

4. One of the conclusions Ulrich Luz draws from the Gospel of Matthew about gentile mission in Matt 28:19–20 is that Matthew saw Jesus as the risen Lord and "was such a living presence that he was able to retract and reverse his earlier command to minister to Israel only" (see Ulrich Luz, *The Theology of the Gospel of Matthew*, trans. J Bradford Robinson [Cambridge: Cambridge University Press, 1995], 143). For Luz, Matthew was either adapting Jesus' saying or writing afresh to meet contemporary needs. However, this author reads the Gospel of Matthew from promise-fulfillment perspective and therefore sees

regarding the nations is both explicit and implicit in Matthew. Some of the relevant passages explored in this chapter in relation to gentile mission include: 1:1–17; 2:1–12; 3:7–9; 4:16–17; 5–7; 8:10–12, 17; 12:18–21, 38–40; 21:12–13, 42–43; 26:26–29. In these passages Matthew alludes to or quotes from the OT. It will be argued that mission to the nations in the Gospel of Matthew has not been given the attention it deserves.[5] This is partly due to "a side effect of the focus on Matthew's relationship to Judaism in current scholarship" which brought about "a relative lack of attention to Matthew's relationship to the gentile world."[6] To address this "lack of attention" the researcher will examine Matthew's interpretation of the mission to the nations from Israel's redemptive events and institutions, prophetic ministry, geographical locations, and intertextual typology.

This chapter is an attempt to answer the question, "How is it that in this Jewish gospel, designed as it is to present Jesus as the Messiah fulfilling Old Testament predictions and typologies, we find a consistent, growing

---

the tension between Jewish and gentile mission as interwoven in the narrative and assumes that mission to Israel is a starting point.

5. A few general works in recent discussion relevant to this chapter include Senior and Stuhlmueller, *The Biblical Foundations for Mission*. In his discussion on foundations for mission in the NT, Senior surveys the mission theology of Matthew and observes that the significant elements of Matthew's mission theology are salvation history and response as a universal principle. With this universal principle, the particularistic proclivity in the Gospel of Matthew gives way to a universal mission. Senior also treats the mission discourse in Matt 10 and the final commission (28:16–20) in which the mission becomes universal. Another contribution in recent times is Wright's *The Mission of God*. In chapter 15, Wright examines God and the nations in the New Testament mission. He treats Jesus and the evangelists in relation to gentile mission as well as gentile-focused quotations. Schnabel is also a significant contributor in this general direction. In his *Jesus and the Twelve,* Schnabel explores Jesus and the gentiles in chapter 12. Walter C. Kaiser Jr., *Mission in the Old Testament: Israel as a Light to the Nations* (Grand Rapids: Baker Academic, 2000), is also significant in this direction as he examines God's intention for Israel as light to the nations. Similarly, John C. Hutchison's article, "Women, Gentiles, and the Messianic Mission in Matthew's Genealogy," *BSac* 158 (April–June 2001), 152–164, is a significant contribution in this direction as he discusses the place and significance of gentile women in Matthew's genealogy. Holwerda's *Jesus and Israel* is an important contribution on promise-fulfillment. His focus on Israel as people of God, temple, land, and law and their realization in the church age shows that the church is included in the promises made to Israel. Another significant contribution is the work of Baker, *Two Testaments, One Bible*. In chapter 8 of his book, Baker examines the fulfillment of God's promises "in the emergence of the Christian community" (215). The promises made to Abraham and his descendants are fulfilled in Jesus and applied to the church.

6. Donald Senior, "Between Two Worlds: Gentiles and Jewish Christians in Matthew's Gospel," *CBQ* 61 (1999): 5.

stream of references to the gentile mission?"[7] Wright believes that Jesus and his followers built on a laid-down edifice that became the mission of the church.[8] As a matter of procedure, the writer treats Matthew's theological and missional interpretation of redemptive events such as the Abrahamic promise, the inclusion of gentile women in Jewish genealogy, God's universal righteousness, the new covenant in the blood of Christ, prophecy, geography, and typology. The writer focuses on these themes from selected fulfillment quotations and other relevant texts with OT motifs to show

---

7. Köstenberger and O'Brien, *Salvation to the Ends of the Earth*, 87. On his part, Warren Carter believes that "Matthew engages the gentile world systematically with a much broader focus on God's just and transforming reign." For him, Matthew is not concerned about individual conversions but the transformation of the gentile world as a way of God demonstrating supremacy over the kingdoms of the world. See Warren Carter, "Matthew and the Gentiles: Individual Conversion and/or Systematic Transformation?" *JSNT* 26.3 (2004): 259–282.

8. Wright, *The Mission of God*, 501. The reasoning of Jesus and his followers, as he says, is anchored to seven cardinal facts. First, the God of Israel is believed to be the God of the whole earth. Second, the nations of the earth, including Israel, stood under God's wrath and judgment. Third, God wills that all the nations of the earth should come to know and worship him. Fourth, God chose Israel to be the means of bringing blessings to all nations. Fifth, the Messiah is the one appointed by God to embody and fulfill the mission of Israel. Sixth, Jesus of Nazareth, the crucified and risen one, is the promised Messiah. Seventh, based on the given facts, the time had now come for the nations to hear the good news (501). See also McKnight, *A Light Among the Gentiles*. He says, "Jews were integrally related to the non-Jewish society in which they were living. Owing largely to the prophets, many Jewish thinkers began to perceive the world as a unity and consequently developed a sense of universalistic religious outlook. If God was the creator of the world and if he had revealed his truth to Israel, then it was the truth also for the whole world, even if Israel was the custodian and tradent of that revelation" (116). John Piper also sees the OT replete with promises and expectations of God being worshipped by all the people from all the nations of the world which form explicit foundation of NT missionary vision. Such foundation, for John Piper, is found in Gen 12:1–3 (see John Piper, *Let the Nations be Glad: The Supremacy of God in Missions* 2nd ed. [Grand Rapids: Baker Academic, 2003], 167). But Wright notes that the centrifugal dimension of the early church mission was something "remarkably new *in practice if not in concept*" (501–502). McKnight arrives at a similar conclusion in his significant work in which he set out to study "the origins of the aggressive missionary behavior of earliest Christianity." McKnight concludes, "Judaism never developed a clear mission to the gentiles that has as its goal the conversion of the world." In effect, then, while Christianity is seen by both Wright and McKnight as a truly missionary religion, Judaism is not, "except in the most general of definitions of missionary" (McKnight, *A Light Among the Gentile*, 116–117). In this connection, Michael F. Bird's point that early Christian mission to Jews and gentiles "did not occur in vacuum and it was indebted to several important contexts, and precedents" may be explored in relation to the milieu from which the early Christian mission developed (see Michael F. Bird, *Crossing Over Sea and Land: Jewish Missionary Activity in the Second Temple Period* [Peabody: Hendrickson Publishers, 2010], 3). But this writer does not intend to pursue Jewish missionary activity in this work.

how Matthew uses them to achieve his theological and missional purposes. After examining the text, the writer will evaluate selected secondary sources dealing with key issues in the light of the evidence of Matthew's text(s).

The writer argues that in Matthew, Israel's redemptive history becomes the story of the nations such that fulfillment of the promises made to the house of Israel is in effect the fulfillment of God's salvific purposes for the world. Jesus Christ, in Matthew, embodies God's saving acts and a "crucial turning point"[9] in his salvific scheme such that response to Jesus' message takes precedence over racial identity. From this line of thought, Matthew sees a common ground in the salvific work of God for both Jews and gentiles. Jesus begins with Israel as people of the covenant through whom God reaches the nations. His mission was first to renew Israel, but is never limited to Israel.[10] Yet in the Great Commission (28:19–20) Matthew does not seem to suggest that gentile mission is dependent upon mission to Israel; each involves the other.

4.2 Redemptive Events, Institutions and Mission

The writer argues that Matthew views the history of the nations within the history of Israel. This may be illustrated from his inclusion of gentile women in Jewish genealogy. Textual evidences and issues that we will explore in this section include: Matthew 1:1, 3:7–9; 8:10–12 (Abrahamic promise and the nations); Matthew 1:3, 5, 6 (gentile women in Jewish genealogy); Matthew 5:1–7:29 (a "single universal righteousness" of the Torah); Matthew 21:12–13 (the temple: a house of prayer [for all nations]); and Matthew 26:17–29 (Jesus and the elect in the blood of the covenant). We will argue that in Matthew's reinterpretation salvation is not exclusively concentrated in Israel's "traditional institutions of salvation," because God now accepts everyone who comes to him by faith, wherever they may be.[11] Therefore, although the exodus, the Torah, the temple, the

---

9. Senior and Stuhlmueller, *The Biblical Foundations for Mission*, 239.
10. Swartley, *Israel's Scripture Traditions*, 65.
11. Hence the command to disciple all nations instead of waiting for people to come to Israel (Schnabel, *Jesus and the Twelve*, 911). Although there is no recorded history of the

Davidic kingdom, and the restoration may not be directly applied to the nations, Matthew provides links that are implicitly, and sometimes explicitly, applied to the nations. The restoration of Israel through the coming of the Messiah provides the ground for the inclusion of the nations in the planned salvific purposes of God rooted in the OT. Matthew's reinterpretation of Israel's faith traditions to the nations will now be examined.

4.2.1 Abrahamic Promise and the Nations

In Matthew 1:1, 3:7–9; 8:10–12 the issue is the person of Abraham and its meaning for Matthew. The writer argues that Matthew 1:1 is to be read alongside 3:7–9 and 8:10–12 and in the light of the gentile mission motif. Matthew mentions the figure of Abraham in the genealogy within the framework of God's redemptive work. This is evident from the key figures and events summarized in 1:1 and 1:17. Matthew connects Jesus Christ to David and Abraham within generations of God's dealings with the people of Israel and the nations (gentile women in the genealogy).[12] Matthew also uses the name of Abraham in 3:7–9 and 8:10–12 to underscore his salvific framework, especially his gentile mission motif.

---

exodus for the nations, the exodus event fulfills the promise made to the patriarch Abraham about his descendants (Gen 15:13–16) and blessing to the nations (Gen 12:1–3). This promise is repeated in Gen 18:18; 22:18; 26:4; 28:14. Therefore, the choice of Israel is an ongoing process through which God brings about the fulfillment of his promises to the nations through Abraham and his seed. According to Bauckham, "The exodus, then, establishes a paradigmatic link between God's particular identity as the God of Israel and God's purpose of universal self-revelation to the nations" (see Bauckham, *Bible and Mission*, 37). As for the Davidic dynasty, "David and his heirs were not merely anointed as kings individually apart from God's larger saving purposes" (Schreiner, *New Testament Theology*, 198). The covenant made with David was that his dynasty would never end (2 Sam 7:11–19; 1 Chr 17:10–27). This Davidic king turns out to be the promised Messiah because the OT anticipated the coming of the anointed king of the Davidic line (Schreiner, *New Testament Theology*, 201). The son of David subdues the nations in inclusion into the salvific purposes of God (Grams, "Geographical and Intertextual Dimensions," 44–45), hence the transformation of the Davidic kingdom into the kingdom of God referred to in chapter 3. See also Baker, *Two Testaments, One Bible*, 80 for the promise in Christ that offers salvation for all who come to him by faith.

12. Paul J. Achtemeier, Joel B. Green and Marianne Meye Thompson argue that Matthew associates Jesus with David and Abraham to show that the salvation this Messiah brings embraces both the gentiles and the Jews. See Paul J. Achtemeier, Joel B. Green and Marianne Meye Thompson, *Introducing the New Testament: Its Literature and Theology* (Grand Rapids: Eerdmans, 2001), 97.

First, Matthew's genealogy underscores his deep knowledge of the Jewish Scriptures[13] and the messianic expectations enshrined in them. The expression Βίβλος γενέσεως in 1:1 is likened to the OT formula אֵלֶּה תּוֹלְדוֹת as in Genesis 2:4; 6:9; 10:1; 11:10, 27; 37:2; and Ruth 4:18 "where in each case it introduces a genealogy that serves as an organizing tool in the narrative history."[14] Not only does Matthew plant Jesus into his Jewish roots by the mention of Abraham and David, it can be argued also that he is aware of the three blessings promised to Abraham in Genesis 12:1–3 making him into a great nation, blessing him so that his name would be great, and that all peoples on earth would be blessed through him.[15] The promise to an individual is so that from the one man the rest of the world would be blessed. Walter Kaiser Jr. traces the choice of Abraham for a blessing from the context of "the three crises" of the fall in the Garden of Eden, the flood, and the Tower of Babel.[16] It is in the history of human failure that God chooses one person through whom his salvific purposes are accomplished. God's salvific purpose for the nations may be illustrated not only by explicit fulfillment of prophecies but also by the implicit mention of the patriarch Abraham in the genealogy whose covenant blessings extend to the nations. In this line of thought, for Jesus to be identified as "son of Abraham" does not simply mean that he was a Jew in the manner that all Jews traced their descent from him (Matt 3:9). Matthew mentions *son of Abraham* "to recall God's promises to Abraham that by his seed all the nations of the earth shall gain blessings (Gen 18:22)."[17] Therefore, the ἐκκλησία that Jesus

---

13. Scholars think the genealogy is a "compressed retelling of the OT story" (Nolland, *The Gospel of Matthew*, 34. According to Nolland, the genealogy echoes Genesis, Ruth 4:18–22 and 1 Chr 3:10–19. All these evoke important aspects of Israel's history). For Gundry, even Matthew's "a record of origins" "reflects OT phraseology, such as that in Gen 2:4; 5:1 LXX" (Gundry, *Matthew*, 13). See also Varner, "A Discourse Analysis of Matthew's Nativity Narrative," 216.

14. See Hutchison, "Women, Gentiles, and the Messianic Mission in Matthew's Genealogy," 162–163.

15. According to Baker, "World mission and blessing for all nations through the chosen people are implicit in Abraham's call (Gen 12:1–13)," stressing that both Testaments recognize the fundamental point that salvation is for Jews and gentiles (see Baker, *Two Testaments, One Bible*), 120.

16. Kaiser Jr., *Mission in the Old Testament*, 16–17.

17. Garland, *Reading Matthew*, 17. Peter and Paul cite this Abrahamic promise (Acts 3:25; Gal 3:6–8). This is a reflection of the understanding of the early believers on this Abrahamic

inaugurates has its roots in the promises of God to the seed of Abraham[18] so that Matthew's genealogy "adumbrates the story of salvation,"[19] for not only does Abraham stand in the genealogy at a decisive point of the origin of the nation of Israel (Gen 12:1–3), but also "at the root of the new people of God (3:9; 8:11)." Some scholars think that the mention of Abraham is an allusion to the patriarchal narrative in Genesis 12–50.[20] But Matthew is also aware that God promised to Abraham and his descendants that they would be a blessing to other nations.[21] Matthew shows that Israel's uniqueness does not mean that God had no concern for other nations.

Second, the mention of Abraham in Matthew 3:9 implies that the Gospel of Matthew is crafted with mission to the nations in view from the beginning. In Matthew 3:7–9, John the Baptist addresses the Pharisees and the Sadducees, the leaders of the people, who seem to have heeded the call for repentance (3:2). But John calls them "brood of vipers" and charges them to produce fruit in keeping with repentance. In Matthew 3:9 John seems to undermine the foundation upon which nominal Jewish faith is built, namely, Πατέρα ἔχομεν τὸν Ἀβραάμ. "For a father, we have Abraham" gives self-confidence to the Jews that the Abrahamic covenant cannot be revoked and that God would have no other children except Abraham's descendants. But John corrects such notion by stating that God could raise up children for Abraham from stones. John seems to say that the identity of τὸν λαὸν αὐτοῦ in 1:21 includes those who were outside of the Abrahamic descent.

Third, this Abrahamic covenant of blessing that flows to the nations is also suggested by the link of the person of Abraham with many who "come from the east and the west and take their places at the feast with Abraham, Isaac, and Jacob in the kingdom of heaven" (8:10–11) as a result of their faith in Jesus. The key concept in Matthew 8:5–13 is the πίστις

---

promise as meaning the inclusion of the gentiles in the church. See also Knowles, *Jeremiah in Matthew's Gospel*, 232.

18. Turner, *Matthew*, 519.

19. John Mark Jones, "Subverting the Textuality of Davidic Messianism: Matthew's Presentation of the Genealogy and the Davidic Title," *CBQ* 56 (1994): 264.

20. Turner, *Matthew*, 59; Robertson, *Christ of the Prophets*, 28.

21. Robertson, *Christ of the Prophets*, 28. According to Verkuyl, God elected Israel with an eye on the nations (see Verkuyl, *Contemporary Missiology*, 90).

of the centurion.[22] His faith draws Jesus' attention. Jesus not only commends the faith of the centurion but immediately links him with Abraham, Isaac and Jacob. Another fascinating observation here is that the mention of Abraham in Matthew 8:11 (and in 3:9) speaks in favor of the "many" (πολλοί) who did not originally form part of the descent from Abraham. In both instances Matthew seems to allude to the Abrahamic blessings of Genesis 12:3. The writer argues that Matthew 8:11 may be interpreted in the light of other references such as Matthew 2:1–12 and Matthew 12:41–42. In the former passage Matthew seems to contrast the faith of the gentile magi with that of the Jews. In the latter passage, the Ninevites and the Queen of the South stand up at the judgment and condemn the generation that heard and saw Jesus' works and yet did not believe.

But the identity of "many from the east and the west" (Matt 8:11) who will feast with Abraham, Isaac and Jacob is subject of debate. Differing from the majority of scholars who believe that the gentiles are in view here, Davies and Allison argue that the assumption of gentiles in the text is "very far from self-evident, whether one is thinking of Jesus or even Matthew."[23] They give six reasons for their position. First, the passage does not explicitly mention gentiles. Second, they see the passage alluding to Psalm 107: 3, which says, "Those he gathered from the lands, from east and west, from north and south." They therefore see the return of the Jewish exiles to their land. Third, they stress that the phrase "east and west" is in Jewish text associated with the coming back of diaspora Jews.[24] For them, therefore, "east and west" refer to Babylon and Egypt.[25] They believe that since the Scriptures do not have instances in which the phrase is used of the eschatological pilgrimage of the gentiles, Matthew 8:11, 12 would not mean the salvation of the gentiles. Instead, Jesus was probably referring to the less privileged diaspora Jews who did not see what Jesus was doing and

---

22. All the Synoptic Gospels portray the centurion(s) in a good light (Matt 8:5–13; 27:54; Mark 15:39–45; Luke 7:1–10; 23:47). A centurion was commended for his faith in Matthew and Luke and as one who loved the Jews and built their synagogue (so Luke). The centurion who witnessed the death of Jesus exclaimed that Jesus was the Son of God (so Matthew and Mark) or a righteous man (so Luke).
23. Davies and Allison, *Matthew*, 121.
24. See *Pss. of Sol.* 11:1–4 on the children of Israel coming from the east and the west.
25. Davies and Allison, *Matthew*, 121.

yet would believe him, as against "the sons of the kingdom" who were the privileged Jews living in Palestine at this time and were witnesses of all the works of Jesus and yet did not believe in him. Fourth, in the OT, the coming of the gentiles is never associated with judgment against Israel. Instead, the gentile pilgrimage serves to exalt Zion. In the light of Matthew 19:28, therefore, Davies and Allison think that "this text presupposes that the scattered tribes have returned to the land."[26] Fifth, "in Israel" (ἐν τῷ Ἰσραὴλ) in the passage could refer either to ethnic unit, namely, the Jewish people, or a geographical entity, that is, the land of Israel. Davies and Allison prefer the latter option.[27] They think that if the "sons of the kingdom" are identified with the Jews as a whole in contrast to gentiles that would consign all Israel to perdition. This is incredible because Jesus, his disciples, and the first evangelists were all Jews. Sixth, although there are many passages in the OT that speak about eschatological pilgrimage of the gentiles to pay homage to Yahweh (cf. Isa 2:1ff), these passages do not speak about the nations participating in the feast of the kingdom of God. Rather, passages like Psalm 107; Isaiah 25–27; 49; and Ezekiel 37–39 connect the pilgrimage of the diaspora Jews to the messianic feast.[28] Therefore, Matthew 8:11–12 draws a contrast between privileged Jews and unprivileged Jews.

However, we will argue here that Abraham serves in this passage as one through whom the nations experience the blessings of God. Abraham also serves *als Glaubensvorbild*[29] for both Jews and gentiles, that is, connection to Jesus and Abraham comes through faith. Therefore, we will advance the following arguments against Davies' and Allison's views. First, Davies and Allison say that "gentiles" are not explicitly mentioned in the text. But it appears unnecessary for Jesus to mention "gentiles" from the east and the west when the subject of discussion is a Gentile—the centurion. Similarly, it appears incongruous for Jesus to contrast the faith of a Gentile (who was present) with the faith of the Jews (who were hearing Jesus) but at the same time refer to diaspora Jews as those coming from the east and west to

---

26. Davies and Allison, *A Critical and Exegetical Commentary*, 2.27.
27. Ibid., 2.24, 25.
28. Ibid., 2.27.
29. See Christoph Joest, "Abraham als Glaubensvorbild in den Pachomianerschriften," *ZNW* 90 (1999), 98–122.

feast with Abraham, Isaac, and Jacob in the kingdom of heaven. Therefore, it seems consistent that the words of Jesus in verse 11 complete the commendation he made of the centurion's faith in verse 10. Second, Davies and Allison allude to Psalm 107 in support of the return of Jewish exile to the land. But are we sure about the text Matthew has in mind? Similarly, although "east and west" echoes eschatological gathering, has Matthew not "economized by mentioning only two of the compass points"?[30] Is not Isaiah 25:6 in which the Lord prepares a feast of rich food for all peoples a better source for Matthew's eschatological banquet? Is Jesus not pointing to those outside Judaism who will become his followers "from the east and the west"?[31] Third, Davies and Allison argue that in the OT the coming of the gentiles is never conceived as a judgment upon Israel or those in the land. Rather, the gentile pilgrimage serves to exalt Zion. But this viewpoint seems to ignore the consequences of lack of faith demonstrated by "the sons of the kingdom" (Matt 8:12) or the larger shape of Matthew's story in which all the nations are discipled for the kingdom of God (Matt 28:19). Fourth, Davies and Allison think that if the "sons of the kingdom" are identified with the Jews as a whole in contrast to gentiles, that would consign all Israel to perdition. This argument is premised on the assumption that "sons of the kingdom" must mean all the Jews in contrast to gentiles. But since Jesus did not say "*all* the sons of the kingdom" in 8:12, would that not mean also that *as many* Jews that will perish due to their lack of faith are "the sons of the kingdom?" There is probably no reason to conclude from the text of Matthew 8:12 that "the sons of the kingdom" are simply identified with the Jews as a whole in contrast to gentiles. Finally, Davies and Allison argue that the many OT passages that speak about eschatological pilgrimage of the gentiles to pay homage to Yahweh do not speak about the nations participating in the feast with Israel in the kingdom of God. Rather, those passages connect the pilgrimage of the diaspora Jews to the messianic feast. But does not Matthew reinterpret and recontextualize the OT texts he cites in the light of Jesus and his mission that extends to the nations? Therefore,

---

30. Nolland, *The Gospel of Matthew*, 357. Cf. Isa 43:5 in which the four corners of the earth are mentioned.

31. Blomberg, *Matthew*, 143.

this writer thinks that if the context of the passage is taken into consideration, one would probably argue for anticipatory gentile inclusion into the kingdom. For Matthew, faith is not only "the door to miraculous powers"[32] but also a door for the nations to feast with Abraham, Isaac, and Jacob in the kingdom of heaven.

Not only is Abraham implicitly mentioned in connection with blessing to the nations in Matthew's genealogy, the inclusion of gentile women is also allusive of the salvific purpose of God for the nations.

4.2.2 Gentile Women in Jewish Genealogy

The writer focuses on Matthew 1:3, 5–6.[33] Matthew mentions the names of gentile women such Tamar, Rahab, Ruth, and Uriah's wife (Bathsheba) in the genealogy. When the genealogy is read within the framework of God's salvific purpose as we established above, it is not difficult to see that these women are included to show that God's salvation includes the nations as well. Reading Matthew 1:2–3 poses some difficulties with regard to the pattern of recording the genealogy. The pattern Matthew follows is: Ἀβραὰμ ἐγέννησεν τὸν Ἰσαάκ, Ἰσαὰκ δὲ ἐγέννησεν τὸν Ἰακώβ, as against Luke's τοῦ Ματθὰτ τοῦ Λευὶ τοῦ Μελχὶ τοῦ Ἰανναὶ τοῦ Ἰωσήφ. But Matthew makes a surprising shift in verses 3, 5, and 6 within his pattern by inserting the phrases ἐκ τῆς Θαμάρ ("from Tamar"), ἐκ τῆς Ῥαχάβ ("from Rahab"), ἐκ τῆς Ῥούθ, ("from Ruth"), ἐκ τῆς τοῦ Οὐρίου, ("from Uriah's [wife]"). Evidently, Matthew ignores all Jewish women in his genealogy except Mary[34] the mother of Jesus. Apart from these four women

---

32. Davies and Allison, *A Critical and Exegetical Commentary*, 2.26.
33. Both Jewish and gentile women play significant role in the Gospel of Matthew. Apart from the gentile women in the genealogy, other instances where women feature prominently include: Peter's mother-in-law (8:14–15); the woman with the issue of blood (9:18–25); Herodias (14:1–11); the Canaanite woman (15:21–28); the mother of James and John, the wife of Zebedee (20:20–28); the woman who anoints Jesus with expensive perfume (26:6–13); the women who had followed Jesus from Galilee to care for his needs (27:54–56); Mary Magdalene and the other Mary at the tomb of Jesus (21:61); and Mary Magdalene and the other Mary on the resurrection day (28:1–11). With the exception of Herodias who caused the death of John the Baptist and the wife of Zebedee whose request was misplaced and displeasing to the other disciples, all the other women display love for Jesus and extraordinary faith in him even in the most challenging circumstances.
34. In both Matt (1:16–24) and Luke (1:26–38), nothing is said about the family background of Mary except that she is a relative of Elizabeth, the wife of Zechariah (so

and Mary, Matthew focuses on the male family heads. Then, why does Matthew mention these particular women and not others? The writer argues that Matthew mentions these gentile women to demonstrate God's salvific purpose for both Israel and the nations.[35]

As noted above, both Matthew and Luke record Jesus' genealogy, except that Luke does not follow Matthew's order, nor does he include the names of women. While Luke traces Jesus' lineage back to Adam to indicate his universal significance, "Matthew does the same through tracing Jesus back to Abraham, the one whom God promised blessing for all nations."[36] Comparatively, one would suggest that both authors speak of God's universal salvific scheme using different approaches: while Luke mentions Adam as father of the human race, Matthew points to Abraham through whom the human race is blessed. The mention of these women in Matthew's genealogy is "a holy irregularity."[37] They serve as reminders about God's mercy and his plan for the nations. According to Wright, "Within the Jewish worldview itself, Israel's vocation is not compromised but is in a sense fulfilled when gentiles come to join the people of God (like Ruth the ancestress of David), listen to his wisdom (like the queen of Sheba), or

---

Luke). It is not clear, therefore, whether she too was a foreigner.

35. Women were not usually included in Jewish genealogy. See Hutchison, "Women, Gentiles, and the Messianic Mission in Matthew's Genealogy,"163. See also Jones, "Subverting the Textuality of Davidic Messianism," 258. Similarly, Bernard Scott notes that patriarchal societies traced lineage through the male and that the purpose of the genealogy is to show the honor to be attributed to the final descendant. See Bernard Brandon Scott, "The Birth of the Messiah," *Semeia* 52 (1990), 87, as cited by Jones, "Subverting the Textuality of Davidic Messianism" 258. According to William Barclay, "By far the most amazing thing about this pedigree is the names of the women who appear in it. It is not normal to find the names of women in Jewish pedigrees at all. The woman had no legal rights; she was regarded, not as a person, but as a thing. She was merely the possession of her father or of her husband, and in his disposal to do with as he liked" (William Barclay, *The Gospel of Matthew*, rev. ed. (Philadelphia: Westminster, 1975), 1:16–17.

36. Wright, *The Mission of God,* 512.

37. Holwerda, *Jesus and Israel,* 35. Holwerda's "holy irregularity" is applied to the inclusion of the four women and to Joseph as husband of Mary and not the father of Jesus since the story that unfolds shows that Jesus was conceived through the Holy Spirit. According to Holwerda, "These four women testify to God's initiative in incorporating outsiders into Israel and to his astonishingly strange providence in placing these women into the royal lineage in which lay the hope of Israel." It is in this sense then that God's election shapes the genealogy of true Israel (35).

otherwise share the life of his people."[38] Therefore, Matthew understands the Messiah as God's overall plan for humanity. He seeks to establish the foundation that Jesus is the Messiah promised by God to his people Israel and the Savior of the whole world.[39]

---

38. Wright, *The New Testament and the People of God*, 267. See Isa 49:6–8; 2:2–4; 11:9–10; 42:1; Mic 4:1–4.

39. According to Hutchison, there are four major views on the inclusion of these matriarchs (Hutchison, "Women, Gentiles, and the Messianic Mission in Matthew's Genealogy," 154–56). First, some scholars look for a common thread in the lives of these four OT women and conclude that their inclusion underlines their sinful background and God's grace in accepting them. In this view the sinful background of these women foreshadow the fact that the Messiah would save his people from their sins. Dorothy Jean Weaver believes that each of the four women "has at least the hint of sexual scandal attached to her name or history", see Dorothy Jean Weaver "Rewriting the Messianic Script: Matthew's Account of the Birth of Jesus," *Int* 9 (October 2000), 378. Hutchison rules out this first option because these women were not more sinful than the rest of the people in the genealogy and not all of the women had sexual scandal. Even in the case of David, the focus is on David's sin (Hutchison, "Women, Gentiles, and the Messianic Mission in Matthew's Genealogy," 156). Second, it is presumed that their inclusion marks the inclusion of gentiles in Messiah's genealogy and mission. It anticipates the Great Commission in which the Messiah is more than Jewish Messiah. Making disciples of all nations is therefore a fulfillment of God's purpose since the call of Abraham. See also Garland who says, "The genealogy contains names that hint of the universality of salvation that will be offered in Jesus." He buttresses this position by the fact that when he was born, gentiles came from the East and that fulfillment quotation from the first division (4:14–16) draws attention to Galilee of the Gentiles (see Garland, *Reading Matthew*, 17). But Hutchison challenges this view because Bathsheba might have been a Jew and the rest of these women were probably regarded as Jews by the Jews (Hutchison, "Women, Gentiles, and the Messianic Mission in Matthew's Genealogy," 159; see also Edwin D. Freed, "The Women in Matthew's Genealogy," *JSNT* 29 [1987]: 4). Third, it is assumed that the inclusion of these four OT women, like Mary, has something to do with their common unusual marital situations and even sexual scandals in their past. As against the first view that focuses on the women's sinful background, this view centers on the women's scandalous background as they either took initiative or were providentially used by God to fulfill his purposes for his people. Therefore, in this view, the mention of the women becomes a response to Mary's story that is also scandalous and serves as encouragement to early Jewish Christians who would have been challenged by unbelievers concerning the Messiah's scandalous birth, see Hutchison, "Women, Gentiles, and the Messianic Mission in Matthew's Genealogy," 154. See also Raymond Brown, *The Birth the of Messiah* (Garden City, NY: Doubleday, 1977), 74, as cited by Hutchison, "Women, Gentiles, and the Messianic Mission in Matthew's Genealogy," 155; J. C. Weren, "The Five Women in Jesus' Genealogy," *CBQ* 59 (April 1997), 290. But on this view, Hutchison questions why the three women were all foreigners rather than Jews and in what ways is Ruth's story scandalous. Furthermore, would Bathsheba be rightly included in the list of gentile women? And if the issue of the circumstances of Mary's birth was not a major concern at the time when Matthew was writing his gospel, "the discontinuity between Mary and the other women is troublesome and leaves one with the sense that a common denominator has not been found" (Hutchison, "Women, Gentiles, and the Messianic Mission in Matthew's Genealogy," 159–160). And fourth, the mention of these

According to Hutchison, Matthew intentionally cites the four women not to bring attention to their persons, but to draw attention to four OT "stories that illustrate a common point." This thesis is a paradigm shift from the position that Matthew mentions these women "because they share something in common in relation to the messianic mission."[40] For Hutchison, the allusions cover the periods of the patriarchs, the conquest, the judges, and David's kingdom, "and in each case a gentile shows extraordinary faith in contrast to Jews, who were greatly lacking in their faith."[41] Hutchison contrasts the faith of Tamar with that of Judah, of Rahab with that of the Israelites in the wilderness, of Ruth with that of the generation of the judges, and Bathsheba who is probably cited as the wife of Uriah in order to focus attention on Uriah's faith in contrast to that of David. Therefore, Hutchison sees the gentiles, in these crucial times, as demonstrating more faith than Jews in response to God.

A "common point" argument is significant for showing the women's "extraordinary faith." Matthew's purpose is to remind the Jews of God's faithfulness to his Abrahamic and Davidic covenant promises, "to lead them to a more accurate understanding of the Messiah's coming kingdom, and to exhort them to forsake the self-righteous attitude toward gentiles who were then joining them in the church, the body of Christ."[42] And Matthew accomplishes this by reminding the Jews of the vital role gentiles played in the Messiah's line. Hutchison makes a significant contribution by ruling out the first four alternative interpretations for the inclusion of women in the genealogy of Matthew,[43] but his conclusion agrees with the second alternative, that is, Matthew's emphasis on Jesus as a universal Messiah. For

---

women is said to have been Matthew's sharing of the Pharisees' viewpoint of his time that the Messiah would come from "Davidic roots which included scandal and gentile blood" (Hutchison, "Women, Gentiles, and the Messianic Mission in Matthew's Genealogy," 155–56). On the gentile blood in the messianic line, Wright says, "Jesus, the Messiah of Israel, had gentile blood in his veins also" (Wright, *The Mission of God,* 512). This Pharisaic viewpoint that Matthew shares is said to contrast with the view then that the Messiah would come from a priestly line. Matthew, therefore, believes Jesus fulfilled the Pharisaic messianic expectations. However, this view is not widely held in scholarly circles.

40. Hutchison, "Women, Gentiles, and the Messianic Mission," 152.

41. Ibid., 152–153.

42. Ibid., 160.

43. See n602 for these alternative views.

in his theological summary of the inclusion of these women he sees, first, God's providential hand in preserving the messianic line even when Israel showed no faith; second, God's heart for the gentiles and the role of their faith; third, the importance of the Abrahamic and Davidic covenants for understanding the messianic mission, with focus on faith and not racial lines; and, fourth, the call to repentance and humility, and the acceptance of gentiles into the body of Christ.[44] Hutchison's significant contribution is his emphasis on the extraordinary faith of gentile women in contrast to Jews. The problem, however, is the case of Bathsheba when Hutchison says that Matthew probably draws attention to Uriah's faith rather than Bathsheba. This appears inconsistent with Matthew's seemingly intentional inclusion of gentile women in Christ's genealogy. Moreover, Hutchison needed to have demonstrated why and how Matthew drew attention to Uriah's faith rather than Bathsheba who is listed along other women.

From this missional standpoint of acceptance of gentiles, Keener notes that from the mixed marriages in the genealogy to the Great Commission Jesus came for all people.[45] And for others, this mixture of races in Matthew's genealogy means that "With Christianity religious identity is fundamentally detached from nation, family and sex."[46] Therefore, in agreement with the view of universal outlook in the Gospel of Matthew, one would conclude that Matthew includes gentile women in his account of the genealogy to show that God's salvific scheme is universal. But in this universal salvific scheme, faith becomes determinative factor.

4.2.3 "A Single Universal Righteousness" of the Torah

The primary objective of this section is to probe each of Jesus' "acts of righteousness" (Matt 6:1) in the Sermon on the Mount (Matt 5–7) and state some of the reasons why this sermon also applies to the nations. An important issue here concerns for whom this sermon is intended. The immediate audience has been discussed in chapter 3, namely, the mixed audience of

---

44. Hutchison, "Women, Gentiles, and the Messianic Mission," 164.
45. See Keener, *A Commentary on the Gospel of Matthew*, 78–81. Luz also believes that Matthew deliberately includes the names of these gentile women to give a universalist perspective (Luz, *The Theology of the Gospel of Matthew*, 26).
46. K. F. Plum, "Genealogy and Theology," *SJOT* 3 (1989), 90.

Jews and, probably, gentiles. This includes the large crowds from Galilee, the Decapolis, Jerusalem, Judea and the region across the Jordan and the disciples that gathered around Jesus (Matt 4:25—5:1). Since the teaching of Jesus in the Sermon on the Mount forms part of what the disciples of Jesus are to teach the nations (Matt 28:19–20), the righteousness taught in the sermon applies to the nations as well. In addition, the researcher presents the view that Jesus' fulfillment of the Torah goes beyond observance of ethical "acts of righteousness." Jesus himself is the embodiment of the Torah, for the Torah finds fulfillment in him as the "perfect sacrifice for sin."[47] As the Torah symbolized the covenant relationship between God and Israel, Jesus who represents the new covenant in his blood (26:28) not only provides a new way of righteousness that requires a transformed heart but also came for the whole world. In addition, the Sermon on the Mount reveals God's character and is therefore intended for all of humanity. Some scholars share this last view.[48] According to Luz, the sermon "supplies the contents of the mission to be proclaimed to the world" by the Matthean community.[49] Similarly, Matthew depicts "a single universal righteousness rooted in creation and intended for the nations of the world" because "Jesus' teaching stands in continuity with the essential righteousness of the Old Testament."[50] Holwerda's argument is that the Sermon on the Mount addresses not only the disciples but the crowds as well, as Matthew 5:1 is linked with the gathering crowds of 4:23–25 and comments made by the crowd at the end of the sermon in 7:28–29. As Holwerda stresses, Jesus intended to teach God's structured righteousness to the whole world and not just to a favored few.[51]

For Holwerda, there is an essential continuity in the teaching and mission of Jesus with the redemptive ethical purpose of the Hebrew Bible, because "the righteousness of God that shaped Israel's ways was intended to shape the ways of the nations."[52] Holwerda argues further that this

---

47. Poythress, *The Shadow of Christ*, 98.
48. See Luz, *Theology of the Gospel of Matthew*, 42–61; Holwerda, *Jesus and Israel*, 140.
49. Luz, *Theology of the Gospel of Matthew*, 44.
50. Holwerda, *Jesus and Israel*, 140; France, *The Gospel of Matthew*, 183.
51. Holwerda, *Jesus and Israel*, 141.
52. Ibid., 138.

Mission to the Nations: Foundations and Framework   161

perspective is articulated in Matthew 28:19–20. The nations are taught not only the message of repentance for salvation, but also instructed on the "structured righteousness of the kingdom of God." This "structured righteousness" is found in Matthew 5:21–7:12. God's universal righteousness is rooted in his being as the only God who exercises dominion in the world he created.

But while Holwerda makes a significant contribution, he leaves out some aspects of the Beatitudes (5:3–12). Purity of the heart [οἱ καθαροὶ τῇ καρδίᾳ] (5:8) as prerequisite for seeing God is applied in the issue of anger (5:22) and lust (5:28) that come from the heart. In the same vein, the Beatitudes emphasize peacemaking [οἱ εἰρηνοποιοί] (5:9) just as the rest of the "sermon" speaks about reconciliation (5:22–23) and love for enemy (5:42–48).[53] This researcher believes, therefore, that the Beatitudes are included in the "acts of righteousness" and provide a better grounding for the single universal righteousness of the Torah. For apart from the mixed audience mentioned earlier, the Beatitudes focus on ἡ βασιλεία τῶν οὐρανῶν (3, 10, 11) in which Jesus reverses "all human evaluations."[54] If the "poor in spirit" (5:3) is interpreted to mean those that are conscious of their spiritual poverty and therefore cry out to God for help, any gentiles who is poor in the spirit is included in ἡ βασιλεία τῶν οὐρανῶν. Similarly, "those who mourn" (5:4)[55] seems to suggest that they are "those who recognize their spiritual bankruptcy"[56] as in the first Beatitude. In all of these Beatitudes, Jesus brings good news of blessings (μακάριοι) to the meek (5:5), to those who hunger and thirst for righteousness 5:6), to the merciful (5:7), to the pure in heart (5:8), to the peacemakers (5:9), and to those who are persecuted because of righteousness (5:11–12). There is no clue to suggest here

---

53. Similarly, Swartley explains this universal righteousness in the light of the love command in Matthew. According to him, the Torah law calls for kindness and help to the enemy in need (Exod 23:4–5; Deut 22:1–4). For this reason Jesus' love command may not be seen as altogether novel. "But when viewed specifically within the exodus and conquest traditions, transformation is apparent" (Swartley, *Israel's Scripture Traditions*, 69). This transformation is understood in the light of Jesus' and Matthew's social worlds in which enmity between Jews and gentiles had socio-racial, political, and religious dimension.

54. Hendriksen, *Matthew*, 264.

55. Hagner believes that this Beatitude alludes to Isa 61:2 (LXX) in which the one anointed by the Spirit comes to comfort those who mourn (see Hagner, *Matthew 1–13*, 92).

56. Hendriksen, *Matthew*, 264.

that it is only the Jews who are the μακάριοι. The universal righteousness of the Torah is demonstrated in the Beatitudes by its universal application.

The next theme is the temple as house of prayer discussed from Matthew's interpretative standpoint.

4.2.4 The Temple: a House of Prayer (for all Nations)

The pericope of Matthew 21:12–13 (cf. Mark 11:15–17; Luke 19:45–46) comes immediately after Jesus' entry into Jerusalem as her king in fulfillment of prophecy (21:1–5). When Jesus entered the temple[57] he found commercial activities that violated the purpose of the temple. Such economic transactions effectively turned the house of prayer (οἶκος προσευχῆς) into a den of robbers (σπήλαιον λῃστῶν) (21:13).

Matthew, like Mark and Luke, cites from two OT passages to make a strong contrast between house of God and den of robbers (Isa 56:7; Jer 7:11). What Matthew omits from Isaiah 56:7 (following Luke) is the phrase "for all peoples" (לְכָל־הָעַמִּים). Matthew's reason for the omission of "for all peoples" is uncertain. However, scholars believe that this selling and buying took place in the outer court, a place the gentiles were permitted to enter.[58] But the significant issue here is the context of Isaiah 56:7 which is about the foreigners who bind themselves with the Lord when the Lord comes to his holy mountain (56:1–7).

Is the text of Matthew 21:13 a sign of judgment and destruction of the temple establishment as Keener and Sanders suggest?[59] Can this be established from Matthew's context? In looking at the cleansing of the temple in the Gospel of Matthew where the phrase "for all nations" is omitted, the

---

57. Some manuscripts add τοῦ θεου to the ἱερόν. According to Metzger, "The addition of τοῦ θεοῦ appears to be a natural expansion, made in order to emphasize the profanation of the holy place. The fact that the parallel passages (Mark 11:15 and Luke 19:45; cf. John 2:14) lack τοῦ θεοῦ would not be an occasion for copyists, if they observed the fact, to delete the words from copies of Matthew, but rather for inserting the words in copies of the other Gospels. Although the Jews had little use for such a phrase (since for them "the temple" could mean only one thing), the longer expression would not be intrinsically objectionable to anyone, and therefore its omission cannot be accounted for on that ground. It appears, therefore, that internal considerations join with strong external evidence in support of the reading ἱερόν" (see Metzger, *A Textual Commentary on the New Testament*, 44).
58. See Keener, *A Commentary on the Gospel of Matthew*, 499–500.
59. Ibid., 495; Sanders, *Jesus and Judaism*, 71.

context of Isaiah 56:7 and the area where the cleansing takes place become important. Moreover, what Jesus does in the temple becomes equally important. The last point is taken first. The blind and the lame came to him in the temple and he healed them there (21:14). He also taught in the temple courts (21:23). By these actions Jesus seems to be suggesting the proper use of the temple. According to the evidence of the text, what he seems to go against here is the buying and selling of merchandise which takes place in the temple. In the Gospel of John, the sellers, the buyers, and the moneychangers angered him because they dared to make his "Father's house into a house of merchandise" (John 2:16).[60] The relevance of John 2:16 for Matthew is that in both Matthew and John, Jesus' anger is directed against merchandise in the temple. This zeal for his Father's house fulfills Psalm 69:9. While Sanders' and Keener's position on this issue is plausible, this researcher thinks that Jesus was not attacking the temple as an institution in itself in the text under consideration. Instead, he believes that by healing and teaching in the temple and also paying the temple tax Jesus was opposing the activities that conflict with the primary purpose of the temple—a house of prayer.

But it also appears that there is a theological tension in Matthew's citation of Isaiah 56:7. He is aware that Jesus' mission is rather centrifugal. Yet he still stresses the essence for which the temple was built. While the text of Isaiah 56:7 still maintains its relevance to this point when Jesus drives out the merchants, its discontinuity is also apparent with Jesus' presence as one greater than the temple (Matt 12:1–14).[61] The temple is judged, according to Swartley, because of "its exclusivity and hierarchically restricted access into God's presence."[62] But this writer believes that the temple is rather cleansed because of the corruption going on in it. Yet Swartley rightly says

---

60. In John 2:18–23, it is Jesus who tells the Jews who were demanding for a sign, to destroy the temple and he would build it in three days. Although his bewildered audience could not comprehend the meaning of this, John as an insider knew that what Jesus meant by the "temple" was his own body and not the destruction of the temple in Jerusalem.

61. As Swartley says, the temple traditions "provide a focus and a foil for the Synoptics' stories of Jesus' pre-passion ministry in Jerusalem" so that Matthew's and Mark's "temple traditions are not only reformed, but set within the paradox of continuity and discontinuity" (Swartley, *Israel's Scripture Traditions*, 255).

62. Swartley, *Israel's Scripture Traditions*, 255.

that the Synoptics view the temple "within the paradox of continuity and discontinuity," which in a way characterizes the whole Gospel of Matthew.

But how is there continuity with the temple tradition[63] in Matthew? On the one hand, when Jesus drives out merchants from the temple and charges them for violating the rightful use of it (21:12–13), continuity with the temple tradition is in view. His attitude is a combination of respect for it "and his awareness of messianic fulfillment and displacement of the temple."[64] As already pointed out, some scholars think that Jesus probably drove out the merchants from the outer Court of the Gentiles.[65] If this assumption is true—although Matthew does not use the word nations in his quotation as does Mark—then, Jesus' words would have been understood by the people to mean that the temple is a house of prayer for all nations. Matthew's citation of Isaiah, then, is an interpretation of the worldwide purposes of God.[66]

On the other hand, some discontinuity is indicated by the episode of 12:1–14. Although there is no fulfillment quotation here, Jesus uses an OT example to support his action. The whole controversy in this pericope is about the Sabbath and the temple. On the charge that the disciples of Jesus were doing what is unlawful to do on the Sabbath, Jesus uses David's breach of the Sabbath law, namely, entering the house of God because of some emergency. Jesus then tells his accusers that the law allows for Sabbath activities of priests in the temple (Num 28:9–10). And "The angle that Matthew takes is to justify priestly behavior on the grounds that the temple is more important than the Sabbath: its needs take precedence."[67] Jesus then tells the Pharisees that he is the one greater than the temple. And since Jesus is greater than the temple he is also greater than the Sabbath, for

---

63. "Temple tradition" is here used as temple institution in the OT rather than in Judaism. The universal outlook of the Gospel of Matthew suggests that he is following the OT tradition in which the temple is a house of prayer for all nations.

64. Holwerda, *Jesus and Israel*, 69–70.

65. Turner, *Matthew*, 499.

66. Piper, *Let the Nations be Glad*, 186.

67. Nolland, *The Gospel of Matthew*, 184. Gundry sees Matthew using *haggadic* argument since it did not include specific reference to violating the Sabbath but "one based on inference from the OT." But 12:6 is *halachic* since it is based on a definite OT reference. (Gundry, *Matthew*, 223).

he is "Lord of the Sabbath." This raises an important question as to whether or not Jesus' presence does away with the need to keep the law in view of his attitude towards it in 5:17–20. According to Nolland, "What Matthew asserts is that Jesus is of such importance that he can arbitrate as to which are the justified violations of the non-work requirements of the Sabbath "rather than obviating the Sabbath laws."[68]

But what is the identity of the "one greater than the temple" in 12:6? Keener and Gundry believe that this is Jesus himself. Keener says, Jesus is "the greater locus of God's presence than the temple."[69] Similarly, Gundry says that Matthew's "christological emphasis insures that μεῖζόν refers to Jesus."[70] But France thinks that the "one greater than the temple" points beyond Jesus himself to a whole new regime focused on him.[71] Although France's position may appear viable, a careful reading of the text suggests that τοῦ ἱεροῦ μεῖζόν is better understood as Jesus himself because of "*I* desire" in 12:7 and "for the Son of Man is Lord of the Sabbath" in 12:8 which both require that the text be understood as putting emphasis on Jesus rather than the disciples or the entire church that makes up the regime after him. On the whole, Matthew's "purpose was to argue that though the disciples profaned the Sabbath, they—like the priests who worked in the temple on Sabbath days—were guiltless because of a higher legal consideration: if the greatness of the temple surpasses the sanctity of the Sabbath, the superior greatness of Jesus surpasses the sanctity of the Sabbath much more."[72]

---

68. Nolland, *The Gospel of Matthew*, 184–185.

69. Keener, *A Commentary on the Gospel of Matthew*, 356. Cf. Gregory K. Beale, "Eden, Temple, and the Church's Mission in the New Creation," *JETS* 48 no.1 (March 2005), 5–31. In this view Christ and his followers are the new temple in the new creation. "For Christ is the temple toward which all earlier temples looked and which they anticipated." He is "the epitome of God's presence on earth as God's incarnate, thus continuing the true form of the old temple, which actually was a foreshadowing of Christ's presence throughout the OT era" (19–20). He therefore sees no possibility for a future physical temple (20).

70. Gundry, *Matthew*, 223. Similarly, Dempster notes that although there are different emphases in the Gospels, the most important is that the meanings of the temple and the Davidic house are merged in the person of Jesus Christ (see Dempster, *Dominion and Dynasty*, 233).

71. France, *The Gospel of Matthew*, 811.

72. Gundry, *Matthew*, 223–224. In the OT, the Sabbath laws came before the establishment of the temple and its regulations. But Matthew presents the Sabbath as subservient to the temple because the priests in the temple desecrate the Sabbath in performing temple duties (Matt 12:5). Since the priests are doing the work of God who established the Sabbath, they

The theological and missional significance of the text for gentile mission is that "In Matthew, Jesus-in-the-church is the new entity of meaning, the 'thing greater' than the temple. Believers meet in the name of Jesus for church matters" (Matt 18:20). This then leads to the next section of Jesus and the elect in the blood of the covenant.

4.2.5 Jesus and the Elect in the Blood of the Covenant

Perhaps no other passage in Matthew brings out the significance of the shed blood of Christ like the Passover narrative (26:17–29; cf. Mark 12–25; Luke 22:7–23; John 13:1–30). The narrative is about Jesus' last hours with his disciples. In its literary context, Jesus is about to leave Bethany (26:6) to go into the city of Jerusalem (26:18). He instructs his disciples just as he did when he was about to enter Jerusalem (26:17–19; 21:1–6).

The Passover celebration takes the reader back to the exodus event (Exod 12:11, 13, 21, 27, 43) that is commemorated annually as God instructed the Israelites (Deut 16:1–2). It is during this Passover feast that Jesus institutes the "Lord's Supper." Of primary significance in the Passover is that Jesus gives special symbolic meaning to the unleavened bread and the wine (the cup in 22:22–23; 26:39).[73] While the broken bread represents Jesus' body, the cup stands for his blood poured out (ἐκχυννόμενον) for the forgiveness of the sins of many people.[74] He calls the cup "my blood of the covenant" (διαθήκη),[75] an allusion to Exodus 24:8 and Zechariah 9:11.[76] Not only is Jesus' celebration of the Passover connected to the Passover in Exodus 12, it is also linked with the בְּרִית חֲדָשָׁה (cf. Jer 31:31–34).

Although the blood of covenant in the OT is limited to the house of Israel, Jesus widens its meaning and scope in the celebration of the Passover

---

are not bound by the rules of the Sabbath but by an order from God. It is in this sense that the Sabbath is subservient to the temple.

73. See Turner, *Matthew*, 625.

74. Cf. Matt 1:21; 20:28; Exod 12:21–27; Isa 53:4, 10, 12.

75. Luke 22:20 and 1 Cor 11:25 have it as "new covenant." According to Metzger, "The word καινῆς has apparently come from the parallel passage in Luke 22:20; he believes if it had been present originally, there is no good reason why anyone would have deleted it" (Metzger, *A Textual Commentary on the Greek New Testament*, 54). Although Matthew does not say "new covenant," he and his disciples will drink this cup "anew" in his Father's kingdom (26:29).

76. See Turner, *Matthew*, 625.

with his disciples. As teacher of the law, Jesus "brings out of his storeroom new treasures as well as old" (Matt 13:52). Matthew does not specify the "many" for whom the blood of the covenant is poured. Jesus' τῆς διαθήκης τὸ περὶ πολλῶν ἐκχυννόμενον (26:28) echoes the πολλοί ("many") in Matthew 8:11; 20:28. In Matthew 20:28 the Son of Man gives his life as a ransom "for many" (ἀντὶ πολλῶν). This seems to prepare the ground for τὰ ἔθνη in Matthew 28:19 who may be included in the "many." In celebrating this last Passover Jesus anticipates his death and resurrection that would open the door for the inclusion of Jews *and gentiles* in the kingdom of God. Matthew's frequent mention of "chosen" (22:14) and "elect" (24:24) evokes God's unique relationship with the house of Israel (Exod 19:5, 6; Amos 3:2). The question, however, is on the identity of the elect in Matthew and by what means they constitute the elect.[77] Most Matthean scholars are agreed that, among other portraits of Jesus, he is the new Israel. In him the promises made to David (such as the *eternal* kingdom) are fulfilled.[78] But the leaders of Israel reject the kingdom of heaven that offers forgiveness of sins as proclaimed by Jesus and his disciples. However, all who believe in Jesus (like the disciples and the centurion) become the new elect of God, comprising both Jews and gentiles. This is explicit in the eschatological discourse of Matthew 24 and Mark 13. The elect, mentioned three times in each of the Gospels,[79] are those who have heard the gospel of the kingdom that is to be preached in the whole world and who will therefore be gathered from all the nations of the earth. The eschatological

---

77. In Isaiah, the Servant of Yahweh is chosen by God (Isa 42:1–4). Jesus fulfills the role of this Servant (Matt 12:18–21). (See Beaton, "Isaiah in Matthew's Gospel," 63–78 and Grams "Narrative Dynamics in Isaiah's and Matthew's Mission Theology," 238–255 for how Isaiah shaped the Gospel of Matthew). Therefore, Matthew's use of Isaiah suggests that the elect in the Gospel of Matthew are all who receive the kingdom of God proclaimed by Jesus and his disciples, both Jews and gentiles. The elect in Matthew are the "little ones" (10:42); the "least" (11:11; 25:40, 45) and "my brothers (12:50; 25:40). By the inclusion of both Jews and gentiles in Matthew's kingdom of heaven, Matthew is working with fulfillment scheme rather than replacement. This will be explored in the 'stone' typology.

78. Holwerda, *Jesus and Israel*, 53; Hagner, *Matthew 1–13*, 36; Keener, *A Commentary on the Gospel of Matthew*, 107.

79. See Matt 24:22, 24, 31; cf. Mark 13:20, 22, 27. They are those for whose sake the days of distress will be shortened; they are those that the false Christs and false prophets would want to deceive along with the rest of the world; and they are those the angels will gather from the four winds, from one end of the heavens to the other when the Son of Man appears with power and great glory.

discourse anticipates the finished work of Jesus the Messiah whose blood of the covenant is poured out for the forgiveness of sins (26:26–29).

The inauguration of the new covenant is understood as fulfillment of the covenant inaugurated by Moses. Here a transition takes place from the symbolic sacrifice of the lamb to the real and final sacrifice through Christ. And the deliverance from Egypt is now deliverance from sin. "We enter not into Canaan but into the kingdom of the Father."[80] The Passover that Jesus celebrated with his disciples is a reminder that Jesus, the new Passover lamb, shed his blood for the forgiveness of sin (εἰς ἄφεσιν ἁμαρτιῶν) for his disciples and the entire world and that this celebration will be done again in his Father's kingdom. "Jesus' body and blood provide a new covenant, the ultimate act of redemption."[81] Those who will participate in the new eschatological celebration include the many who come from the east and the west and take their places at the feast with Abraham, Isaac and Jacob in the kingdom of heaven (8:11) or "his elect from the four winds, from one end of the heavens to the other" (24:31).

From these redemptive events and institutions, how Matthew views prophetic ministry with respect to the nations will be explored.

4.3 Prophetic Ministry and Mission

It is argued here that what the prophets said about the gentiles shaped Matthew's understanding of God's dealings with the nations.[82] This is explored from the standpoint of prophetic ministry before John the Baptist and the ministry of John the Baptist.

---

80. Poythress, *The Shadow of Christ*, 278.
81. Keener, *A Commentray on the Gospel of Matthew*, 627.
82. Wright discusses on prophecy concerning the nations in the Gospel of Matthew in chapter 15 of his *The Mission of God*. His emphasis is on quotations from the book of Isaiah that focus on the gentiles (see Wright, *The Mission of God*, 513–514). Similarly, the contribution of Kaiser Jr. is also significant in this direction. In chapter 4 of his *Mission in the Old Testament*, he talks about Isaiah's universalism and draws the conclusion that God's call to Israel is to be the light of the nations. Particularly important for Kaiser Jr. are the passages in Isaiah that Matthew cites as having been fulfilled in the life of Jesus. Keener also believes that Matthew's citation from Isaiah's Servant Song reinforces Matthew's theme of gentile mission (Keener, *A Commentary on the Gospel of Matthew*, 360–361)

4.3.1 Prophetic Ministry Prior to John the Baptist

As noted earlier in this chapter, Matthew calls Jesus "son of Abraham" in his genealogy. Implicitly, Matthew is aware of the blessings made to Abraham that would embrace the nations. This understanding continues with the inclusion of gentiles in the genealogy. In Matthew 2:1–12 the magi worship the Savior while the Jews seek to kill him. These appear to prepare the way for the direct prophecies to come regarding the gentiles. In this section, we will explore Matthew's citation of Isaiah 53:4–5 in Matthew 8:17 and Isaiah 42:1–4 in Matthew 12:18–21.

4.3.1.1 Yahweh's Servant Heals both Jews and Gentiles

In discussing how Matthew (8:17) handles Isaiah's prophecy (53:4–5), we will first examine the relevant texts from the OT background.

Table 12: *Matthew's Servant of Yahweh*

MT	LXX	NT
Isa 53:4-5 ⁴אָכֵן חֳלָיֵנוּ הוּא נָשָׂא וּמַכְאֹבֵינוּ סְבָלָם וַאֲנַחְנוּ חֲשַׁבְנֻהוּ נָגוּעַ מֻכֵּה אֱלֹהִים וּמְעֻנֶּה: ⁵וְהוּא מְחֹלָל מִפְּשָׁעֵנוּ מְדֻכָּא מֵעֲוֹנֹתֵינוּ מוּסַר שְׁלוֹמֵנוּ עָלָיו וּבַחֲבֻרָתוֹ נִרְפָּא־לָנוּ:	Isa 53:4-5 οὗτος τὰς ἁμαρτίας ἡμῶν φέρει καὶ περὶ ἡμῶν ὀδυνᾶται καὶ ἡμεῖς ἐλογισάμεθα αὐτὸν εἶναι ἐν πόνῳ καὶ ἐν πληγῇ καὶ ἐν κακώσει ⁵ αὐτὸς δὲ ἐτραυματίσθη διὰ τὰς ἀνομίας ἡμῶν καὶ μεμαλάκισται διὰ τὰς ἁμαρτίας ἡμῶν παιδεία εἰρήνης ἡμῶν ἐπ' αὐτόν τῷ μώλωπι αὐτοῦ ἡμεῖς ἰάθημεν	Matt 8:17 ὅπως πληρωθῇ τὸ ῥηθὲν διὰ 'Ησαΐου τοῦ προφήτου λέγοντος, Αὐτὸς τὰς ἀσθενείας ἡμῶν ἔλαβεν καὶ τὰς νόσους ἐβάστασεν.
Surely **he took up our infirmities and carried our sorrows**, yet we considered him stricken by God, smitten by him, and afflicted. ⁵ But he *was* wounded for our transgressions, *he was* bruised for our iniquities: the chastisement of our peace *was* upon him; and with his stripes we are healed.	⁴ Surely he **took up our infirmities [sins] and carried our sorrows**, yet we considered him stricken by God, smitten by him, and afflicted. ⁵ But he was pierced for our transgressions, he was crushed for our iniquities; the punishment that brought us peace was upon him, and by his wounds we are healed.	This was to fulfill what was spoken through the prophet Isaiah: "**He took up our infirmities and carried our diseases.**"

Three OT quotations in the Gospel of Matthew have been traditionally associated with gentile mission. These include 4:15–16, 12:18–21 and 21:42. Most scholars ignore Matthew 8:17 in this direction. The writer argues that Jesus' healing ministry (8:17) as a fulfillment of Isaiah 53:4–5 needs to be explored in relation to Jesus' salvific work for both Jews and gentiles. The four Servant Songs in Isaiah are found in 42:1–4, 49:1–6, 50:4–9, and 52:13—53:12.[83] The "servant" is sometimes equated with Israel (41: 8–10; 44: 1–2; 45:4; 49:3).[84] Attention is on God's chosen servant who brings justice and blessings to the gentiles.[85]

The context of Matthew 8:17 is significant. Matthew reviews all the healings that took place and then cites Isaiah 53:4. The writer argues that Matthew sees Yahweh's servant as healer of both Jews and gentiles. From the table above, Matthew deviates slightly from the LXX and follows the MT, "or may well be Matthew's own" translation.[86] Matthew renders the Hebrew כְּאֵבֵינוּ ("our sorrows", 53:4) literally as ἡμῶν νόσους ("our diseases", 8:17). Why does Matthew equate "sorrows" with "diseases" in his translation? According to Carson when the NT quotes a brief OT passage, it usually refers to the entire context of the OT text. In this case the entire Servant Song (Isa 52:13—53:12) is in view. Carson also notes that both Scripture and Jewish tradition understand that all sickness is caused by sin, directly or indirectly. The emphasis of the Servant Song is substitutionary atonement so that the servant bears the sicknesses of others through suffering and death. For Matthew, therefore, Jesus' vicarious death lays the foundation for destroying sicknesses.[87]

---

83. It is noteworthy that these chapters say much about the gentiles, especially in their inclusion in the salvific purpose of God.
84. Blomberg, "Matthew," in *Commentary on the New Testament Use of the Old Testament*, 31. According to him, "Isaiah explicitly identified the servant in earlier Servant Songs as Israel, but increasingly used imagery that was impossible for a nation to fulfill. Matthew recognized this, and may have known of an already existing messianic interpretation of what remained unfulfilled, and drew on the holistic understanding of affliction and redemption throughout Isaiah to introduce one of his distinctive and characteristic fulfillment formulas here," 32, 33.
85. Blomberg, "Matthew," in *Commentary on the New Testament Use of the Old Testament*, 31.
86. Hagner, *Matthew 1–13*, 210.
87. Carson, "Matthew," 40.

Matthew's "in order that it might be fulfilled" (ὅπως πληρωθῆ) in 8:17 is a summary of all of the healing ministry of Jesus that had just taken place, beginning from the healing of the leper to the "many who were demon-possessed" and "all the sick."[88] We have treated the significance of ἵνα and ὅπως clauses in the Gospel of Matthew in chapter 3. "In order that" (ὅπως) indicates purpose, which Matthew uses for fulfillment quotations. Although it may be argued that the "many who were demon-possessed" and "all the sick" could include a number of gentiles, the healing in this context that directly involved a non-Jew is the centurion's servant. The miracles of 8:1–15 all have parallels in Mark or Luke as observed. However, only Matthew explicitly says that in the healings that have taken place Jesus now fulfills a prophecy.

One of those healed is the centurion's servant (8:5–13). Jesus is amazed (ἐθαύμασεν) at the profound faith of this centurion (8:10)—a Gentile. Jesus showed similar astonishment when a Canaanite woman expressed such faith in Jesus (15:28). Jesus then turns to those following him and says, "I tell you the truth, I have not found anyone in Israel with such great faith" (8:10).[89] Here Jesus speaks to the children of the kingdom who have less faith than the pagan centurion. It is this Gentile who obtains healing for his servant along with the children of the kingdom in fulfillment of Isaiah 53:4–5. But one may argue further from the "many who were demon-possessed" (δαιμονιζομένους πολλούς·) and "all the sick" (πάντας τοὺς κακῶς ἔχοντας) in Matthew 8:16 that some gentiles might be included, besides the centurion. This assumption appears plausible because of Matthew's portrayal of this region as Galilee of the Gentiles (Matt

---

88. Gundry observes that Matthew's quotations from Isa (4:14; 12:17) "all occur in summaries of Jesus' salvific work" (Gundry, *Matthew*, 151).

89. Among two other variants readings, the reading οὐδὲ ἐν τ Ἰσραὴλ τοσαύτην πίστιν εὗρον, according to Metzger, "besides being clearer and easier than the text, is doubtless an assimilation to the parallel in Luke 7:9. The other two readings probably arose through inadvertence on the part of copyists." See Metzger, *A Textual Commentary on the Greek New Testament*, 17.

4:15–16). In addition, the healing of the centurion's servant might have encouraged other gentiles to bring in their sick ones to Jesus.[90]

A rather striking example of Jesus' healing of gentiles is the issue of the Canaanite woman who requests a miracle on behalf of her demon-possessed daughter (15:21–28). The context is Jesus' withdrawal from the Pharisees and the teachers of the law (14:13) "and contrasts their approach to the Messiah with that of this gentile woman."[91] Jesus withdraws to a pagan territory, a region of Tyre and Sidon. While Mark describes this woman as a "Syrophoenician" (Mark 7:26), Matthew calls her a "Canaanite woman." Matthew's use of OT geographical names as he does here is meant to conjure "up their evil connotation from bygone eras."[92] The Canaanites were Israel's ancient enemies. It is rather surprising that even when Jesus restricts his mission to Israel (10:5–6; 15:24), he seems to violate this restriction and grants the request of a Canaanite woman because of her great faith (15:28). This pagan woman calls Jesus "Lord" and "Son of David." She recognizes the Messiah of the Jews. Since this miracle takes place in Tyre and Sidon (Matt 11:22), this suggests that "with the coming of Jesus, these cities receive another opportunity to repent."[93] Therefore, the healing ministry of Jesus in fulfillment of Isaiah 53:4–5 extends to these gentiles as well. For when Jesus drove out the evil spirits and healed all the sick in Matthew 8:16–17 it was in fulfillment of Isaiah's prophecy.

The theological and missional significance of Matthew 8:17 is that the kingdom of heaven has come in power. For Matthew the Messiah has come to all, including the leper (8:1–4), the Gentile centurion (8:5–13), a woman in Israel (8:14–16), and the Canaanite woman (15:21–28). Jesus'

---

90. Jesus' healing of the two demon-possessed in the region of the Gedarenes (Matt 8:28–34), a primarily gentile region, gives further support to the idea that gentiles might have been included in the demon-possessed and all the sick in Matt 8:16).
91. Carson, "Matthew," 75.
92. Blomberg, *Matthew*, 242.
93. Ibid.

ministry cuts across social class, gender, and racial divide.[94] The reference to those from the east and west who feast with Abraham in the kingdom of heaven is, therefore, Matthew's way of saying that Abraham is a father of all believers. As noted earlier, Matthew echoes in this text the promise of God to bless all the people of the earth through him (Gen 12:3). Matthew saw in Jesus' substitutionary death the power not only to save from sins but to also heal the sick, both Jews and gentiles.

4.3.1.2 The Nations Put their Hope in His Name

The focus here is on Matthew 12:18–21. Just as in the citations in 4:14–16 and 8:17, Matthew mentions that what happens here fulfills Isaiah's prophecy. Matthew stresses that Jesus' salvific ministry extends to the nations. The immediate literary context of this passage is Jesus' withdrawal from the crowd because of the threat to his life by the Pharisees who accused Jesus of violating the Sabbath by healing a man with a withered hand.[95] Although he withdraws from the crowd, many (πολλοί)[96] more people continue to come to him and he heals them (12:15). This publicity was generating more tension, so he warns the healed people not to tell who he was—"the

---

94. Therefore, "scrup about ritual purity, ethnic exclusivism, and gender stereotypes must not hinder this mission" (Turner, *Matthew*, 237). The text is therefore "a paradigm for extension of the Gospel of Israel's Messiah to include also those who had no natural claim on him" (France, *The Gospel of Matthew*, 310).

95. For a good treatment of Jesus' retreats in face of danger beginning from Matt 2, see Rainer Metzer, "Der Rückzug Jesu im Matthäusevangelium: Ein literarisches Déjà-vu-Erlebnis," *ZNW* 94 (2003): 258–268.

96. Some manuscripts add crowds to the "many." As Metzger explains, "While it is possible that through homoeoteleuton ὄχλοι may have accidentally fallen out, it is slightly more probable that scribes, influenced by the familiar phrase 'many crowds' or 'great crowds' (e.g. 4:25; 8:1; 13:2; 15:30; 19:2), strengthened the simple πολλοί (a reading that is supported by early Alexandrian and Western witnesses) by adding ὄχλοι, either before or after πολλοί" (Metzger, *A Textual Commentary on the Greek New Testament*, 26).

famous messianic secret motif."[97] Jesus' withdrawal from the crowd and his avoidance of undesirable publicity is now interpreted in Matthew as a fulfillment of Isaiah 42:1–4. But the quotation also anticipates the conflict with the Pharisees and teachers of the law in the following narrative in which they oppose and misinterpret Jesus' source of power. Matthew now "reads Jesus as Isaiah's 'servant of Yahweh'" although "Judaism in Jesus' day rarely applied the servant passages to the Messiah."[98] Keener argues that despite the skepticism of Matthew's critics, "it is not too hard to see how Matthew interprets Isaiah 42" in the light of Isaiah's larger context from which Matthew derives his meaning of the passage.[99]

What, then, is the larger context of this Servant Song of Isaiah from which Matthew finds correspondence in Jesus' ministry? Further analysis of Matthew 12:18–21 continues from an investigation of Matthew's citation of Isaiah 42:1–4 as highlighted in the following table.

---

97. Blomberg, "Matthew," in *Commentary on the New Testament Use of the Old Testament*, 42. The so-called messianic secrets began with the work of William Wrede (1859–1906) who argued in his *The Messianic Secret*, trans. J. C. G. Greig (Cambridge: James Clark, 1971) that the book of Mark is not a reliable account of the life of the historical Jesus, but "was actually an elaborate theological interpretation devised (by the Marcan community, not by a single individual) to bring the historical Jesus into line with the dogmatic Christ of the church's faith". See Robert B. Strimple, *The Modern Search for the Real Jesus: An Introductory Survey of the Historical Roots of Gospels Criticism* (Phillipsburg: P&R Publishing, 1995), 60. See also Richard N. Soulen and R. Kendall Soulen, *Handbook of Biblical Criticism*, 3rd ed. (Louisville: WJK, 2001), 110.
98. Keener, *A Commentary on the Gospel of Matthew*, 360.
99. Ibid.

Table 13: *The Chosen Servant of Yahweh*

MT	LXX	NT
Isa 42:1-4 הֵן עַבְדִּי אֶתְמָךְ־בּוֹ בְּחִירִי רָצְתָה נַפְשִׁי נָתַתִּי רוּחִי עָלָיו מִשְׁפָּט לַגּוֹיִם יוֹצִיא׃ ² לֹא יִצְעַק וְלֹא יִשָּׂא וְלֹא־יַשְׁמִיעַ בַּחוּץ קוֹלוֹ׃ ³ קָנֶה רָצוּץ לֹא יִשְׁבּוֹר וּפִשְׁתָּה כֵהָה לֹא יְכַבֶּנָּה לֶאֱמֶת יוֹצִיא מִשְׁפָּט׃ ⁴ לֹא יִכְהֶה וְלֹא יָרוּץ עַד־יָשִׂים בָּאָרֶץ מִשְׁפָּט וּלְתוֹרָתוֹ אִיִּים יְיַחֵלוּ׃	Isa 42:1-4 Ιακωβ ὁ παῖς μου ἀντιλήμψομαι αὐτοῦ Ισραηλ ὁ ἐκλεκτός μου προσεδέξατο αὐτὸν ἡ ψυχή μου ἔδωκα τὸ πνεῦμά μου ἐπ' αὐτόν κρίσιν τοῖς ἔθνεσιν ἐξοίσει ² οὐ κεκράξεται οὐδὲ ἀνήσει οὐδὲ ἀκουσθήσεται ἔξω ἡ φωνὴ αὐτοῦ ³ κάλαμον τεθλασμένον οὐ συντρίψει καὶ λίνον καπνιζόμενον οὐ σβέσει ἀλλὰ εἰς ἀλήθειαν ἐξοίσει κρίσιν ⁴ ἀναλάμψει καὶ οὐ θραυσθήσεται ἕως ἂν θῇ ἐπὶ τῆς γῆς κρίσιν καὶ ἐπὶ τῷ ὀνόματι αὐτοῦ ἔθνη ἐλπιοῦσιν	Matt 12:18-21 Ἰδοὺ ὁ παῖς μου ὃν ᾑρέτισα, ὁ ἀγαπητός μου εἰς ὃν εὐδόκησεν ἡ ψυχή μου· θήσω τὸ πνεῦμά μου ἐπ' αὐτόν, καὶ κρίσιν τοῖς ἔθνεσιν ἀπαγγελεῖ. ¹⁹ οὐκ ἐρίσει οὐδὲ κραυγάσει, οὐδὲ ἀκούσει τις ἐν ταῖς πλατείαις τὴν φωνὴν αὐτοῦ. ²⁰ κάλαμον συντετριμμένον οὐ κατεάξει καὶ λίνον τυφόμενον οὐ σβέσει, ἕως ἂν ἐκβάλῃ εἰς νῖκος τὴν κρίσιν. ²¹ καὶ τῷ ὀνόματι αὐτοῦ ἔθνη ἐλπιοῦσιν.

"Behold, My Servant, whom I uphold; My chosen one in whom My soul delights. I have put My Spirit upon Him; He will bring forth justice to the nations. He will not cry out or raise His voice, Nor make His voice heard in the street. A bruised reed He will not break, And a dimly burning wick He will not extinguish; He will faithfully bring forth justice. He will not be disheartened or crushed, Until He has established justice in the earth; And the coastlands will wait expectantly for His law." (NAS)	"Behold, [Jacob] My Servant, whom I uphold; My chosen one in whom My soul delights. I have put My Spirit upon Him; He will bring forth justice to the nations. He will not cry out or raise His voice, Nor make His voice heard in the street. A bruised reed He will not break, And a dimly burning wick He will not extinguish; He will faithfully bring forth justice. He will not be disheartened or crushed, Until He has established justice in the earth; And the coastlands will wait expectantly for His law" [And in his name the nations will hope]. (NAS)	"Behold, My Servant whom I have chosen; My Beloved in whom My soul is well-pleased; I will put My Spirit upon Him, And He shall proclaim justice to the Gentiles. He will not quarrel, nor cry out; Nor will anyone hear His voice in the streets. A battered reed He will not break off, And a smoldering wick He will not put out, Until He leads justice to victory. 'And in His name the Gentiles will hope'." (NAS)

A closer examination of this passage reveals that Matthew departs from the LXX for the most part and does not fully follow the MT in some of the wordings. Perhaps Matthew may be doing his own translation of the Hebrew text.[100] Where he follows the MT he appears to provide a literal rendering of the text.[101] In citing Isaiah 42:1, Matthew (12:18) omits the

---

100. Turner, *Matthew*, 316; Hagner, *Matthew 1–13*, 336; Blomberg, "Matthew," in *Commentary on the New Testament use of the Old Testament*, 43.
101. Blomberg, "Matthew," 43.

LXX's Ιακωβ ὁ παῖς μου ("my servant Jacob", 42:1) and rather follows the MT's עַבְדִּי אֶתְמָךְ־בּוֹ ("my servant whom I uphold", 42:1). What the LXX has done is to equate the "servant" with the nation Israel by inserting the word Jacob.[102] Matthew also departs from the LXX's ἔδωκα ("I have placed") to future θήσω ("I will place"), construing the MT's נָתַתִּי as a prophetic perfect.[103] The Lord places his Spirit upon his servant with whom his soul is well pleased. He will proclaim (ἀπαγγελεῖ) justice to the gentiles instead of LXX's "will bring" (ἐξοίσει) or the MT's יוֹצִיא ("he will bring forth"). Some think that Matthew uses "proclaim" instead of "bring forth" because Jesus and his persecuted disciples do not seek for justice but rather proclaim it.[104] Matthew translates the MT's "In faithfulness he will bring forth justice" in verse 3 as "till he leads justice to victory." He omits the first part of MT's Isaiah 42:4, that is, "he will not falter or be discouraged till he establishes justice on the earth" (לֹא יִכְהֶה וְלֹא יָרוּץ עַד־יָשִׂים בָּאָרֶץ מִשְׁפָּט) which the LXX follows. And Matthew translates the MT (42:4) "In his law the islands will put their hope" (וּלְתוֹרָתוֹ אִיִּים יְיַחֵלוּ) as "In his name the nations will put their hope," following the LXX (42:4) this time except that he omits the LXX's ἐπι ("upon"). Why does Matthew change "law" for "name" and the "islands" for "nations"? What is evident here is that Matthew reworks the original text. In the final line he pursues the theme of gentile mission of 12:18 by his καὶ τῷ ὀνόματι αὐτοῦ ἔθνη ἐλπιοῦσιν (12:21).[105] Therefore the LXX suits his purpose.

Matthew (12:18) portrays Jesus as the *servant*[106] of Isaiah in whom God delights, on whom God puts his Spirit, who brings justice to the nations (Isa 42:1).[107] Although he is filled with the Spirit and brings justice to the

---

102. Ibid.
103. Archer and Chirichigno, *Old Testament Quotations in the New*, 113.
104. Blomberg, "Matthew," 43.
105. Keener, *A Commentary on the Gospel of Matthew*, 360.
106. B. Gerhardson draws attention to the theme of servive in the entire Gospel of Matthew and especially as Matthew cites from Isa 42:1–4 (see B. Gerhardson, "Gottes Sohn als Diener Gottes: Messias, Agape und Himmelsherrschaft nach dem Matthäusevangelium," *ST* 27 (1973): 73–106.
107. For a good treatment of the concept of מִשְׁפָּט in Isa 42:1–4, see Richard Beaton, "Messiah and Justice: A Key to Matthew's use of Isa 42:1–4," *JNST* 75 (1999): 5–23. His whole argument is that Matthew's citation of Isaiah is to demonstrate Jesus' just treatment of the poor and oppressed as against the unjust treatment of the people by the Pharisees.

nations, 12:19, 20 suggest that he will act in humility and quietness such that no one will hear his voice in the streets. Matthew shows that Jesus did not come as political leader "or warrior messiah for the present time; he humbled himself as a suffering servant until the time when he would lead 'justice to victory.'"[108] He therefore emphasizes the lowly character of Jesus' earthly ministry. But "this Messiah's mission displays divine power and ultimately will lead to the universal triumph of God's kingdom."[109]

In 12:21 Matthew goes back to 12:18 on Jesus' mission to the nations. Matthew shows keen interest in the servant's proclamation of justice to the nations. This is apparent as noted in the textual analysis. Matthew translates the MT "in his law the islands will put their hope" as "in his name the nations will put their hope," in accordance with the LXX's rendering.

But what is the context of Isaiah 42:1–4? In Isaiah 41 the nation Israel is threatened with the judgment of God, using "one from the north," a prediction of the Babylonian captivity. But in Isaiah 42, a ray of hope is provided by God who announces salvation for God's people through his servant. And who is this servant? When Isaiah 42:1–4 is read in context, it is clear that Israel as a nation is in view. Matthew views the text from the larger context. God chose an individual within Israel to replace Israel and to restore the rest of his people (49:5–7) because Israel failed in its mission (42:18–19). This individual would now bear the punishment (cf. 40:2) that is due Israel (52:13–53:12). "As in 12:1–14, Matthew provides a hermeneutical key for his entire Gospel; his interpretation of Isaiah may

---

He therefore translates both מִשְׁפָּט in Isaiah and κρίσις in Matthew as "justice" rather than "judgment." It is noted that the word κρίσις "refers primarily to the activity of judging, and then derivatively to the bringing of justice, to the body that makes judgment (a court), to the sentence of condemnation, or even to the punishment resulting." However, "condemnation" is to be excluded in Matthew's usage (12:18) "on the basis of the language of hope in 12:21. Perhaps best is the establishment of a just order in place of the manifest injustices of the present life" (see Nolland, *The Gospel of Matthew*, 493). Nolland is in agreement with Beaton on the understanding of the concept of κρίσις in the text, although he applies the injustice rather broadly as societal injustice of the present age rather than the narrower Pharisaic injustice of Beaton.

108. Keener, *A Commentary on the Gospel of Matthew*, 361.
109. Blomberg, "Matthew," 42.

explain the Israel typology predominant in texts cited in the editorial asides of his infancy narratives."[110]

As mentioned earlier, Isaiah's Servant Song "reinforces Matthew's theme of gentile mission (2:1–12; 4:15; 24:24; 28:19)."[111] Not only does he show compassion to the "bruised reed" and the "smoldering wick," that is, "the weakened and shattered Judeans" in its initial context "but more implicitly and ironically to Egypt and Babylon in Isaiah's larger context of assuring Israel of their ultimate consolation"[112] or "the 'little ones,' whom Jesus treats tenderly (cf. 9:36; 11:28–30),"[113] but he also proclaims or announces (ἀπαγγελεῖ) justice (κρίσιν) to the nations (12:18) and "In his name the nations will put their hope" (12:21). According to Nolland, the recurrence of "nations" and "justice" takes the reader back to the final clause of 12:19 in which the role of the servant was first identified. Nolland reasons that although minor intimidations of the potential significance of Jesus for those outside the historical people of God are made in the Gospel of Matthew, 12:18, 19 go beyond these "minor intimidations." God was known to be the judge of all humanity in Jewish theology, but the thought that he would also be the savior of all the nations was far beyond normal Jewish thought.[114] Matthew claims here that the action God initiated through the Isaianic servant reaches the entire human race.[115]

---

110. Keener, *A Commentary on the Gospel of Matthew*, 360–361. On this "larger context" and God's choice of one person within Israel to restore the rest of the people, Blomberg sees Matthew employing double fulfillment as his hermeneutic key. As he says, "Matthew recognizes that Isaiah envisioned a servant role for Israel corporately throughout OT times and later, greater messianic fulfillment" (Blomberg, "Matthew," 43). For the rejection of the concept of double-fulfillment, see Kaiser Jr., *The Uses of the Old Testament in the New*, 88, 209–210. And this fulfillment through "an anointed prophet" is necessitated by "the inability of Israel ever to bring justice to all the nations of the earth" so that "more long-term fulfillment in an individual, a Davidic king or messiah" is in view in the text" (44). Matthew shows repeatedly (1:1; 2:15, 18; 4:1–12) that Jesus' mission rooted in the history of Israel and not a new event. And for Matthew, "the servant songs greatly define Jesus' identity (3:17; 8:17; 20:28)" (Keener, *A Commentary on the Gospel of Matthew*, 361).

111. Keener, *A Commentary on the Gospel of Matthew*, 360.

112. Blomberg, "Matthew," 44.

113. Gundry, *Matthew*, 230.

114. Nolland, *The Gospel of Matthew*, 495.

115. According to Nolland, "The universal mission to invite people to participate in this hope is anticipated in 24:14 and established in 28:19–20." And this language of hope is said to be "suggestive of a process underway, which fits well with the way the kingdom of

4.3.2 Prophetic Ministry of John the Baptist[116]

How does John the Baptist's ministry relate to gentile mission? The researcher argues that the message of John the Baptist in Matthew 3:7–10 (cf. Luke 3:7–9) has some indirect significance for gentile inclusion in the salvific purpose of God. It has been argued earlier that the genealogical record of Matthew 1:1–17 signaled a new era in which the definition of Israel goes beyond correct genealogical connections since the gracious intervention by God to save the chosen people was necessary, and even using women who were not properly connected to Abraham. 'Abraham' occurs five times in the Gospel of Matthew (1:2, 17; 3:9; 8:11; 22:32). In both Matthew 3:9 and 8:11, the name challenges ancestral descent. Matthew presents John the Baptist as one who is aware of a new era in which God looks beyond Abrahamic descent. In calling the people to repentance John the Baptist challenges the priority of race[117] because they were "unfaithful to their heritage."[118] He shows that racial privilege would not be beneficial in the coming kingdom.[119] If Israel as a nation fails to bear fruit God would raise children for Abraham from stones.[120] Davies and Allison focus atten-

---

God is conceived in Matthew" such that "Matthew may well intend his readers to link hope in the servant's name here with the significance of the name Jesus and Immanuel in 1:21, 23" (Nolland, *The Gospel of Matthew*, 495. See also Gundry, *Matthew*, 360 on the emphasis on gentile mission in this passage). Similarly, as Hagner (*Matthew 1–13*, 338) points out, Matthew includes the last line of Isa 42:4, skipping over parts of the verse to indicate that God has been faithful to Israel and that he grants salvation to the nations through Jesus (cf. 8:11–12; 21:43; 24:14; 28:19). Summarizing the text in its context, "Jesus retiring from persecution and pursuing itinerant evangelism rather than defending himself exemplify his disciples' flight from place to place in a persecuted ministry that results in conversion of gentiles" (Gundry, *Matthew*, 230).

116. For the crucial nature of John's ministry as a bridge, see the treatment of Matthew 11:12–13 in chapter 3.

117. Edgar Krentz, "None Greater Among Those Born From Women: John the Baptist in the Gospel of Matthew," *CurTM* (ATLAS, n. d.), 335.

118. Craig S. Keener, "'Brood of Vipers' (Matthew 3:7; 12:34; 22:33)," *JSNT* 28.1 (2005), 11.

119. In other words, "this ethnic chosenness is insufficient to guarantee salvation unless it is accompanied by righteousness" (Keener, *A Commentary on the Gospel of Matthew*, 124). John speaks to Jewish leaders, the Pharisees and Sadducees. Matthew is consistent in his invectives against the Jewish leaders.

120. Keener notices that pagans had stories of people formed out of stones, but that John spoke from Jewish Palestinian setting such that "children" and "stone" might have been word play in Aramaic. Furthermore, it is noted that the use of stones as symbol of God's people (Exod 24:4; 28:9–12; Josh 4:20–21; 1 Kgs 18:31) or covenants (Gen 31:46; Josh

tion on Matthew's citation of Isaiah at the beginning in relation to gentile mission. According to them, "Throughout Matthew, Isaiah's name (Matt 6–7; Mark 2; Luke 2) is associated on the one hand with Jesus' ministry to a blind Israel that rejects him and, on the other hand, with the salvation held out to the gentiles (8:17; 13:14(?); 35(?); 15:7; and 4:14 and 12:17 respectively)."[121] Therefore they view the challenge to Abrahamic descent here "for Matthew an allusion to the salvation soon to come to the gentiles."[122]

Thus in the new era inaugurated by the coming of the Messiah, both John and Jesus emphasize the bearing of fruit.[123] This demand for fruit comes in the context of impending judgment, and Abrahamic descent could not save one from this judgment. The imagery of a tree cut or burnt, applied to the judgment of a nation is rooted in the OT.[124] In this case, it is the tree that fails to bear fruit. If Israel fails to bear fruit God would raise children for Abraham from stones. Similarly, in Matthew 8:11–12 Jesus shows that it is faith in God that counts in the kingdom he inaugurates and not a matter of genetic privileges.

But not only does prophetic ministry play a decisive role in Matthew's mission theology, some of these prophecies are significantly linked with geographical locations.

4:20–24) is a common feature in the OT. "John's hearers thus would have understood his language clearly; he savaged their sense of security. Other early Jewish Christian texts echo this view that God is sovereign that he can choose the elect even on a basis that contradicts Israel's view of covenant (cf. Rom 9:6–29) (Keener, *A Commentary on the Gospel of Matthew*, 125).

121. Davies and Allison, *A Critical and Exegetical Commentary*, 1.293.

122. Ibid. On the contrary, James D. G. Dunn does not think that John the Baptist has gentiles in mind. He believes that John is addressing the factionalism in Second Temple Judaism that seem to ignore the fact that the choice of Israel is by God's sovereign freedom, see James D. G. Dunn, *Christianity in the Making*, vol. 1: *Jesus Remembered* (Grand Rapids/ Cambridge: Eerdmans, 2003), 365. But Dunn's position does not seem to take into account the gentile mission motif in the Gospel of Matthew, especially in Matthew's citation of Isaiah as Davies and Allison noted above.

123. See 3:8; 7:16–17; 12:33; 13:22–23; 21:34, 43; cf. John 15:6; Jude 12.

124. Keener, *A Commentary on the Gospel of Matthew*, 123. See Ezek 31:12–18; Dan 4:23; Ps 80:16; Jer 11:16; cf. 2 Sam 23:6–7.

4.4 Geography and Mission

In the Gospel of Matthew, God's salvation is beyond the geographical borders of Israel, for some will come from the east and the west (8:11; 25:31). From the genealogical record the nations are represented. At Jesus' birth, pagans from the east worship him.[125] We will therefore examine some of these geographical areas as Matthew represents them.

4.4.1 Magi from the East

The writer examines Matthew 2:1–12. This pericope has been treated in chapter 3 in relation to the Davidic shepherd-king. We will now present the significance of the story for gentile mission in the light of the text. According to this narrative, a star (ἀστήρ) guides the Magi from the East to the place Jesus is born (2:2).[126] A gentile motif surfaces. The mission of the magi is to worship Jesus (2:2).[127] From the beginning of the Gospel of Matthew, Jesus who is identified as the king of the Jews is worshipped

---

125. Keener, *A Commentary on the Gospel of Matthew*, 97. And by this "Matthew forces his audience to identify with the pagan magi rather than Herod or Jerusalem's religious elite, and hence to recognize God's interest in the gentile mission" (97–98).

126. Keener sees in this guidance by a star a probable allusion to the pillar of cloud that guided Israel in the wilderness, "suggesting that however the astrologers viewed the star, God used it in a manner reminiscent of Israel's salvation history" (Keener, *A Commentary on the Gospel of Matthew*, 104).

127. Jack Dean Kingsbury, *Matthew as Story* (Philadelphia: Fortress Press, 1886), 46.

by the Magi[128] from the East.[129] The three occurrences of προσκυνῆσαι in the text point to its significance (2:2, 8, 11).[130] Herod is acting deceptively (2:8); but the Magi from the East act with genuine intention (2:2, 11). They worship him and present him gifts (2:11). God also uses them to preserve the life of Jesus (2:12). On the presentation of gifts by the magi, France believes that the story is "modeled in parts on the words of Isaiah 60:1–6, where it is to the people of God in Zion that the gentiles will bring their gold and frankincense."[131] J. Duncan M. Derrett also points to the biblical prophecies that the nations would come to the Messiah bringing

---

128. *Magos*, a word with both negative and positive connotations in the NT, is said to be originally the title of Medes and Persian priestly caste with esoteric skills of dream interpretation. Their role was to advise the king. The term was later applied widely to learned men and priests who were skilled astrologers and interpreters of dreams, and sometimes performed magical arts and soothsaying. In the LXX, the term is applied to the "court magicians" (Dan 1:20; 2:2, 10, 27) whose functions included the interpretation of dreams. The magi in Matt 2 seem to have interest in astrology because of the fact that they were guided by a star, although the term magi, as noted here, is used in a variety of ways. It is said that although the magi were to be found all over the Roman Empire, they were linked with Babylonia. Therefore, Matthew's portrait of Magi from the East might point to the fact that they were from Babylon, a common understanding of the East by the Palestinians. It is believed that although the gifts they brought are associated with Arabia, it cannot be concluded that they were from there, although some scholars like Tony T. Maalouf argue in favor of Arabian origin, (see Tony T. Maalouf, "Were the Magi from Persia or Arabia?" *BSac* 156 [October–December 1999]: 423–42). For identity of the magi see also France, *The Gospel of Matthew*, 66; Turner, *Matthew*, 79; Nolland, *The Gospel of Matthew*, 108; Hendriksen, *Matthew*, 150–52; D. Mark Davis, "Matthew 2:1–12," *Int* (October 2003): 420–422. As Turner says, "The inclusion of the pericope about the magi does not amount to a sanction of astrology, which is condemned and forbidden in the Bible (e.g. Isa 47:13–13; Jer 10:1–2). Rather, Matthew includes the incident to contrast the mysterious insight of the magi with the obtuseness of Herod and the religious leaders" (Turner, *Matthew*, 79; see also Davis, "Matthew 2:1–12," 420 for the strong condemnation of astral cults in the OT). According to Keener, the historicity of this story, against many who see it as a tale, is rather strengthened by the fact that Matthew would probably not make up a story about magi believing Jesus, knowing official Jewish polemic against astrology (Keener, *A Commentary on the Gospel of Matthew*, 98).

129. Maalouf's article, "Were the Magi from Persia or Arabia?" 423–442, explores the ethnic origin of the magi and the reason for their interest in the King of the Jews. The interest of this author lies in the fact that they are gentiles who have come to worship the Jewish king. As such their ethnic origin lies outside the scope of the research.

130. According to Keener, the threefold repetition of *worship* in 2:2, 8, 11 reinforces the point of Matthew's narrative that if the Jews failed to honor and worship Jesus, the gentiles would, and that the narrative is a reflection of Jesus' identity in his royal authority as equal with the Father (28:9, 17–20). See Keener, *A Commentary on the Gospel of Matthew*, 105.

131. See France, *Matthew: Evangelist and Teacher*, 208. Cf. Ps 72:10.

him gifts.[132] Derrett says, "The nations would come one day to Jerusalem and claim to be enrolled as worshippers of the Jewish deity."[133]

Similarly, Weaver observes, "Through the story line of the magi (2:1–12), the narrator refutes traditional understandings of the vocation of the Messiah and in so doing redefines the categories of "outsider" and "insider.""[134] The traditional viewpoint is established through the genealogy that agrees with Jewish history and the fulfillment in the rest of chapter 1 of Matthew. But after that Matthew sets about rewriting the messianic script. According to Weaver, this rewriting begins by the portrayal of the Jewish people as being unaware of the Messiah in their midst "and singularly unreceptive to his presence when they learn of it."[135] King Herod and all Jerusalem did not know that the Messiah was born "until alerted to this fact by foreign astrologers newly arrived in town" and were terrified by the news of the birth of the Messiah. "And the collective response of the Jewish people to the arrival of their Messiah can be seen in the deadly character of the 'worship' that Herod, the king of Judea, seeks to offer 'the one who has been born king of the Jews.'"[136]

The theological and missional import of the pericope is that the Magi from the East who are "outsiders" demonstrate keen interest and faith in Jewish scriptural prophecies. And when the magi saw the star they followed it all the way from the East. They were able to locate the place where the Jewish Messiah was born, while the Jewish scribes and teachers of the law could only tell where the Messiah was to be born. Most importantly, while the Messiah's life is threatened by Herod and the Jewish people, he receives true worship from the gentiles. It means that Jesus' mission reaches beyond

---

132. J. Duncan M. Derrett, "Further Light on the Narratives of the Nativity," *NovT* 17.2 (n.d.), 97. See Mic 5:4; Ps 68:30, 31; 72:11. Derrett's point is that since messianic expectations existed in many eastern lands, "messianic movements in Israel will have found leadership." Furthermore, Jewish and pagan people in the Middle East looked to the East for wisdom (97–8). Similarly, Hendriksen points to the widely spread expectation of a deliverer in those days (John 4:25) and that the wise men might have been taught by the Jews to expect the coming of the Messiah (Hendriksen, *Matthew*, 153).
133. Derrett, "Further Light on the Narratives of the Nativity," 103.
134. Weaver "Rewriting the Messianic Script," 381.
135. Ibid.
136. Ibid., 382.

the Jewish nation and the borders of Judea.[137] Similarly, the story challenges prejudice against pagans.

4.4.2 Galilee of the Gentiles

The textual analysis of Matthew 4:15–16 has been treated in chapter 3. As we noted in chapter 3, Matthew sees Jesus' ministry in Galilee of the Gentiles as an era of the restoration of Israel. But we will argue here that Matthew's interpretative viewpoint is that a restored Israel also means that salvation has come to the nations. Therefore, Galilee, "the despised, sorely afflicted, and largely ignorant masses, a mixed gentile-Jewish population,"[138] not only represents "the land of reception"[139] but also a significant opening of the message of the kingdom for the gentiles as Jesus' encounters with the gentiles and their positive responses portray.

The pericope (4:12–17) is a transition and introduces Jesus' Galilean ministry. The preparatory role of John the Baptist appears to have been completed by his arrest and imprisonment. Jesus had also prepared for his own ministry through his victory in the desert temptation by the devil. This Galilean ministry is backed up by a quotation from Isaiah 9:1–2 (8:23–9:1, MT, LXX). It is noteworthy that in the phrase Γαλιλαία τῶν ἐθνῶν "both the geographic and the ethical elements are significant for Matthew's theology. Jesus brings light to a dark place and his message is ultimately for all the nations (24:14; 28:19)."[140] Although Galilee is the

---

137. Weaver, "Rewriting the Messianic Script," 381. Keener sees this narrative fitting Matthew's theme of the gentile mission (1:3, 5–6; 3:9; 4:15; 8:10–12, 28). See Keener, *A Commentary on the Gospel of Matthew*, 98. Putting this story in its background, Keener noted that leaders usually sent official representatives to congratulate leaders in other domains (Jos. *War* 2:309; 4:498–501; Acts 25:13). "Without condoning astrology, Matthew's narrative challenges his audience's prejudice against outsiders to their faith" and demonstrates that "even the most pagan of pagans may respond to Jesus if given the opportunity" (100). Similarly, looking at response to the message of Jesus as a universal principle, Senior says, "Throughout his story Matthew illustrates how disciples, outcasts, and occasional gentiles responded to Jesus with faith and conversion, while the Jewish leaders—and ultimately the people themselves—rejected him" (Senior and Stuhlmueller, *The Biblical Foundations for Mission*, 243).
138. Hendriksen, *Matthew*, 243. For the mixed population, see also France, *The Gospel of Matthew*, 142, 143.
139. Swartley, *Israel's Scripture Traditions*, 40.
140. Turner, *Matthew*, 132.

starting point for mission to Israel and mission to the nations,[141] the significance of Galilee for the nations is much more than a mere starting point of mission to the nations. In the Gospel of Matthew, Jesus began his ministry in Galilee (4:12–25). And when he rose from the dead he went back to Galilee (26:32). The angel who appeared to the women told them that Jesus would go ahead of the disciples into Galilee (28:5–6). When he met them in Galilee he told them to go into the world and make disciples of all nations (28:19–20). The prominence given to Galilee of the Gentiles both before and after the resurrection of Jesus is a clue that the nations play a crucial role in the Gospel of Matthew. Schnabel's position that sees Galilean ministry as primarily a ministry to Israel as noted in chapter 3 is less convincing in the light of what Galilee stands for in the universal mission of Jesus. The passage under consideration and the entire Gospel of Matthew seem to place more prominence to the universal mission of Jesus than mission to Israel, especially when Galilee is viewed in the light of the Great Commission. Swartley observes that the phrase 'Galilee of the Gentiles' "contributes an important interpretative perspective to Jesus' entire Galilean ministry."[142] This perspective is that Matthew includes the gentiles in the mission of God.

But does the social world of Galilee also support the notion that Matthew's quotation of Isaiah has the gentiles in mind? Freyne examined the Galilean social world and what influence that might have had on contours of Jesus' ministry. While the cultural and social identity of the Galileans is usually measured by the description of Isaiah 9: 1 and 1 Maccabees 5: 15, Freyne maintains, "The case for a pagan Galilee is poorly supported by the literary evidence and receives no support whatsoever from archaeological explorations," yet he admits that "in principle there is nothing to preclude the Galilean population from including Israelite, Iturean,

---

141. Garland, *Reading Matthew*, 43. See 1 Macc 5:15; 1 Enoch 48:4.
142. Swartley, *Israel's Scripture Traditions*, 61. Swartley compares Jesus' Galilean ministry to the exodus tradition and says that the miracles of chapters 8–9 in Matthew may be compared to the ten plagues in Egypt. The miracles of Matthew, however, show fulfilled missional intention in Jesus. Instead of judgment upon the pagans, they are blessed (Gen 12:3). Conversely, Israel is judged for rejecting the miracles of Jesus (8:11–13; 11:20–24; 12:38–42). It is in this respect that mission only to Israel rather clarifies Israel's spurned opportunity (67).

Judean, and even Babylonian strands in the ethnic mix by the first century C. E."[143] It is on the weight of the second position, namely, "the ethnic mix by the first century C. E." and in the light of prevailing scholarly position on Galilee as an area influenced by gentile elements, that this sub-section is treated. Contrary to Freyne's view concerning lack of evidence for a gentile Galilee, Hagner argues that the phrase Galilee of the Gentiles "was a common designation for Galilee, resulting from what had historically been a rather large gentile population."[144] Therefore, Matthew (4:15–16) cites Isaiah 9:1–2 about Jesus' ministry in the region of Galilee.[145]

Following the position that Jesus did not seek gentiles in the Galilean ministry, Schuyler Brown says that Jesus' openness to them may be indicated by the miracles he performed on their behalf, although there is no evidence that Jesus sought them out.[146] For Brown, "even when such

---

143. Freyne, "Galilee and Judea," 26. For more on the Galilean social world, see Karl-Heinrich Ostmeyer, "Armenhaus und Räuerhöhle? Galiläa zur Zeit Jesu," *ZNW* 96 (2005): 147–170.

144. Hagner, *Matthew 1–13,* 73. He adds that here Matthew does not refer to mission of Jesus to the gentiles, "but Matthew's readers may well have seen in these words a foreshadowing of what would occur after the resurrection (28:19; cf. 24:14). It is again for Matthew no accident that despite his limitation of his ministry to the Jews, Jesus began his ministry in a region that had gentile association" (73).

145. Capernaum, a place Jesus made his home, was a village in Galilee on the north shore of the lake (Matt 4:12–17). History has it that it was Herod Antipas who moved people to form a city on the west side of the lake, Tiberias. This happened before Jesus began his ministry in Galilee. Grams notes that it was perhaps this movement that facilitated Jesus' own relocation to the area (Grams, "Geographical and Intertextual Dimensions" 52). Jesus' hometown, Nazareth, is also in the Galilean region, only two miles from the pro-Roman city of Sepphoris. Tiberias and Sepphoris were the leading cities of Galilee. These cities were important at the time of Jesus' ministry. According to Grams, "while the Gospels nowhere mention Jesus' ministry in either Tiberias or Sepphoris, Matthew does record Jesus' ministry in 'all the cities' and the towns (9:35)" (52). Grams states that Matthew could not have written this if he had in mind that Jesus did not enter these two greatest cities of Galilee (52). He submits that Jesus' location may often have been necessitated by the political threats he faced from those who opposed his ministry, but "Matthew saw a deeper reason for Jesus' move back to Galilee and to the northern shores of the Sea of Galilee in particular: Jesus was positioning his ministry where it might expand to the nations" (53).

146. Schuyler Brown, "The Matthean Community and the Gentile Mission," *NovT* XXII.3 (July 1980): 194–195. Brown's position is representative of those who do not see mission to the nations interwoven in Matthew's narrative. But Harvey rightly suggests that Jesus' particularistic statements "must be weighed against aspects of his teaching and practice that suggest a more universal scope" (Harvey, Mission in Jesus' Teaching" 38). Harvey sees Jesus' statements in Matt 10:5–6; 15:24 as suggesting that during his lifetime Jesus limited his mission to Jewish people. But other references such as Matt 8:11–12; 22:1–14, 43; Luke

exceptional cases of restoration of physical health to gentiles are understood as an exercise of Jesus' 'saving ministry,' they do not constitute a precedent for the gentile mission."[147] Jesus' mission among the people, in Brown's view, is an expression of his concern for the "people of the land" (עַם הָאָרֶץ). Brown's premise is that "The teaching and practice of the historical Jesus provided the post-Easter community with no clear directive with regard to missionizing gentiles" and that "Matthew's inclusion of the particularistic form of the mission mandate in his Central Section suggests that the gentile mission was controverted at the time of the gospel's composition."[148] For Brown, the only thing that could have authorized gentile mission was Jesus' "expectant universalism" found in passages of Matthew like 8:11–12.[149] Swartley, however, says, "Granted, chapter 10 indicates that Jesus' mission was first and foremost to bring renewal to Israel, but Jesus' ministry, as presented in Matthew, is never limited to Israel."[150] Dorothy J. Weaver's point that nowhere does Matthew record the actual fulfillment of the commission in chapter 10 and that the mission to Israel cannot be separated from mission to the rest of the world is noteworthy.[151]

Isaiah 9:1–2 is key to understanding Jesus' mission to the nations in the Gospel of Matthew (4:15–16). For "Jesus' positioning of himself on the north shore of the Sea of Galilee had as much relevance in Isaiah's day as in his own if someone wished to minister to gentiles in the region."[152] Josephus also says that both Upper and Lower Galilee are home for foreign nations.[153] So both Isaiah and Matthew see this Galilee as a Jewish region surrounded by gentiles. For Swartley, the mention of Syria, the Decapolis

---

13:28–29; 14:16–24, etc., suggest that "Israel would be replaced as the exclusive inheritors of the kingdom" (38).

147. Brown, "The Matthean Community and the Gentile Mission," 195.

148. Ibid., 220.

149. Brown thinks that the first missionaries to the gentiles were the Hellenists who were suited for this work through their ability to use Greek and their attitude toward Jewish ritual law (220).

150. Swartley, *Israel's Scripture Traditions*, 65.

151. D. J. Weaver, *Matthew's Missionary Discourse: A Literary-Critical Analysis* (JSNTSS 38; Sheffield: JSOT, 1990), 124–53, as cited by Swartley, *Israel's Scripture Traditions*, 65. Therefore, the disciples' commission "stays open literally through 11:2–28:16–20" (65).

152. Grams, "Geographical and Intertextual Dimensions," 53.

153. Jewish War 3:41.

and beyond the Jordan in Matthew 4:24–25 signify Jesus' "ministry of liberation was not confined to Jews, but included gentiles also."[154]

But perhaps the most significant point that most scholars seem to ignore is Matthew's own emphasis concerning gentile mission in this territory. Matthew twice quotes from the OT (4:15–16; 12:18–21) concerning the nations and reworks those texts to underscore his gentile mission motif. One would even suggest that a missional structure of the Gospel of Matthew is inclined toward Galilean ministry and gentile mission: Jesus' pedigree and preparation for ministry (1:1–4:11); Jesus' ministry in Galilee (4:12–16:20); Jesus' ministry on the way to Jerusalem (16:21–20:34); Jesus' ministry in Jerusalem, death and resurrection (21:1–28:15); Jesus' post-Easter ministry in Galilee (28:16–20). Therefore, Galilee stands prominent in this structure. Josephus' brief reference to Jesus' ministry indicates that "He drew over to him both many of the Jews, and many of the gentiles."[155] Therefore, we will assume that Matthew 4:15–16 underscores gentile mission.

We will now examine the significance of Mount Zion for gentile mission.

4.4.3 Mount Zion[156] and Eschatological Pilgrimage

The text and context of Matthew 21:1–11 on Mount Zion has been treated in chapter 3. We discussed that in Jerusalem the people received Jesus as Son of David who comes in the name of the Lord (21:9). This text (21:1–11) does not mention the nations except that Jesus is a prophet from Nazareth in Galilee (21:11). But the entry into Jerusalem occurs as fulfillment of Zechariah 9:9. The connecting thread here is what *Zion* meant for the prophets in the eschatological age and how Matthew might have interpreted this. Some scholars have attempted to connect this event with the gathering of the nations, namely, the eschatological pilgrimage. According to Brown, Jesus' "expectant universalism" which reflects "a positive attitude

---

154. Swartley, *Israel's Scripture Traditions*, 64.
155. *Antiquities,* XVIII, iii, 3. The authenticity of the reference to Jesus by Josephus is questioned on the unproven ground that the work is edited.
156. See Levenson, *Sinai and Zion,* 111–184. Mount Zion replaced Mount Sinai as the mountain of God (Ps 50:2–3). Zion also became the mountain of the temple. But in the Psalms and the prophets, the idea of Zion as a cosmic mountain, a sacred space, where the restored Israel and the nations come together in the new temple is a dominant theme.

Mission to the Nations: Foundations and Framework 191

towards the inclusion of gentiles in eschatological salvation" is said to be drawn from Matthew 8:11–13 as a classic text, although this text "leaves unresolved *how* the gentiles are to come to the worship of the one true God"[157] (emphasis original). The *how* of gentile mission that Brown considers unresolved is based on his position that the "historical Jesus provided the post-Easter community with no clear directive with regard to missionizing gentiles" and that "Matthew's inclusion of the particularistic form of the mission mandate in his Central Section suggests that the gentile mission was controverted at the time of the gospel's composition."[158] Brown makes an important connection between Matthew 8:11–12 and the eschatological pilgrimage of the nations (Isa 2:2f; Mic 4:1f) "and their share in the eschatological banquet" (Isa 25:6f).[159] But Brown argues that Matthew alludes to texts that are centripetal rather than centrifugal.

Brown's point, though well argued, is less convincing because it does not consider the change from the centripetal viewpoint of the eschatological pilgrimage of the OT to the centrifugal dimension of mission in Matthew. Although Mount Zion is connected to the idea of the eschatological pilgrimage, Matthew does not connect Zion with the nations, but an unnamed mountain in Galilee (Matt 28:16). Furthermore, the context of Zechariah 9:9 shows that although this king rightly proclaims peace to the nations, his rule extends to the ends of the earth (9:10).[160] This, therefore, explains

---

157. Brown, "The Matthean Community and the Gentile Mission," 196.
158. Ibid., 220.
159. Ibid., 196. According to Brown, Jesus' conception of the eschatological pilgrimage "takes on particular relevance in view of Jesus' *presentist* eschatology according to which the moment for the coming of the gentiles would seem already to have arrived" (196, emphasis original. Cf. Matt 12:28; Luke 17:21). However, Brown says that the OT texts alluded to in Matthew's eschatological pilgrimage do not indicate the participation of human agents or missionary activities. Instead the gentiles would come to Mount Zion "either spontaneously, having been drawn by Israel's prosperity to inquire as to its cause, or else as the result of God's action. Thus the very conception which might seem to *call* for the gentile mission ('since the kingdom of God is present, the time for the coming of the gentiles has arrived') appears on closer inspection to *prohibit it*" (196, emphasis original. Cf. Isa 19:21; 25:6f; 45:20f; 51:4; 66:18; Zeph 3:9).
160. Schnabel says, the Hellenistic, Greek-speaking Jewish Christians of Jerusalem "understood and proclaimed the consequences of the death and resurrection of Jesus the Messiah for the identity of Israel the people of God" (Schnabel, *Jesus and the Twelve*, 911). They believed that what the Bible says about God who does not dwell in temples made by human hands has come to effect in the time of the Messiah which ushered in the arrival of

Matthew 28:18, 19. God was now reaching out to the nations instead of waiting for the nations to come to Jerusalem as pilgrims. And all the nations of the earth could now find their place in God's salvific plan.[161]

It is important to highlight briefly other references in connection with the expectant universal outreach in the Gospel of Matthew in support of 8:11–12. We will not treat them in detail here as priority is given to texts with OT motifs. Matthew 13:38 identifies the field as the world. This has universal mission motif.[162] In the parable of the tenants (21:33–46), discussed fully in the section of typology in relation to the "stone," and the parable of the wedding banquet (22:1–14), inclusion of gentiles in the kingdom is in view. Similarly, in Matthew 24:14 Jesus reveals that before his coming back, the gospel of the kingdom will be preached to the whole world. This is bringing the whole of humanity in God's program of salvation. The nations' gathering before the Son of Man at the eschatological judgment has been treated in the previous chapter, and the expectant universal viewpoint is also indicated by Jesus' comments about the woman who anointed him (26:6–14). This universal prospect is climaxed in the Great Commission (28:16–20). Therefore, Matthew 21:1–11 seems to be primarily concerned about Jesus coming to his people Israel and not the gathering of the nations.

We will now examine the final section dealing with intertextual typology in Matthew's gospel with respect to gentile mission.

---

the kingdom. "They understood that God had revealed himself for the salvation of Israel and the world in Jesus of Nazareth, the Messiah from Galilee, who died on the cross and rose from the dead on the third day" (911). Salvation is now possible only in connection with Jesus and the temple has ceased to be the place of God's atoning sacrifice. "If the Torah is no longer the normative center for Israel's relationship with Yahweh, if the temple is no longer the central place of Yahweh's atoning presence, if Judea is no longer holier than any other land, if God's salvation is no longer concentrated exclusively on Israel and its traditional institutions of salvation, if God's merciful presence can now be experienced wherever people repent and depend on Jesus the Messiah for salvation—if these convictions are held deeply and consistently and joyfully, then the path to world mission has been opened up" (911).

161. And "this new, revolutionary mode of realizing God's promise to Abraham, in whose name all families of the earth were to be blessed, was a theological consistent corollary of the redefinition of the significance and the role of the temple and the Torah in the messianic era that had dawned" (Schnabel, *Jesus and the Twelve*, 911–12).

162. Hagner, *Matthew 1–13*, 393; France, *The Gospel of Matthew*, 535; Turner, *The Gospel of Matthew*, 559. Hendriksen, *Matthew,* 571.

4.5 Intertextual Typology and Mission

The meaning of typology and intertextuality has been explored in chapter 3.[163] This section examines how the typological use of the mountain, the sign of Jonah, and the stone[164] are applied to gentile mission.

4.5.1 The Mountain

The mountain (τὸ ὄρος) motif has been referred to in chapters 2 and 3 as a significant element in the mission of Jesus. This discussion focuses on the last mountain of Matthew 26:32; 28:5–7, 16. What is significant about the last mountain in Matthew is that it is where Jesus meets with his disciples after his resurrection and the location where the Great Commission takes place. It is a mountain in Galilee,[165] a region Matthew links with the gentiles (4:15–16). It is on this mountain that Jesus instructs his disciples to go and make disciples of all nations and to teach them to observe all that he commanded them,[166] presumably the contents of the Sermon on the Mount and everything else he taught them. This mountain of meeting with the disciples after the resurrection seems to suggest that it is a mountain in which the nations are gathered instead of Mount Zion where Jesus fulfills his role as king of the Jews (Matt 21:1–12). The writer suggests, therefore, that Matthew's earlier description of this region as "Galilee of the Gentiles"

---

163. Similarly, recent scholars' contributions on intertextual typology in chapter 3 also apply.

164. Left out here is the wilderness motif (treated in the previous chapter), which can hardly be applied directly to the nations but probably indirectly since there is no direct reference indicating such a connection. If an application could be made, this may be derived from the meaning Matthew intended to communicate to his church, comprising Jews and gentiles. Perhaps the story is recorded to encourage the church to endure the trials and temptations they were passing through as their Lord had endured. Similar references in the NT that cites the wilderness experiences as warnings and encouragement could be found. In warning against unbelief, the writer of Hebrews says, "So the Holy Spirit says: 'Today, if you hear his voice, do not harden your hearts as you did in the rebellion, during the time of testing in the desert, where your fathers tested and tried me and for forty years saw what I did" (3:7, 8). The apostle Paul also speaks about this wilderness temptation in 1 Cor 10:1–11 and concludes that those events happened as example for the church. Could it be that Matthew also had similar intention by his use of the wilderness motif?

165. According to Swartley, "Matthew clearly identifies the risen Jesus' return to Galilee as culminating in the commissioning of the disciples to go in mission to the nations, the gentiles" (Swartley, *Israel's Scripture Traditions,* 41).

166. See also Hagner, *Matthew 14–28,* 883.

(4:15–16) is in pursuit of the gentile mission motif and is intended to portray this mountain as the mountain of gathering the nations.[167]

But as noted in chapters 2 and 3, some scholars generally interpret Matthew's mountain motif as either a Moses typology (so Allison) or the Son-Christology, namely, the Son on Mount Zion where his sovereign power over the nations is affirmed (so Grams and Donaldson). According to Allison, "Jesus' appearance on a mountain is joined to the new Moses theme."[168] However, Terrence L. Donaldson believes that some of the mountain motifs in Matthew have no Sinai background and are devoid of Mosaic connection. Donaldson's position is that the mountain motif in Matthew depicts Jesus as Son of God gathering the nations unto God. For him, Psalm 2:6 is Mount Zion where the son's sovereign power over the nations is affirmed. But in the third temptation and the Great Commission remarkable relationship is established with Psalm 2 in which the royal son is seen as sovereign and worthy of worship.[169]

A parallel drawn from the mountain motif in Matthew with eschatological significance is Isaiah 2:2–4 and Jeremiah 31:12, 31–34. On the mountain of the Lord God draws all the nations of the earth to himself. Just as Jesus gave instruction to the people on the Mount of Beatitudes so also instructions from the Lord come from the mountain in these OT references. On the Mount of Beatitudes, although in Galilee and not Mount Zion, Jesus is seen as gathering the nations in fulfillment of OT prophecies. In a similar way, the Great Commission is said to picture Jesus as involving "gathering the nations under his sovereignty."[170]

This writer takes a harmonizing position of the two views above. He believes that the mountain motif could be cast into both Moses typology and Son-Christology depending on which mountain is in view. He assumes this position from the fact that in Matthew the allusions to both

---

167. Carson shares a similar view. For him, "Galilee of the Gentiles" foreshadows the commission to "all nations" in Matt 28:19 (Carson, "Matthew," 20).

168. Allison, *The New Moses,* 263. For him, "of all the figures in the Christian Bible, Moses and Jesus are the two whose narratives, from beginning to end, are most punctuated by significant mountain scenes" (263). See 4:8; 5:1–2; 15:29; 17:1–2; 24:3; 28:16–20.

169. Terence L. Donaldson in his *Jesus on the Mountain: A Study in Matthean Theology,* JSNTSS 8 (Sheffield: JSOT Press, 1985), 101ff.

170. Grams, "Geographical and Intertextual Dimensions," 55.

the Son of God and Moses can hardly be missed (e.g. Matt 2:13–15; 5:1). If Jesus, the Son of God, is the new Moses, it is possible for him to give the new law on the mountain (in Moses typology) and also gather the nations on the mountain (in Son typology). This is supported by the fact that the mountains in Matthew do not seem to play the same role and neither does their typological significance as we noted in chapter 3. The second reason this researcher gives for a different viewpoint is that types and antitypes do not seem to fit into a single meaning all the time. It appears that while Jesus may be depicted as the new Moses in the Gospel of Matthew, he may also fill the role of Israel as God's son in the same Gospel.

In summary, Matthew makes a theological and missional connection between Galilee and the Mountain of the Great Commission. Therefore, while the Mount of Beatitudes (5:1) and Mount Zion (21:5) may represent Jesus as the new Moses, the last mountain (26:32; 28:5–7, 16) appears to be the mountain of gathering the nations. That the mountain is unnamed is also significant for this researcher. It is perhaps Matthew's disassociation of Jesus from being a solely Jewish Messiah that corresponds to his portrayal of Jesus as Savior of both Jews and gentiles.[171]

Next in the discussion of typology in Matthew is the sign of Jonah.

4.5.2 The Sign of Jonah

The typological significance of Jonah has been treated in chapter 3 regarding the resurrection of Jesus in relation to Israel. But Jesus' resurrection as typified by Jonah could be applied to gentile mission as well. Matthew specifically uses Jonah's example to show gentile responsiveness to the message of the kingdom (12:41–42). The uniqueness of Jonah among all the other OT prophets is that he is the only prophet called to go to a gentile nation to preach. Although other prophets were also given messages to preach to the nations they remained in the land of Israel.[172] Another important distinction in the book of Jonah is that all the characters encountered in it are

---

171. Köstengerger and O'Brien think that "by omitting reference to the name of the mountain in Galilee where the event took place and by providing no description of Jesus' external appearance, Matthew focuses attention on Jesus' words uttered on this occasion" (Köstengerger and O'Brien, *Salvation to the Ends of the Earth,* 102.

172. See Jer 46–51; Ezek 25–26; Amos 1–3.

gentiles except Jonah the Jewish prophet. A notable irony in the book of Jonah is that a disobedient and reluctant prophet of God from the nation Israel preaches to a gentile nation that eagerly responds in fear and obedience to the voice of God.[173]

The attempt here is to draw the connections that Matthew makes between Jonah and the nations. The repentance of the Ninevites fits Matthew's theme of gentile responsiveness in the Gospel of Matthew. In Jonah 3:5 the men of Nineveh believed God (וַיַּאֲמִינוּ אַנְשֵׁי נִינְוֵה בֵּאלֹהִים) and they turned away from their evil ways as mark of repentance (3:9, 10). Matthew urges repentance and turning away from evil (3:1–8; 4:17). Matthew now contrasts the Ninevites with those who heard Jesus and saw his miracles and yet did not believe (12:22–24). Matthew shows those who are least expected to put their faith in the God of Israel demonstrate greater faith than the children of the kingdom. Similarly, Matthew uses the example of the Queen of Sheba (1 Kgs 10:1–13) to reinforce the contrast he is making between the faith of the gentiles and the unbelief of his generation. The Queen of Sheba came because she "heard about the fame of Solomon and his relation to the name of the Lord" (1 Kgs 10:1). But Jesus is one greater than Solomon, yet the people of his generation did not believe him. Jesus makes a similar charge against the Jews of his generation in Matthew 11:20–24. The gentile nations would have repented if they had seen the miracles performed by Jesus among the Jews.

One explicit theological and missional significance in the book of Jonah is the fact that God is not concerned with only one ethnic nationality but with all who respond[174] to him in repentance. The story of Jonah comes

---

173. Scholars are divided on the significance of the book of Jonah in relation to gentile mission in the OT. Although this is outside the scope of discussion in this work, it is important to mention that while scholars like Kaiser Jr. see in Jonah God's deliberate plan to reach out to the nations through Israel, others like Bosch think differently (cf. Kaiser Jr., *Mission in the Old Testament*, 65–74 and Bosch, *Transforming Mission*, 17. For Bosch, "even the book of Jonah has nothing to do with mission in the normal sense of the word").

174. According to Senior and Stuhlmueller, "The massive emphasis on right response in Matthew's gospel makes of this motif not only a pattern of history but a criterion of salvation itself. Regardless of social or religious background, whoever responds with faith and obedience to the gospel of Jesus Christ becomes thereby a member of God's people" (Senior and Stuhlmueller, *The Biblical foundations for Mission*, 247). Senior and Stuhlmueller say that "there is a sweeping universalism inherent in this principle" (247).

as a contrast to the exclusive nationalism of the Jews[175] and their refusal to repent. In his theological and missional scheme, Matthew uses Jonah as a type of Jesus and example of gentile inclusion into the kingdom of heaven.

The *stone* motif is also significant for Matthew's mission theology. This forms our next discussion.

4.5.3 The Stone

The writer examined the theological and missional import of the stone motif for mission to Israel in chapter 3 with regard to Israel's religious leaders. The stone imagery in Matthew and its significance to gentile mission may be properly understood against the background from which it is drawn. An interesting observation about the stone motif in Matthew 3:9 and 21:43 is that both occurrences speak against the leaders of Israel. While in Matthew 3:9 the stone (ὁ λίθος) represents lifeless objects from which God could raise up children for Abraham to replace the unfruitful natural descendants of Abraham, the stone in Matthew 21:42 is Jesus himself whom the leaders have rejected and yet becomes the capstone. The writer focuses here on the cornerstone from the parable of the tenants (21:33–46), an echo of vineyard allegory of Isaiah 5:1–7 as noted in chapter 3. In this parable Matthew indicts Jerusalem's "religious establishment,"[176] "the builders of Israel."[177] The writer has commented on the MT and LXX texts in chapter 3, that the LXX agrees with the MT and that Matthew follows both. Therefore, he rather focuses here on the text of Matthew and evaluates scholars' positions on the key issues arising from the pericope. The attention is primarily on what Jesus means by taking away the kingdom and giving to people who will produce its fruit (21:43). Of particular significance here is the meaning of ἔθνος. For some scholars, the *nation* represents the "Matthean community as an eschatological messianic remnant whose leaders will replace the current Jerusalem religious establishment and lead Israel in bearing the

---

175. Arturo Bravo, "Jonah and Jesus," *Theology Diggest* 51, no. 2 (Summer 2004): 130.
176. Turner, *Matthew*, 518.
177. Snodgrass, *Stories with Intent*, 295.

fruit of righteousness for God."[178] Therefore, Turner rejects *replacement* as later theology with its attendant anti-Semitism.

However, according to France, "the mention of another 'nation' to replace 'you' in the tenancy of the vineyard takes us to the heart of the issue of the true Israel which underlies this whole section of the gospel."[179] France's observation is that interpreting Jesus' words "as a prediction of imminent regime change in Jerusalem" is confronted with the "unexpected term" ἔθνος which suggests something more radical. But what alternative regime does France propose? According to him, the clue lies in the quotation of Psalm 118:22. For "after the tenants' rejection of the son in the parable the builders' rejection of the stone is not hard to interpret."[180] Just as the rejected stone will become the cornerstone, so also the rejected Son will be vindicated "and replace the present leadership." For this reason, the addition of the quotation point beyond the death of Christ is to the resurrection. The ἔθνος therefore refers to people who follow the risen Jesus. "There is thus inherent in this parable with its appended Psalm quotation a bold Christology of rejection and vindication, of death and resurrection, and it is focused in the parable character of the owner's son."[181] Sharing France's view is Keener who sees the "nation" in verse 43 "to whom it would be given undoubtedly refers to a holy nation of a new exodus"[182] and Hendriksen who sees the "nation" as "a church international, gathered from both Jews and gentiles."[183] According to Keener, the "crushing" power of the stone

---

178. Turner, *Matthew*, 518. Therefore, the parable is about ethics and not ethnicity, and is concerned about Jewish remnant as against gentile replacement of the Jews. This interpretation follows the depiction of 21:29 of Israel as the repentant son and of 22:9–10 as responsive guests, and should never, therefore, be interpreted in ethnic terms. In his view, the idea of replacement here is reading into the text a later theology and is responsible for anti-Semitism. The passage "should, rather, be interpreted as an intramural transfer of leadership from the fruitless Jerusalem religious establishment to the fruitful Matthean Christian Jewish community, led by the apostles." In this view the church is the "eschatological remnant of Israel that continues its mission to Israel while expanding its horizons to all the nations. This Jewish remnant becomes the nucleus of the nascent church" (519).

179. France, *The Gospel of Matthew*, 808.

180. Ibid., 811.

181. Ibid.

182. Keener, *A Commentary on the Gospel of Matthew*, 515. See Exod 19:5–6; 1 Pet 2:9.

183. Hendriksen, *Matthew*, 786.

probably refers to Daniel 2:44 and the stumbling aspect of it may have been an allusion to Isaiah 8:15 and 28:16.[184]

Turner makes two significant points. First, the possibility of reading into the text a later theological viewpoint is noteworthy. Second, the anti-Semitism that follows from a wrong interpretation of a text is unhealthy. However, the rejection of replacement[185] theology is one thing, and to see the ἔθνος in the text as the disciples of Jesus is quite another, especially if "disciples" here does not include all believers. We will examine the text from the entire context of the Gospel of Matthew. Matthew shows that those who demonstrate faith and respond to Jesus' message will have a place in the kingdom of heaven regardless of their ethnic background (8:10–12). Therefore, the writer argues that the ἔθνος in Matthew 21:43 is probably to be understood as Matthew's new people, the ἐκκλησία. The new nation "is not to the exclusion of Jews as such but only of those whose lack of faith has debarred them from the kingdom of heaven."[186] The writer finds replacement theology difficult to accept, in spite of the use of the word ἔθνος, based on the evidence of the text, especially on reading Matthew as a whole. Unlike Nickelsburg who argues that Israel stands under judgment because of their rejection of Jesus, and that she has been stripped of her status as God's people, "while the church, largely gentile in constituency, is bestowed this favored position,"[187] the writer offers some reasons why such view is less convincing. First of all, it is the chief priests and the Pharisees who were offended by the parable because they knew that Jesus was speaking against them. And although they wanted to arrest Jesus they were afraid of the

---

184. Keener, *A Commentary on the Gospel of Matthew*, 516.

185. "Replacement theology" is defined here as the acceptance of the gentiles into the kingdom of God in place of the entire Jewish race due to its rejection of Jesus. (See Nickelsburg's view below).

186. France, *The Gospel of Matthew*, 816. Therefore, "This new 'nation' is neither Israel nor the gentiles, but a new entity, drawn from both, which is characterized not by ethnic origin but by faith in Jesus (816–817). According to Anthony J. Saldarini, *"ethnos* should not be translated in 21:43 as 'nation' because the followers of Jesus were not a nation or ethnic group." Matthew uses the term in the sense of "a voluntary organization or small social group." This group is the ἔθνος that believes in Jesus and produces fruit. They are not "a new or true Israel, nor a replacement for Israel" (Anthony J. Saldarini, "Reading Matthew without Anti-Semitism," in *The Gospel of Matthew in Current Study*, ed. David E. Aune [Grand Rapids/Cambridge: Eerdmans, 2001], 172–173).

187. Nickelsburg, "Good News/Bad News," 326.

crowd (Matt 21:45–46). Therefore, the crowd is not part of those who reject the stone at this point. Second, throughout the Gospel of Matthew, both John the Baptist and Jesus directed their invectives against the religious and political leaders and not the crowds (3:7–10; 23:1–39) that were like sheep without a shepherd (9:36). Third, Matthew suggests that it is the Pharisees and the teachers of the law who "shut the kingdom of heaven in men's faces" (Matt 23:13). These leaders abused the privileged position of the "keys" of the kingdom entrusted to them and hindered "the would-be followers of Christ."[188] Finally, the word *builders* in the text suggest prominent people or leaders and shows that Jesus is rather speaking against the leaders of Israel. Therefore it is tenable to assume that Jesus is referring to the replacement of the religious leaders and all the Jews who reject Jesus through unbelief rather than the entire nation of Israel. Similarly, unless one excludes the nation Israel from τὰ ἔθνη of Matthew 28:19–20, it is logical to understand the ἔθνος in Matthew 21:43 as a new view of God's people that Matthew depicts in the entire gospel. Therefore, theological and missional import of the text is that Matthew speaks of the new assembly of God's people who are made up of both Jews and the gentiles. Jesus is the cornerstone of the ἐκκλησία, made up of all who accept the Son (21:37).

4.6 Summary and Conclusion

A fascinating observation in this chapter is how Matthew interwove the whole narrative with gentile mission. Not only is this gentile mission motif implicit in the genealogy and in 2:1–12, but also in the explicit citations of 4:15 and 12:18–21, all culminating in the Great Commission of 28:19 which implies that the Abrahamic blessing "to all the peoples on earth" (Gen 12:3) has come to fulfillment. Matthew seems to have achieved his objective by a number of methods. First, Matthew's narrative is framed with

---

188. Keener, *A Commentary on the Gospel of Matthew*, 547. According to Hagner, the correct teaching of the Torah by the Pharisees and the teachers of the law should have been the key to open the door for others to enter and enjoy the kingdom. But they failed through their false teaching of the Torah (see Hagner, *Matthew 14–28*, 668).

contrasts, irony,[189] and paradox, all intended to demonstrate that gentile mission is also legitimate. In the Jewish genealogy gentile women surface prominently (1:5–6). Jesus, the king of the Jews, is rejected and handed over to be crucified by the Jews (27:12–26), while he is received and worshipped by the gentile magi (2:1–12). Similarly, many from the east and west take their places and feast with Abraham, Israel's father, while the heirs of the kingdom are thrown outside (8:10–12). Abraham's children could also be replaced by stones for failure to bear fruit (3:7–9). Jesus finds greater faith among the gentiles (8:10; 15:21–28). Jesus' healing ministry is received by the gentiles (8:13; 15:28) but repudiated by the Jews (12:24). The Jews constitute "a wicked and adulterous generation" whom the men of Nineveh stand up at the judgment and condemn (12:39, 41). The stone the builders rejected has become the cornerstone (21:42). Zion/Jerusalem, the city of God and of the great temple is now "your house is left to you desolate (23:38)," while the despised Galilee of the Gentiles becomes the location where light dawns and the place of the Great Commission (4:15–16; 28:16).

Second, Matthew legitimized gentile mission by his unparalleled passages that allude to gentile inclusion in the kingdom of God like the account of the magi (2:1–12), the Galilee of the Gentiles (4:15–16), the Servant of Yahweh who proclaims justice to the nations and in whose name the nations put their hope (12:17–21), and the Great Commission (28:16–20). In these passages, Matthew's theological and missional viewpoint is apparent and interwoven in the entire gospel such that the Great Commission is like an inclusio.

Third, Matthew deals with the question of continuity and discontinuity in his gospel. The mention of Abraham in the genealogy would appeal to Israel as the descendants of Abraham. But the mention of the same name in Matthew 3:9 and 8:11 suggests that there is both continuity and discontinuity. Matthew 8:11 especially evokes God's covenant blessings to Abraham that extends to the nations. Abraham now assumes the role of a father to many from the east and the west. Matthew pursues this continuity and discontinuity by including gentile women in the Abrahamic and

---

189. Irony is here used in the sense of something that happens that is incongruous with what might have been expected.

Davidic genealogy to show that Abrahamic blessing is intended for the nations as well. In this continuity and discontinuity scheme, Jesus cleanses and restores the temple and, along with his disciples, pays the temple tax; but he also shows that he is the one greater than the temple and that the new community gathers in his name, not necessarily in the temple in Jerusalem. Continuity and discontinuity also touches on the issue of the gentiles in relation to the Torah. Implicitly, Matthew shows that God established a single universal righteousness for all humankind because the teachings of the Sermon of the Mount cannot be fully realized within the confines of the disciples' community, for the disciples were instructed to go and make disciples of all the nations by teaching them to obey what Jesus commanded them (Matt 28:19).

Fourth, in polemic and apologetic mode, Matthew demonstrates that the prophets also played a decisive role as God worked through them to announce his plans concerning the nations. God is the ultimate agent in prophetic ministry. Matthew demonstrates deep insight into this prophetic ministry. He does this through reshaping, reinterpretation, and recontextualization of OT texts he cites. For him, God spoke through Isaiah concerning the Galilee of the Gentiles and his chosen and anointed servant who would be the light of the nations and in whose name the nations put their hope.

Finally, typologically Matthew sees the nations being gathered on the mountain of the Lord, not in Jerusalem but in Galilee. He also sees God at work through the prophet Jonah as representative of what God purposed to do for the nations through Christ. Not only would Jesus die for the world, the Ninevites would also stand up on the day of judgment and condemn the heirs of the kingdom because they (Ninevites) repented at Jonah's preaching. In addition, the "stone the builders rejected" becomes the cornerstone of the church, which comprises both Jews and gentiles.

On the whole, then, what Matthew has done in his gospel is to present a universal view of God's salvific purpose within the same OT foundations and framework by a careful transformation and recontextualization of the materials at his disposal. He realized the objective of an instructed teacher of the law "who brings out of his storeroom new treasures as well as old." And having examined wide-ranging issues and themes in chapters 2 through 4, the writer draws some general conclusions in chapter 5.

CHAPTER 5

Conclusions and Recommendations

5.1 Conclusions

The writer examined hermeneutics of mission in the Gospel of Matthew in relation to Israel and the nations. This missional hermeneutic is connected to other themes. The major themes and issues in Matthean studies in the recent past include: the setting for the Gospel of Matthew or his community (that touches on the relationship between Matthew and the historical Jesus); the sources and structure of the Gospel of Matthew; theology and salvation history; the relationship between Jewish and gentile mission; Matthew's use of the OT; Matthew's attitude to the Torah (including Matthew's place in early Christianity); Christology in Matthew; Matthew and Paul, especially on law and grace; Matthew's *ekklēsia* and discipleship.[1] These themes and issues enriched Matthean studies from the 1960s to the present. Some of the vital issues that remain unresolved in Matthean studies, however, include: the question of whether Matthew respected the context of the OT texts he cited;[2] Matthew's relationship to the historical Jesus (that is, is Matthew an eye witness of the events in the

---

1. For trajectory of directions in Matthean studies, see chapter 1 n10 and n11. See also Donald Senior, "Directions in Matthean Studies," in *The Gospel of Matthew in Current Study,* ed. David E. Aune (Grand Rapids: Eerdmans, 2001), 5–21; idem, *What are they saying about Matthew?*
2. See S. V. McCasland, "Matthew Twists the Scriptures," in *The Right Doctrines from the Wrong Texts?* 146–152; Kaiser Jr., *The Uses of the Old Testament in the New.*

life of Jesus or merely a detached redactor?);³ the community of Matthew (namely, did Matthew write his gospel for all Christians or for a particular community?);⁴ Matthew and Paul;⁵ and whether Matthew is working with a replacement or fulfillment scheme in his mission to Israel and the nations. This touches on the issue of one covenant or many covenants and the theology of Christian-Jewish relations.⁶

From the major themes and issues above, the writer focused on Matthew's use of the OT from a missional standpoint. He treated the critical issue of mission to Israel and the nations under the framework of promise-fulfillment, which inevitably touched on other relevant issues in Matthean studies. Following this missional approach, the seemingly irreconcilable themes in the Gospel of Matthew are interwoven in the grand mission of God. This is believed to be the distinctive contribution to the subject of mission in the Gospel of Matthew. It is hoped that this approach provides a viable direction for Matthean studies, namely, a missional reading of the Gospel of Matthew. As we suggested in chapter 1, all the themes in Matthew are to be treated in the light of the primary focus of mission because Christ comes as a fulfillment of God's mission on earth.⁷ Throughout the study, the writer attempted to connect some of the divergent themes of the Gospel of Matthew into theological and missional perspectives. The

---

3. For this continuing debate, see Richard Bauckham, *Jesus and the Eyewitnesses: The Gospels as Eyewitness Testimony* (Grand Rapids: Eerdmans, 2006).

4. This ongoing discussion is illustrated by Richard Bauckham's, (ed.), *The Gospel for All Nations: Rethinking the Audiences* (Grand Rapids: Eerdmans, 1998); Anthony J. Saldarini, *Matthew's Christian-Jewish Community* (Chicago: The University of Chicago Press, 1994); David C. Sim, *The Gospel of Matthew and Christian Judaism: The History and Social Setting of the Matthean Community* (Edinburgh: T & T Clark, 1998).

5. See David C. Sim, "Matthew, Paul and the origin and nature of the gentile mission: The great commission in Matthew 28:16–20 as an anti-Pauline tradition," *HTS* 64.1 (2008): 377–392.

6. See Gavin D'Costa, "One Covenant or Many Covenants? Toward a Theology of Christian-Jewish Relations," *Readings in Modern Theology*, ed. Robin Gill (London: SPCK, 1995), 173–185; Holwerda, *Jesus and Israel*; Turner, *Matthew*, 518; France, *The Gospel of Matthew*, 808, 816–817.

7. For although the Gospel of Matthew deals with seemingly divergent themes, a growing consensus among Matthean scholars is that "no single facet of Matthew's theology stands on its own" (Senior, *What are they saying about Matthew?*, 62). The writer made a similar assumption at the beginning of this intriguing study concerning the connectedness of the divergent themes of the Gospel of Matthew and how these various themes converge upon the mission of God.

writer believes that these various themes converge upon Matthew's single story of the mission of God to save both Israel and the nations. Having demonstrated this in the course of the study he now presents a synthesis of results as well as concluding thoughts for consideration.

First, Matthew offers a mission theology that is remarkably influenced by Israel's "faith traditions" which he considered precursive to the coming of the Messiah. But as observed from a reading of the original texts in their contexts, Matthew seems to have transformed some of these "faith traditions" by way of reinterpretation and recontextualization; a transformation that underscores his theological and missional purposes. But the most important point for consideration in relation to Matthew's use of Israel's "faith traditions" is that reading his mission theology as a concept that is rooted in OT foundations and framework undermines the notion that Matthew 28:19–20 is an afterthought in God's salvific scheme for Matthew. For if the inclusion of the gentiles as the subjects of the kingdom of God also fulfills God's promises in the OT, the Great Commission is an expansion of the kingdom of God foreseen by God himself.

Second, most scholars who engage in the discussion on Jews and gentiles in the Gospel of Matthew usually ignore the theme of promise-fulfillment and capitalize on the existing tension between Matthew 10:5, 6 and 28:19–20. This approach ignores Matthew's overriding purpose and the harmony that the theme of promise-fulfillment brings into the narrative. It is therefore argued that the theme of promise-fulfillment puts Jewish and gentile mission into proper perspective by the way Matthew demonstrated that gentile mission is also in the salvific scheme of God.

Third, based on the theme of promise-fulfillment, the Gospel of Matthew is a synthesis of the different OT expectations concerning the Messiah. Jesus is the Son of David who, as corporate Israel represents, leads and restores Israel. He is also the Son of God like Israel and could therefore fulfill Hosea 11:1. As Son of God, not only is God pleased with him, but the disciples (and the world) are to listen to him. Jesus is also Son of Man who heals and forgives sins. Furthermore, he is the expected prophet and teacher of the law. Not only that, he is the Messiah who saves his people from their sins and is equally light to the nations. From this salvific standpoint, Matthew presents a missional Christology in which Jesus' titles are connected to his functions.

Fourth, John the Baptist and Jesus began their ministry by calling people to repent in view of the coming kingdom of heaven that Jesus inaugurated (Matt 3:1–2; 4:17). The gospel of the kingdom is preached in the whole world before the end comes (Matt 24:14). Therefore, the goal of mission is the expansion of the kingdom of God through proclamation and disciple making. As such, disciple making in Matthew 28:19–20 is the *method* by which the primary goal is realized. This is the responsibility of the disciples. It is through the method of proclamation and discipleship that both Israel and the nations are brought together into the kingdom of God through faith in the risen Lord. By discipling the nations, the Abrahamic blessings intended for the nations (Gen 12:3) are fulfilled. In other words, the mission of God is the establishment of his kingdom through disciple making. The emphasis on the kingdom of God does not relegate the method Jesus employs for reaching the goal. Therefore, the so-called missionary texts of the Gospel of Matthew need to be read from this perspective, namely, that Jesus came as a fulfillment of OT promises to establish the kingdom of God through disciple making.

Fifth, although the command of Matthew 28:19–20 comes after the resurrection, this command does not mean that Jesus retracted and reversed his earlier command in 10:5, 6.[8] The position this writer advances is that mission to the nations is anticipated and demonstrated before the resurrection of Jesus, and this anticipation and demonstration is not only illustrated by passages like the magi and the centurion episodes but also by explicit fulfillment quotations substantiating gentile inclusion into the kingdom of God that Matthew interweaves throughout his narrative. Therefore Matthew harmonizes the exegetical and theological crux of the perplexing relationship between mission to Israel and mission to the nations by his use of promise-fulfillment framework such that both Jewish and gentile mission are prior to the Easter experience.

---

8. For the view that Jesus retracted and reversed his earlier command, see Luz, *The Theology of the Gospel of Matthew*, 143.

Sixth, Matthew presents the mission of the Triune God as fulfillment of promise made in the OT concerning the Davidic kingdom and Jesus as the embodiment of this promise. Jesus who comes as the Davidic king also inaugurates the new exodus and fulfills the Torah and represents the presence of God as one greater than the temple. His coming therefore brought restoration to the people of Israel. He ushered in the kingdom of heaven as fulfillment of the Davidic kingdom that would last forever. However, the ministry of Jesus not only fulfills the time of God's visitation of his people Israel but also the salvation of the nations—for while Jesus came to gather the lost sheep of Israel (Matt 15:24; Luke 4:43), he also commissioned his disciples to make disciples of all nations (28:16–20). In Jesus, therefore, the rest of the world is restored along with Israel. For this reason, Matthew presents a double dimension of mission in keeping with prophecy: the restoration of Israel and the nations. As the king returns to Zion he draws the nations (Zech 2:7–13; 9:9–10), yet in a centrifugal sense (Matt 28:19–20). Therefore, the seemingly opposing mission to Israel and mission to the nations is resolved by the concept of continuity and discontinuity embedded in the Gospel of Matthew which he describes under the rubric "new treasure as well as old" (Matt 13:52).

Seventh, the earthly manifestation of the coming kingdom is characterized by works of miracles and healings and the proclamation of the good news. The healing ministry demonstrates that Jesus is the powerful Son of Man who also has authority to forgive sins (Matt 9:1–8). Matthew presents repentance and child-like faith (18:1–5) as the prerequisites for entry into the kingdom and not merely through the ticket of Jewish ancestry. Receiving the benefits of the kingdom is also obtained by faith. Some of the healing accounts of Jesus stress the importance of this faith (8:10–13; 17:14–20; cf. Mark 9:23; 9:19–22; cf. Mark 5:23–34; Luke 842–48; 20:29–34; cf. Mark 10:46–52; Luke 18:35–43). In Matthew, the idea of *people* and *nation* are therefore radically transformed to mean that whoever has faith in Jesus is included in the people of God. This faith that Jesus demands is both trust in God's gracious rule and trust in Jesus as mediator of God's rule. It is those who have eyes to see and ears to hear that believe in the message of Jesus regarding the kingdom of heaven (13:16).

5.2 Recommendations

The following recommendations and suggestions are offered for further study. First, most NT scholars who move beyond the level of anthropocentric and ecclesiocentric views of mission in the Gospel of Matthew dwell on the messianic mission of Jesus. But such approach seems to fall short of the foundation of mission from Matthew's perspective. For Matthew, mission is rooted in the work of the Triune God. Therefore, the writer contends that a better way for understanding mission in Matthew is a Trinitarian model. This model deserves more attention in scholarly circles.

Second, Matthew presents the OT as a book of promise whose fulfillment is in Christ. We have argued that for Matthew the entire OT is divinely orchestrated toward the life and ministry of the Messiah. Matthew shows that without the coming of the long awaited Messiah the OT would lose its purpose and significance. In Jesus Christ the OT finds confirmation and consummation. Therefore, while the study of the OT in its own right has yielded significant results such as renewed appreciation of the OT milieu and context, the growing pursuit of OT discipline almost as an end in itself is challenged in the Gospel of Matthew, the most Jewish of the gospels. For this reason, Christian scholars may need to develop more objective ways of understanding Matthew's demand for reading the OT in light of the NT.

The writer also offers the following recommendations for the church. First, we observed from the conclusions Matthew's strong emphasis on disciple making as the method for the expansion of the kingdom of God. Therefore, disciple making in the Gospel of Matthew is deemed an area of priority for both the global and the African church in the twenty-first century. Although the African church is recognized the world over for its numerical growth, and this numeric strength is used in support of the concept of the center-of-gravity shift, disciple making has remained inadequate. But without disciple making, the church in Africa stands at a crossroads because of global anti-Christian culture and values. The church in Africa needs to explore a better method of disciple making in which the concept of the Lordship of Christ is clearly explained to all who profess faith in Jesus Christ. The kind of disciple making we recommend here is the community disciple-making model just as Matthew addressed a diaspora Christian community. Matthew's diaspora Christian community proclaims the gospel to the unbelieving Jewish community and the entire world. Similarly, it is this diaspora Christian community that acts as salt and light (Matt 5:13–16) and as catalyst of change. Therefore, this communal and relational aspect of disciple making and accountability will help in the spiritual nurture that is desired for African churches because the spiritual growth of the individual becomes the responsibility of the entire community of believers. While church leaders "prepare God's people for works of service" (Eph 4:11–12), the entire community of believers engages in building the body of Christ with the more mature believers on the lead in mentoring younger ones. This model does not replace, but complements, the conventional method in which a single mentor disciples one person or a group of people at a time.

Third, the Gospel of Matthew speaks against racial, religious, social, political, and ethnic divides, especially in the final commission to disciple all the nations. This underlines the need for the church to reach out to the entire world—to Jews and non-Jews—across racial, religious, social, and political barriers. The church exists to "mirror" Jesus' "compassion for the outcasts and disenfranchised of our world."[9] Similarly, the Great Commission speaks about church unity. Both the priestly prayer of Jesus for the church in John 17:20–23, and the one Spirit and one baptism that Paul underscores in Ephesians 4:4–6 point to the direction of Christian unity. This unity is connected to the baptismal formula in Matthew 28:19–20 in which all believers are baptized in the name of the same Triune God. However, the African church suffers from an unhealthy ethnic divide such that its power is weakened and its influence has become disproportionate to its numerical growth. Yet the kingdom of God has the potential to advance more forcefully in Africa if the church were united in facing the task of evangelism and discipleship (Matt 28:19–20). African church leaders must therefore figure out ways of focusing on fundamental elements of the

---

9. Craig L. Blomberg, *Jesus and the Gospels: An Introduction and Survey* (Leicester: Apollos, 1997), 412.

Christian faith that unite rather than emphasizing minor doctrinal issues, liturgical differences, and divisive ethnicity.[10]

Fourth, mission in Matthew is carried out in the context of great hostility, rejection and threats to life. But one of the key messages Jesus gave in the Sermon on the Mount for his would-be disciples is love for the enemy and the persecutor (Matt 5:43–48). It is the obligation of the twenty-first-century church in Africa to figure out how to reach out to groups and nations that are antagonistic toward the Christian faith without letting hatred replace love for the perceived enemy. Loving the enemy and carrying out Jesus' mandate to disciple the nations is therefore probably the most important external challenges facing the church in Africa. But the church in Africa needs to work from the premise that the problems of rejection, persecution and antagonism against the Christian faith can hardly be solved with the same level of thinking that created these problems. The church must embrace Jesus' method of dealing with the enemy in the first place. Although he sends out his disciples into the world "like sheep among wolves," he tells them to "be as shrewd as snakes and as innocent as doves" (Matt 10:16). This level of thinking and behavior is what the church in Africa needs to embrace in the face of rejection and persecution in order to fulfill her mission as peacemaker (Matt 5:9) and the salt and the light of the world (Matt 5:13–16).

Fifth, the proclamation of the kingdom of God in the Gospel of Matthew remains the message of the church. And just as the church's prayer is "thy kingdom come," the church's message is the kingdom of God. Jesus as the way to the kingdom has to be stressed in the twenty-first century. This proclamation comes as a unique voice in a pluralistic and relativistic world. Similarly, the church has to emphasize the claims of Jesus for authority in heaven and on earth in the contemporary society. But the twenty-first-century church in Africa must figure out how this message will address to the African Traditional Religion, the Muslim, the atheist, the pluralist, and

---

10. See Yusufu Turaki, *Tribal Gods of Africa: Ethnicity, Racism, Tribalism and the Gospel of Christ* (Nairobi: Ethics, Peace and Justice Commission of the Association of Evangelicals, 1997); Barje S. Maigadi, *Divisive Ethnicity in the Church in Africa* (Kaduna: Baraka Press, 2006); Elie A. Buconyori (ed.), *Tribalism and Ethnicity* (Nairobi: The AEA Theological and Christian Education Commission, 1977).

the relativist as the church in Africa proclaims the gospel of Christ within and beyond its borders. This calls for contextualization without diluting the essential content of the gospel message.

Sixth, for effectively reaching out to the world, the message of the kingdom in its ethical dimension of salt and light in a corrupt world of violence, injustice, terrorism, and gender discrimination needs to be demonstrated in the life of the proclaimers and disciplers. Therefore, African church leaders and followers need to match their faith and practice and be vanguards of good virtues and morality in order to "make the teaching about our God and Savior attractive" (Tit 2:10) and to "Let your light shine before men, that they may see your good deeds and praise your Father in heaven" (Matt 5:16). It is in this manner that the church functions as God's agent of transformation in the African society and the entire world until the kingdom of God comes. For the mission of God in the Gospel of Matthew is "your kingdom come, your will be done on earth as it is in heaven" (Matt 6:10).

Bibliography

Accad, Martin and John Corrie. "Trinity." In *Dictionary of Mission Theology: Evangelical Foundations,* edited by John Corrie, et al. Nottingham: IVP, 2007, 396–401.

Achtemeier, Paul J., Joel B. Green, and Marianne Meye Thompson. *Introducing the New Testament: Its Literature and Theology.* Grand Rapids: Eerdmans, 2001.

Aland, Barbara, Kurt Aland, Johannes Karavidopoulos, Carlo M. Martin, and Bruce M. Metzger, eds. *The Greek New Testament.* 4th rev. ed. D-Stuttgart: Deutsche Bibelgesellschaft, 1998.

Allison Jr., Dale C. *The New Moses: A Matthean Typology.* Minneapolis: Fortress, 1993.

Alsup, John E. "Typology." In *ABD.* Vol. 6. Edited by David Noel Freedman, et al. New York: Doubleday, 1992, 682–685.

Archer, Gleason L. and Gregory Chirichigno. *Old Testament Quotations in the New Testament.* Chicago: Moody Press, 1983.

Aune, D. E., T. J. Geddert, and C. A. Evans. "Apocalypticism." In *Dictionary of New Testament Background,* edited by Craig Evans and Stanley Porter. Downers Grove: IVP, 2000, 45–58.

Aune, D. *Prophecy in Early Christianity and Ancient Mediterranean World.* Grand Rapids: Eerdmans, 1983.

Bailey, Mark L. "The Parable of the Sower and the Soils." *BSac* 155 (April–June 1998), 172–188.

Baker, D. L. *Two Testament, One Bible: The Theological Relationship Between the Old and the New Testaments.* 3rd edition. Downers Grove: IVP, 2010.

———. *Two Testaments, One Bible: A study of some modern solutions to the theological problem of the relationship between the Old and the New Testaments.* Downers Grove: IVP, 1976.

———. "Typology and the Christian Use of the Old Testament. In *The Right Doctrine from the Wrong Texts? Essays on the Use of the Old Testament in the*

New, edited by G. K. Beale. Grand Rapids: Baker Academic, 1994, 313–330.

Barclay, William. *The Gospel of Matthew.* Philadelphia: Westminster, 1975.

Barker, Kenneth L. and John R. Kohlenberger III. *The Expositor's Bible Commentary.* Abridged edition. Grand Rapids: Zondervan, 1994.

Bartholomew, Craig G. and Michael W. Goheen. *The Drama of Scripture: Finding our Place in the Biblical Story.* Grand Rapids: Baker Academic, 2004.

Bauckham, Richard, ed. *God Will be All in All: The Eschatology of Jürgen Moltmann.* Edinburgh: T & T Clark, 1999.

———. *Bible and Mission: Christian Witness in a Postmodern World.* Grand Rapids: Baker Academic, 2003.

———. *Jesus and the Eyewitnesses: The Gospels as Eyewitness Testimony.* Grand Rapids: Eerdmans, 2006.

———, ed. *The Gospel for All Nations: Rethinking the Audiences.* Grand Rapids: Eerdmans, 1998.

Bauer, David. R. "Son of David." In *Dictionary of Jesus and the Gospels,* edited by J. Green, S. McKnight and I. H. Marshall. Downers Grove: IVP, 1992, 766–775.

———. "The Major Characters of Matthew's Story: Their Functions and Significance." *ATLAS* (n.d.), 357–363.

———. *The Structure of Matthew's Gospel: A Study in Literary Design.* Sheffield: Sheffield Academic Press, 1996.

Baxter, Wayne. "Healing and the 'Son of David': Matthew's Warrant." *NovT* 48, no. 1 (2006): 36–50.

Beale, G. K. "Did Jesus and his Followers Preach the Right Doctrine from the Wrong Texts? An Examination of the Presuppositions of the Apostles' Exegetical Method." *Themelios* 14 (April 1989), 89–96.

———. *The Temple and the Church's Mission: A Biblical Theology of the Dwelling Place of God.* Edited by D. A. Carson. NSBT 17. Leicester: IVP, 2004.

———, ed. *The Right Doctrine from the Wrong Texts? Essays on the Use of the Old Testament in the New.* Grand Rapids: Baker Academic, 1994.

———. "Eden, Temple, and the Church's Mission in the New Creation." *JETS* 48, no. 1 (March 2005), 5–31.

Beale, G. K. and D. A. Carson, eds. *Commentary on the New Testament Use of the Old Testament.* Grand Rapids: Baker Academic, 2007.

Beaton, Richard. "Isaiah in Matthew's Gospel." In *Isaiah and the New Testament,* edited by Steve Moyise and Maarten J. J. Menken. London: T & T Clark International, 2005, 63–78.

———. "Messiah and Justice: A Key to Matthew's use of Isaiah 42:1–4." *JNST* 75 (1999): 5–23.

Bird, Michael F. *Crossing Over Sea and Land: Jewish Missionary Activity in the Second Temple Period*. Peabody: Hendrickson Publishers, 2010.

Blenkinsopp, Joseph. *Prophecy and Canon: A Contribution to the Study of Jewish Origins*. Notre Dame: University of Notre Dame Press, 1977.

———. *A History of Prophecy in Israel: From the Settlement in the Land to the Hellenistic Period*. Philadelphia: Westminster, 1983.

Blomberg, Craig. L. "The Unity and Diversity of Scripture." In *New Dictionary of Biblical Theology*, edited by T. Desmond Alexander and Brian S. Rosner. Downers Grove: IVP, 2000, 64–72.

———. "Matthew." In *Commentary on the New Testament Use of the Old Testament*, edited by G. K. Beale and D. A. Carson. Grand Rapids: Baker Academic, 2007, 1–109.

———. *Matthew*, The New American Commentary Series. Nashville: Broadman Press, 1992.

———. *Jesus and the Gospels: An Introduction and Survey*. Leicester: Apollos, 1997.

Bock, Darrell L. "Evangelicals and the Use of the Old Testament." *BSac 142* (July–September, 1985), 209–223.

———. "Single Meaning, Multiple Contexts and Referents." In *Three Views on the New Testament use of the Old Testament*. Grand Rapids: Zondervan, 2008, 105–151.

———. "Scripture Citing Scripture: Use of the Old Testament in the New." In *Interpreting the New Testament Text: Introduction to the Art and Science of Exegesis*, edited by Darrel L. Bock and Buist M. Fanning. Wheaton: Crossway Books, 2006, 255–276.

Bock, Darrell L. and Buist M. Fanning, eds. *Interpreting the New Testament Text: Introduction to the Art and Science of Exegesis*. Wheaton: Crossway Books, 2006.

Bohlen, Maren. "Die Einlasssprüche in der Reich-Gottes-Verkündigung Jesu. " *ZNW* 99 (2008), 167–184.

Bosch, David. *Transforming Mission: Paradigm Shift in Theology of Mission*. Maryknoll: Orbis Books, 1991.

Bravo, Arturo. "Jonah and Jesus." *TD* 51.2 (Summer 2004), 129–132.

Broer, I. "Versuch zur Christologie des ersten Evangeliums." In *The Four Gospels 1992: FS F. Neirynck*. Edited by F. Van Seybroeck *et al*. Leuven: University Press, 1992, 125–182.

Brown, Raymond. *The Birth of the Messiah.* Garden City: Doubleday, 1977.

———. *The Sensus Plenior of Sacred Scripture.* Baltimore: St Mary's University Press, 1955.

Brown, Schuyler. "The Matthean Community and the Gentile Mission." *NovT* XXII, no. 3 (July 1980), 192–221.

Buchanan, George Wesley. *Typology and the Gospel.* New York: University Press of America, 1987.

Buconyori, Elie A., ed. *Tribalism and Ethnicity.* Nairobi: The AEA Theological and Christian Education Commission, 1977.

Bultmann, Rudolf. *Theology of the New Testament.* 2 vols. New York: Scribners', 1951, 1955.

Buono, Giuseppe. *Missiology: Theology and Praxis.* Nairobi: Paulines Publications Africa, 2002.

Burer, Michael H. "Narrative Genre: Studying the Story." In *Interpreting the New Testament Text: Introduction to the Art and Science of Exegesis*, edited by Darrel L. Bock and Buist M. Fanning. Wheaton: Crossway Books, 2006, 197–219.

Burger, C. *Jesus als Davidssohn.* Göttingen: Vandenhoeck & Ruprecht, 1970.

Burton, De Witt. *Syntax of the Moods and Tenses in New Testament Greek.* Grand Rapids: Kregel Publications, 1976.

Carson, D. A. *God with Us: Themes from Matthew.* Ventura: Regal Books, 1985.

———. "Matthew." In *The Expositor's Bible Commentary.* Abridged edition. Edited by Kenneth L. Barker and John R. Kohlenberger. Grand Rapids: Zondervan, 1994, 1–135.

———. *When Jesus Confronts the World: An Exposition of Matthew 8–10.* Grand Rapids: Baker Book House, 1987.

Carson, D. A. and Douglas J. Moo. *An Introduction to the New Testament.* 2nd ed. Leicester: Apollos, 2005.

Carter, Warren. "Matthew and the Gentiles: Individual Conversion and/or Systematic Transformation?" *JSNT* 26, no. 3 (2004), 259–282.

———. *Matthew and Empire: Initial Explorations.* Harrisburg: Trinity Press International, 2001.

———. "Evoking Isaiah: Matthean Soteriology and an Intertextual Reading of Isaiah 7–9 and Matthew 1:23 and 4:15–16." *JBL* 119, no. 3 (Autumn, 2000), 503–520.

Charette, Blaine. "A Harvest for the People? An Interpretation of Matthew 9:37f." *JSNT* 38 (1990), 29–35.

———. *Restoring Presence: The Spirit in Matthew's Gospel.* JPTSup 18. Sheffield: Sheffield Academic Press, 2000.

Childs, Brevard S. *The Struggle to Understand Isaiah as Christian Scripture.* Grand Rapids/Cambridge: Eerdmans, 2004.

———. *The Book of Exodus.* Philadelphia: Westminster, 1974.

Chilton, B., P. W. Comfort and M. O. "Temple, Jewish." In *Dictionary of New Testament Background,* edited Craig A. Evans and Stanley E. Porter. Downers Grove: IVP, 1992, 1167–1183.

Chilton, Bruce D. *A Galilean Rabbi And His Bible: Jesus' Use of the Interpreted Scripture of His Time.* Wilmington: Michaels Glazier, 1984.

———, ed. *The Kingdom of God in the Teaching of Jesus.* Philadelphia: Fortress Press, 1984.

———. *Pure Kingdom: Jesus' Vision of God.* Grand Rapids: Eerdmans, 1996.

Chisholm Jr., Robert B. "The Christological Fulfillment of Isaiah's Servant Songs." *BSac* 163 (October–December 2006), 387–404.

Christensen, N. Nepper. Das Matthäusevangelium: ein juden-christliches Evangelium? Aarhus: Universitetsforlaget, 1958.

Clark, K. W. "The Gentile Bias in Matthew." *JBL* 66 (1947), 165–172.

Clowney, Edmund P. *The Unfolding Mystery: Discovering Christ in the Old Testament.* Leicester: IVP, 1988.

Combrink, Bernard. "Teaching and Living the Good News: Mission According to Matthew." In *Missionary Perspectives in the New Testament: Pictures from Chosen New Testament Literature,* edited by Johann du Plessis, Eddie Orsmond, and Hennie van Deventer. Wellington: Bible Media, 2009, 81–92.

Connor, John S. "Toward a Trinitarian Theology of Mission." *Missiology: An International Review* 9, no. 2 (April 1981), 155–169.

Conrad, Edgar W. "The Annunciation of Birth and the Birth of the Messiah." *CBQ* 47 (1985), 656–663.

Cullmann, Oscar. *Salvation in History.* London: SCM Press, 1967.

Cunningham, Scott S. "Ephesians 2:19–22: The Temple Motif." In *Interpreting the New Testament Text: Introduction to the Art and Science of Exegesis,* edited by Darrell L. Bock and Buist M. Fanning. Wheaton: Crossway Books, 2006, 387–400.

Cuvillier, Elian. "Torah Observance and Radicalization in the First Gospel; Matthew and the First-Century Judaism: A Contribution to the Debate." *NTS* (2009), 144–159.

Danker, Frederick W. "God With Us: Hellenistic Christological Perspectives in Matthew." *ATLAS* (n.d.), 433–439.

D'Costa, Gavin. "One Covenant or Many Covenants? Toward a Theology of Christian-Jewish Relations." In *Readings in Modern Theology*, edited by Robin Gill. London: SPCK, 1995, 173–185.

Daugherty, Kevin. "*Missio Dei*: The Trinity and Christian Mission." *ERT* 31, no. 2 (2007), 151–168.

Davies, G. I. "Wilderness Wanderings." In *ABD*. Vol. 6. Edited by David Joel B. Freedman. New York: Doubleday, 1992, 912–914.

Davies, W. D. and Dale C. Allison, Jr. *A Critical and Exegetical Commentary on the Gospel According to Saint Matthew*. 3 vols. The International Critical Commentary. New York: T & T Clark, 2000, 2001.

———. *Matthew: A Shorter Commentary*, edited by Dale C. Allison, Jr. New York: T & T Clark International, 2004.

Davis, D. Mark. "Matthew 2:1–12." *Int* (October 2003), 420–422.

Day, Dan. "A Fresh Reading of Jesus' Last Words: Matthew 28:16–20." *RevExp* 104 (Spring 2007), 375–384.

De Ridder, Richard R. *Discipling the Nations*. Grand Rapids: Baker Book House, 1971.

Dearborn, Tim. "Beyond Duty." In *Perspectives on the World Christian Movement*, edited by Ralph D. Winter and Steven C. Hawthorne. Pasadena: William Carey Library, 1999, 44–47.

Dempster, Stephen G. *Dominion and Dynasty: A Theology of the Hebrew Bible*, edited by D. A. Carson. NSBT 15. Downers Grove: IVP, 2003.

Derrett, J. Duncan M. "Further Light on the Narratives of the Nativity." *NovT* 17, no. 2 (n.d.), 81–108.

deSilva, David A. *An Introduction to the New Testament: Contexts, Methods & Ministry Formation*. Leicester: Apollos, 2004.

Deutsch, Celia M. *Lady Wisdom, Jesus, and the Sages: Metaphor and Social Context in Matthew's Gospel*. Valley Forge: Trinity Press International, 1996.

Dillard, Raymond B. *2 Chronicles*, Word Biblical Commentary. Edited by John D. W. Watts. Nashville: Nelson Reference and Electronic, 1987.

Dodd, C. H. *According to the Scriptures: The Sub-Structure of New Testament Theology*. London: Nisbet, 1952.

———. *Apostolic Preaching and Its Developments*. New York: Harper and Brothers Publishers, 1962.

Donaldson, Terence L. *Jesus on the Mountain: A Study in Matthean Theology*. JSNTSS 8. Sheffield: JSOT Press, 1985.

Dunne, Tad. "Trinity and History." *TS* 45 (1984), 139–152.
Dunn, James D. G. *Christianity in the Making*. Vol. 1. *Jesus Remembered*. Grand Rapids/Cambridge: Eerdmans, 2003.

———. *Jesus and the Spirit: A Study of the Religious and Charismatic Experiences of Jesus and the First Christians as Reflected in the New Testament*. Grand Rapids: Eerdmans, 1973.

Dupont, Dom Jacques. "Vous n'aurez pas achevé les villes d'Israël avant que le fils de l'homme ne vienne" (Matt 10:23)." *NovT* 2, no. 3/4 (October, 1958), 228–244.

Edersheim, Alfred. *Prophecy and History in Relation to the Messiah*. Grand Rapids: Baker Book House, 1955.

———. *The Life and Times of Jesus the Messiah*. Peabody: Hendrickson, 1993.

Eichrodt, Walter. *Theology of the Old Testament*. Vol. 1. Translated by J. A. Baker. London: SCM Press, 1961.

Elliger, K. and W. Rudolph, eds. *Biblia Hebraica Stuttgartensia*. Stuttgart: Deutsche Bibelgesellschaft, 1977.

Ellis, E. Earle. *The Making of the New Testament Documents*. Boston/Leiden: Brill Academic Publishers, 2002.

———. *The Old Testament in Early Christianity: Canon and Interpretation in the Light of Modern Research*. Eugene: Wipf and Stock Publishers, 2003.

Eloff, Mervyn. "From the Exile to the Christ: Exile, Restoration and the Interpretation of Matthew's Gospel." ThD diss., University of Stellenbosch, December 2002.

Elwell, Walter A. and Robert W. Yarbrough. *Encountering the New Testament: A Historical and Theological Survey*. 2nd ed. Grand Rapids: Baker Academic, 2005.

Enns, Peter. "Fuller Meaning, Single Goal: A Christotelic Approach to the New Testament Use of the Old in Its First-Century Interpretive Environment." In *Three View on the New Testament use of the Old Testament*. Grand Rapids: Zondervan, 2008, 167–217.

Evans, Craig A. "New Testament Use of the Old Testament." In *New Dictionary of Biblical Theology*, edited by T. Desmond Alexander and Brian S. Rosner. Downers Grove: IVP, 2000, 72–80.

———."From Language to Exegesis." In *The Interpretation of Scripture in Early Judaism and Christianity: Studies in Language and Tradition*. Edited by Craig A. Evans. London: T & T Clark International, 2004, 19–23.

———. "Jesus and Justice: We Can't Have One without the Other." *Sapientia Logos* 1, no. 2 (2009): 194–221.

———. "Jesus and the Continuing Exile of Israel." In *Jesus and the Restoration of Israel: A Critical Assessment of N. T. Wright's Jesus and the Victory of God,* edited by Carey C. Newman. Carlisle: Paternoster, 1999, 77–100.

———. "Jesus' Action in the Temple: Cleansing or Portent of Destruction?" *CBQ* 51, 1989, 237–270.

———. "From 'House of Prayer' to 'Cave of Robbers': Jesus' Prophetic Criticism of the Temple Establishment." In *The Quest for Context and Meaning: Studies in Biblical Intertextuality in Honor of James A. Sanders,* edited by C. A. Evans and S. Salmon. Biblical Interpretation Series 28. Leiden: Brill, 1997, 417–442.

Faierstein, Morris M. "Why Do the Scribes Say that Elijah Must Come First?" *JBL* 100, no. 1, 1981, 75–86.

Fanning, Buist. "Theological Analysis: Building Biblical Theology." In *Interpreting the New Testament Text: Introduction to the Art and Science of Exegesis,* edited by Darrell L. Bock and Buist M. Fanning. Wheaton: Crossway Books, 2006, 277–291.

Fee, Gordon D. and Douglas Stuart. *How to Read the Bible for All Its Worth.* 2nd edition. Grand Rapids: Zondervan, 1993.

Fernando, Ajith. "Grounding Our Reflections in Scripture: Biblical Trinitarianism." In *Global Missiology for the 21st Century: The Iguassu Dialogue,* edited by William D. Taylor. Grand Rapids: Baker Academic, 2000, 189–238.

Finkelstein, Israel and Neil Asher Silber. "Temple and Dynasty: Hezekiah, the Remaking of Judah and the Rise of Pan-Israelite Ideology." *JSOT* 30, no. 3 (March 2006), 259–285.

Fishbane, Michael. *Biblical Interpretation in Ancient Israel.* Oxford: Clarendon Press, 1985.

Foulkes, Francis. "The Acts of God: A Study of the Basis of Theology in Old Testament." In *The Right Doctrine from the Wrong Texts? Essays on the Use of the Old Testament in the New,* edited by G. K. Beale. Grand Rapids: Baker Academic, 1994, 342–371.

France, R. T. *Jesus and the Old Testament: His Application of Old Testament Passages to Himself and His Mission.* London: The Tyndale Press, 1971.

———. *Matthew: Evangelist and Teacher.* Grand Rapids: Zondervan, 1989.

———. *The Gospel According to Matthew: An Introduction and Commentary.* Tyndale New Testament Commentaries. Edited by Leon Morris. Leicester: IVP, 1985.

———. *The Gospel of Matthew*. In *The New International Commentary on the New Testament*. Grand Rapids: Eerdmans, 2007.

———. "The Formula-Quotations of Matthew 2 and the Problem of Communication." In *The Right Doctrine from the Wrong Texts? Essays on the Use of the Old Testament in the New*, edited by G. K. Beale. Grand Rapids: Baker Academic, 1994, 114–134.

Frankemölle, H. *Jahweh-Bund und Kirche: Studien zur Form- und Traditionsgeschicte des "Evangeliums" nach Matthäus*. Münster: Aschendorff, 1984.

Freed, Edwin D. "The Women in Matthew's Genealogy." *JSNT* 29 (1987), 4–19.

Freyne, Sean. "Galilee and Judea: The Social World of Jesus." In *The Face of New Testament Studies: A Survey of Recent Research*. Edited by Scot McKnight and Grant R. Osborne. Grand Rapids: Baker Academic, 2004, 21–35.

Garland, David E. *Reading Matthew: A Literary and Theological Commentary*. Macon: Smyth & Helwys Publishing, 2001.

Gaston, L. "The Messiah of Israel As Teacher of the Gentiles: The Setting of Matthew's Christology." *Int* 29 (1975), 24–40.

Gelardini, Gabriella. "Religion and Ethnicity: Toying with Two Related Concepts in 19th and 20th Century German Jesus Scholarship: A Socio-historical Analysis." *Sapientia Logos* 1, no. 2 (2009), 162–193.

Gerhardson, B. "Gottes Sohn als Diener Gottes: Messias, Agape und Himmelsherrschaft nach dem Matthäusevangelium." *ST* 27 (1973), 73–106.

Gibbs, Jeffrey A. "Israel Standing with Israel: The Baptism of Jesus in Matthew's Gospel (Matt 3:13–17)." *CBQ* 64 (2002), 511–526.

Goldsmith, Martin. *Matthew and Mission: The Gospel Through Jewish Eyes*. Carlisle: Paternoster Press, 2001.

Goppelt, Leonhard. *Typos: The Typological Interpretation of the Old Testament in the New*. Translated by Donald H. Madvig. Grand Rapids: Eerdmans, 1982.

Grams, Rollin G. "Narrative Dynamics in Isaiah's and Matthew's Mission Theology." In *Transformation* 2, no. 4 (October 2004), 238–255.

———. "Some Geographical and Intertextual Dimensions of Matthew's Mission Theology." In *Bible and Mission: A Conversation Between Biblical Studies and Missiology*, edited by Rollin G. Grams et al. Schwarzenfeld: Neufeld Verlag, 2008, 42–73.

Guder, Darrell L., ed. *Missional Church: A Vision for the Sending of the Church in North America*. Grand Rapids: Eerdmans, 1998.

Gundry, Robert H. "Salvation in Matthew." *SBLSP* 39. Atlanta: SBL, 2000.

———. *Matthew: A Commentary on His Literary and Theological Art.* Grand Rapids: Eerdmans, 1982.

———. *The Use of the Old Testament in St. Matthew's Gospel: With Special Reference to the Messianic Hope.* Leiden: Brill, 1967.

Gundry, Stanley N., Kenneth Berding, and Jonathan Lunde, eds. *Three Views on the New Testament use of the Old Testament.* Grand Rapids: Zondervan, 2008.

Guthrie, Donald. *New Testament Introduction.* Leicester: Apollos, 1990.

Hagner, Donald A. *Matthew 1–13.* Word Biblical Commentary. Edited by Ralph P. Martin. Nashville: Thomas Nelson, 1993.

———. *Matthew 14–28.* Word Biblical Commentary. Edited by Ralph P. Martin. Nashville: Thomas Nelson, 1995.

Hahn, Ferdinand. *Mission in the New Testament,* Studies in Biblical Theology 47. Naperville: Alec R. Allenson, 1965.

Hare, Douglas R. A. and Daniel J. Harrington. "Make Disciples of All the Gentiles' (Matt 28:19)." *CBQ* 37 (1975), 359–369.

Harvey, John D. "Mission in Jesus' Teaching." In *Mission in the New Testament: An Evangelical Approach,* edited by William J. Larkin Jr. and Joel F. Williams. Maryknoll: Orbis Books, 1998, 30–49.

Hays, Richard B. "Victory over Violence: The Significance of N. T. Wright's Jesus for New Testament Ethics." In *Jesus and the Restoration of Israel: A Critical Assessment of N. T. Wright's Jesus and the Victory of God,* edited by Carey C. Newman. Downers Grove: IVP, 1999, 142–158.

Hays, Richard B. and Joel B. Green. "The Use of the Old Testament by New Testament Writers. In *Hearing the New Testament: Strategies for Interpretation*, edited by Joel B. Green. Carlisle: The Paternoster Press, 1995, 222–237.

Heckle, Reik. "Der biblische Begründungsrahmen für die Jungfrauengeburt bei Matthäus: Zur Reception von Gen 5, 1 in Mt 1." *ZNW* 95 (2004), 161–180.

Heil, John Paul. *The Death and Resurrection of Jesus: A Narrative-Critical Reading of Matthew 26–28.* Minneapolis: Fortress Press, 1991.

Heim, S. Mark. "Witness to Communion: A Trinitarian Perspective on Mission and Religious Pluralism." *Missiology: An International Review* 33, no. 2 (2005), 192–199.

Hendricksen, William. *Exposition of the Gospel According to Matthew,* New Testament Commentary. Grand Rapids: Baker Book House, 1973.

Hengel, Martin. *The Cross of the Son of God: Containing the Son of God, Crucifixion, the Atonement.* London: SCM Press, 1986.

Hill, David. "Son and Servant: An Essay on Mattean Christology." *JSNT* 6 (1980), 2–16.

———. *The Gospel of Matthew*, The New Century Bible Commentary, edited by Ronald E. Clements and Matthew Black. Grand Rapids: Eerdmans, 1972.

Hoekema, Anthony A. *The Bible and the Future*. Grand Rapids: Eerdmans, 1994.

Hoffmeyer, John F. "The Missional Trinity." *Dialog: A Journal of Theology* 40, no. 2 (Summer 2001), 108–111

Holman, Charles L. *Till Jesus Comes: Origins of Christian Apocalyptic Expectations*. Peabody: Hendrickson Publishers, 1996.

Holwerda, David E. *Jesus and Israel: One Covenant or Two?* Grand Rapids: Eerdmans, 1995.

Horn, F. W. "Holy Spirit." In *ABD*. Vol. 3. Edited by David Joel B. Freedman. New York: Doubleday, 1992, 260–280.

House, Paul R. "Biblical Theology and the Wholeness of Scripture: Steps Toward a Program for the Future." In *Biblical Theology: Retrospect and Prospect*, edited by Scott J. Hafemann. Downers Grove: IVP, 2002, 267–279.

Howell, David B. *Matthew's Inclusive Story: A Story in Narrative Rhetoric of the First Gospel*. JSNTSS 42. Sheffield: JSOT Press, 1990.

Hugenberger, G. P. "Introductory Notes on Typology." In *The Right Doctrine from the Wrong Texts? Essays on the Use of the Old Testament in the New*, edited by G. K. Beale. Grand Rapids: Baker Academic, 1994, 331–341.

Hutchison, John C. "Women, Gentiles, and the Messianic Mission in Matthew's Genealogy." *BSac* 158 (April–June 2001), 152–164.

Ijatuyi-Morphé, Randee O. *Community and Self-Definition in the Book of Acts*. Bethesda: Academica Press, 2004.

Jaeger, David-Maria. "Toward Redefining Our Mission—With Respect to the Jewish People." *Missiology: An International Review* 7, no. 4 (October 1979), 461–476.

Joest, Christoph. "Abraham als Glaubensvorbild in den Pachomianerschriften." *ZNW* (1999), 98–122.

Jones, John Mark. "Subverting the Textuality of Davidic Messianism: Matthew's Presentation of the Genealogy and the Davidic Title." *CBQ* 56 (1994), 256–272.

Kaiser Jr., Walter C. *Mission in the Old Testament: Israel as Light to the Nations*. Grand Rapids: Baker Academic, 2000.

———. "Single Meaning, Unified Referents: Accurate and Authoritative Citations of the Old Testament by the New Testament." In *Three Views on the New Testament use of the Old Testament.* Grand Rapids: Zondervan, 2008, 45–89.

———. *The Uses of the Old Testament in the New.* Eugene: Wipf and Stock Publishers, 2001.

———. *Toward Old Testament Theology.* Grand Rapids: Zondervan, 1978.

———. *Toward Rediscovering the Old Testament.* Grand Rapids: Zondervan, 1991.

Kamlah, E. "Spirit, Holy Spirit." In *NIDNTT.* Vol. 3. Grand Rapids: Zondervan, 1986, 689–693.

Kapolyo, Joe. "Matthew." In *Africa Bible Commentary,* edited by Tokunboh Adeyemo. Nairobi: WordAlive Publishers, 2006, 1105–1170.

Karrer, Martin. "Jesus, der Retter (*Sôtêr*): Zur Aufnahme eines hellenistischen Prädikats im Neuen Testament." *ZNW* 93 (2000), 153–176.

Keck, Leander E. *Who is Jesus? History in Perfect Tense.* Edinburgh: T & T Clark, 2001.

Keener, Craig S. *A Commentary on the Gospel of Matthew.* Grand Rapids/Cambridge: Eerdmans, 1999.

———. *Gift and Giver: The Holy Spirit for Today.* Grand Rapids: Baker, 2001.

———. *Matthew,* The IVP New Testament Commentary Series. Edited by Grant R. Osborne. Downers Grove: IVP, 1997.

———. "'Brood of Vipers' (Matthew 3:7; 12:34; 22:33)." *JSNT* 28, no. 1 (2005), 3–11.

Kent, Homer A. Jr., "Matthew's Use of the Old Testament." *BSac* (January 1964), 34–43

Kingsbury, Jack Dean. *Gospel Interpretation: Narrative-Critical & Social-Scientific Approaches.* Edited by Jack Dean Kingsbury. Harrisburg: Trinity International Press, 1997.

———. *Matthew: Structure, Christology, Kingdom.* Philadelphia: Fortress Press, 1975.

———. "A Profile of a Ministry of Healing." *ATLAS* (n.d.), 102–107.

———. *Matthew as Story.* Philadelphia: Fortress Press, 1986.

Kistemaker, Simon. *The Parables of Jesus.* Grand Rapids: Baker Book House, 1980.

Klein, William W., Craig L. Blomberg, and Robert L. Hubbard, *Introduction to Biblical Interpretation.* Melbourne: Word Publishing, 1993.

Knowles, Michael P. "Scripture, History, Messiah: Scriptural Fulfillment and the Fullness of Time in Matthew's Gospel." In *Hearing the Old Testament in the New Testament,* edited by Stanley E. Porter. Grand Rapids/Cambridge: Eerdmans, 2006, 59–82.

———. *Jeremiah in Matthew's Gospel: The Rejected-Prophet Motif in Matthean Redaction.* JSNTSup 68. Sheffield: Sheffield Academic Press, 1993.

Koester, Helmut. "Suffering Servant and Royal Messiah from Second Isaiah to Paul, Mark, and Matthew." *TD* 51, no. 2 (Summer 2004), 103–128.

Köstenberger, A. J. "Mission." In *New Dictionary of Biblical Theology,* edited by T. D. Alexander, et al. Leicester: IVP, 2000.

———. *The Mission of Jesus and the Disciples According to the Fourth Gospel.* Grand Rapids: Eerdmans, 1998.

———. *John,* Baker Exegetical Commentary on the New Testament. Grand Rapids: Baker Academic, 2004.

Köstenberger, Andreas J. and Peter T. O'Brien. *Salvation to the Ends of the Earth: A Biblical Theology of Mission.* Edited by. D. A. Carson. Downers Grove: IVP, 2001.

Krentz, Edgar. "'Make Disciples'"—Matthew on Evangelism." *CurTM* 33, no. 1 (February 2006), 23–41.

———. "Christ's Assembly: Community Identity in Matthew." *CurTM* 35, no. 2 (April 2008), 118–122.

———. "None Greater Among Those Born From Women: John the Baptist in the Gospel of Matthew." *CurTM* (ATLAS, n.d.), 333–338.

———. "Missionary Matthew: Matthew 28:16–20 as Summary of the Gospel." *CurTM* 31, no. 1 (February 2004), 24–31.

Kupp, David. *Emmanuel: Divine Presence and God's People in the First Gospel.* SNTSMS 90. Cambridge: Cambridge University Press, 1996.

Ladd, G. E. *A Theology of the New Testament.* Edited by Donald A. Hagner. Grand Rapids: Eerdmans, 1993.

Larkin Jr., William J., and Joel F. Williams, eds. *Mission in the New Testament: An Evangelical Approach.* Maryknoll: Orbis Books, 1998.

Levenson, Jon D. *Sinai and Zion: An Entry into the Jewish Bible.* New York: HarperCollins, 1985.

Levin, Yigal. "Jesus, 'Son of God' and 'Son of David': The Adoption of Jesus into the Davidic Line." *JNST* 28, no. 4 (June 2006), 415–442.

Levine, Amy-Jill. "Matthew and Anti-Judaism." *CurTM* 34, no. 6 (December 2007), 399–416.

Levison, John R. *The Spirit in Early Judaism.* Boston/Leiden: Brill, 1997.

Liefeld, Walter L. "Theological Motifs in the Transfiguration Narrative." In *New Dimensions in New Testament Study,* edited by Richard N. Longenecker and Merrill C. Tenney. Grand Rapids: Zondervan, 1974, 162–179.

Lindars, Barnabas. "The Place of the Old Testament in the Formation of New Testament Theology: Prolegomena" In *The Right Doctrine from the Wrong Texts? Essays on the Use of the Old Testament in the New,* edited by G. K. Beale. Grand Rapids: Baker Academic, 1994, 137–145.

Longenecker, Richard N. "'Who is the Prophet Talking About'? Some Reflections on the New Testament's use of the Old." *Themelios* 13 (October/November 1997), 4–8.

———. *Biblical Exegesis in the Apostolic Period.* Grand Rapids: Eerdmans, 1975.

Lunde, Jonathan. "Introduction." In *Three View on the New Testament use of the Old Testament,* edited by Stanley N. Gundry, Kenneth Berding, and Jonathan Lunde. Grand Rapids: Zondervan, 2008.

Luz, Ulrich. "Eine thetische Skizze der matthäischen Christologie," *Anfänge der Christologie:FS fü F. Hahn.* Edited by C. Breytenbach and H. Paulsen; Göttingen: Vandenhoeck & Ruprecht, 1991, 221–235.

———. *The Theology of the Gospel of Matthew.* Translated by J. Bradford Robinson. Cambridge: Cambridge University Press, 1995.

Maalouf, Tony T. "Were the Magi from Persia or Arabia?" *BSac* 156 (October–December 1999), 423–442.

MacArthur, John. *Matthew 1–7,* The MacArthur New Testament Commentary. Chicago: Moody Press, 1985.

———. *Matthew 24–28,* The MacArthur New Testament Commentary. Chicago: Moody Press, 1989.

Maigadi, Barje S. *Divisive Ethnicity in the Church in Africa.* Kaduna: Baraka Press, 2006.

Marguerat, D. *Le jugement dans l'Evangile de Matthieu.* Geneva: Labor er Fides, 1981, 266–267.

Marshall, I. Howard. *New Testament Theology: Many Witnesses, One Gospel.* Downers Grove: IVP, 2004.

———. "Church." In *Dictionary of Jesus and the Gospels,* edited by J. Green, S. McKnight and I. H. Marshall. Downers Grove: IVP, 1992, 122–125.

Martínez, Florentino García. *The Dead Sea Scrolls Translated.* 2nd ed. Translated by Wilfred G. E. Watson. Leiden: Brill, 1996.

Mbiti, John. *African Traditional Religions and Philosophy.* Portsmouth: Heinemann, 1998.

McCasland, S. V. "Matthew Twists the Scriptures." In *The Right Doctrine from the Wrong Texts? Essays on the Use of the Old Testament in the New,* edited by G. K. Beale. Grand Rapids: Baker Academic, 1994, 146–152.

McConnel, Richard S. "Law and Prophecy in Matthew's Gospel: The Authority and Use of the Old Testament in the Gospel of St. Matthew." ThD diss., University of Basel. Basel: Friedrich Reinhart Kommissionsverlag, 1969.

McDaniel, Ferris. "Mission in the Old Testament." In *Mission in the New Testament: An Evangelical Approach,* edited by. William J. Larkin Jr. and Joel F. Williams. Maryknoll: Orbis Books, 1998, 11–29.

McKenzie, John L. "Problems of Hermeneutics in Roman Catholic Exegesis." *JBL* 77 (September 1958), 197–204.

McKnight, Scot. *A Light Among the Gentiles: Jewish Missionary Activity in the Second Temple Period.* Minneapolis: Fortress Press, 1991.

Mead, James. *Biblical Theology: Issues, Methods, and Themes.* Louisville/London: Westminster John Knox Press, 2007.

Meier, John P. *Law and History in Matthew's Gospel.* AnaBib 71. Rome: Biblical Institute Press, 1976.

———. *The Vision of Matthew: Christ, Church, and Morality in the First Gospel.* New York: Crossroad, 1979.

———. "Salvation History in Matthew: In Search of a Starting Point." *CBQ* 37 (1975), 203–215.

Metzger, Bruce M. *A Textual Commentary on the Greek New Testament.* 2nd ed. Stuttgart: Deutsche Bibelgesellschaft/German Bible Society, 1994.

Metzer, Rainer. "Der Rückzug Jesu im Matthäusevangelium: Ein literarisches Déjà-vu-Erlebnis." *ZNW* 94 (2003), 258–268.

Mickelsen, A. B. *Interpreting the Bible.* Grand Rapids: Eerdmans, 1963.

Moltmann, Jürgen. *The Trinity and the Kingdom.* New York: HarperCollins Publishers, 1991.

———. *Theology of Hope: On the Ground and Implications of a Christian Eschatology.* New York: HarperSanFrancisco, 1991.

Moo, D. J. "The Problem of *Sensus Plenior.*" In *Hermeneutics, Authority and Canon,* edited by D. A. Carson and J. D. Woodbridge. Grand Rapids: Zondervan, 1986, 179–211.

Moreau, A. Scott, Gary R. Corwin, and Gary R. McGee. *Introducing World Mission: A Biblical, Historical, and Practical Survey.* Grand Rapids: Baker Academic, 2004.

Morris, Leon. *New Testament Theology.* Grand Rapids: Zondervan, 1990.

Motyer, Alec. *Look to the Rock: An Old Testament Background to our Understanding of Christ.* Leicester: IVP, 1996.

Mounce, Robert H. *Matthew,* New International Biblical Commentary. Carlisle: Hendrickson Publishers, 1991.

Moxnes, Halvor. "Patron-Client Relations and the New Community in Luke-Acts." In *The Social World of Luke-Acts: Models for Interpretation,* edited by Jerome H. Neyrey. Peabody: Hendrickson, 1991, 241–268.

Na, Kyung Soo. "Understanding the Great Commission Against the Background of Matthew's Gospel as a Whole." ThD diss., University of Stellenbosch, August 1998.

Neusner, Jacob. *Recovering Judaism: The Universal Dimension of Judaism.* Minneapolis: Fortress Press, 2001.

———. "Money-Changers in the Temple: The Mishnah's Explanation." *NTS* 35 (1989), 287–290.

Newbigin, Lesslie. *The Open Secret: An Introduction to the Theology of Mission.* Grand Rapids: Eerdmans, 1995.

Nickelsburg, George W. E. "Good News/Bad News: The Messiah and God's Fractured Community." *ATLAS* (n.d.), 324–332.

Nolland, John. *The Gospel of Matthew,* NIGTC. Edited by I. Howard Marshall and Donald A. Hagner. Grand Rapids/Cambridge: Eerdmans, 2005.

———. "The Sources for Matthew 2:1–12." *CBQ* 60 (1998), 283–300.

Notley, R. Steven. "The Kingdom of Heaven Forcefully Advances." In *The Interpretation of Scripture in Early Judaism and Christianity: Studies in Language and Tradition,* edited by Craig A. Evans. London: T & T International, 2004, 279–311.

Novakovic, Lidija. *Messiah, Healer of the Sick: A Study of Jesus as the Son of David in the Gospel of Matthew.* Tübingen: Mohr Siebeck, 2003.

Okure, T. "The Significance Today of Jesus' Commission to Mary Magdalene." *International Review of Mission* 81 (1992), 177–188.

Ostmeyer, Karl-Heinrich. "Armenhaus und Räuberhöhle? Galiläa zur Zeit Jesu." *ZNW* 96 (2005), 147–170.

Overman, J. Andrew. *Church and Community in Crisis: The Gospel According to Matthew.* Valley Forge: Trinity Press International, 1996.

Pate, Marvin C. *Communities of the Last Days: The Dead Sea Scrolls, the New Testament and the Story of Israel.* Downers Grove: IVP, 2000.

Phillips, Peter. "Casting out the Treasure: A New Reading of Matthew 13:52." *JNST* 13.1 (2008), 3–24.

Piper, John, *Let the Nations be Glad: The Supremacy of God in Missions.* 2nd edition. Grand Rapids: Baker Academic, 2003.

Plum, K. F. "Genealogy and Theology." *SJOT* 3 (1989), 90.

Plummer, Alfred. *An Exegetical Commentary on the Gospel According to Matthew.* Grand Rapids: Eerdmans, 1960.

Porter, Stanley E., ed. *Hearing the Old Testament in the New Testament.* Grand Rapids: Eerdmans, 2006.

Powell, Mark Allan. *God With Us: A Pastoral Theology of Matthew's Gospel.* Minneapolis: Fortress, 1995.

Poythress, Vern S. *The Shadow of Christ in the Law of Moses.* Phillipsburg: P&R Publishing, 1991.

Punt, Jeremy. "Paul, Hermeneutics and the Scriptures of Israel." *Neot* 30, no. 2 (1996), 377–425.

Rahlfs, Alfred, ed. *Septuaginta.* Stuttgart: Deutsche Bibelgesellschaft, 1979.

Riches, John, William R. Telford, and Christopher M. Tuckett. *Synoptic Gospels: With an Introduction by Scot McKnight.* Sheffield: Sheffield Academic Press, 2001.

Ridderbos, H. N. *Matthew.* Bible Student's Commentary. Translated by Ray Togman. Grand Rapids: Zondervan, 1987.

———. *Redemptive History and the New Testament Scriptures.* 2nd edition. Translated by H. De Jongste. Phillipsburg: P&R Publishing, 1988.

Riesner, R. "Archaeology and Geography." In *Dictionary of Jesus and the Gospels*, edited by J. Green, S. McKnight, and I. H. Marshall. Downers Grove: IVP, 1992, 33–46.

Robertson, O. Palmer. *The Christ of the Prophets.* Phillipsburg: P&R Publishing, 2004.

———. *The Israel of God: Yesterday, Today, and Tomorrow.* Phillipsburg: P&R Publishing, 2000.

Rogers, Cleon. "The Great Commission." *BSac* (July 1973), 258–267.

Roxburgh, Alan. "Rethinking Trinitarian Missiology." In *Global Missiology for the 21st Century: The Iguassu Dialogue,* edited by William D. Taylor. Grand Rapids: Baker Academic, 2000, 179–188.

Sahlin, Harald. "The New Exodus of Salvation According to St. Paul." In *The Root of the Vine,* edited by A. Fridrichsen. London: Dare, 1953.

Saldarini, Anthony J. *Matthew's Christian-Jewish Community.* Chicago: The University of Chicago Press, 1994.

———. "Reading Matthew without Anti-Semitism." In *The Gospel of Matthew in Current Study,* edited by David E. Aune. Grand Rapids, /Cambridge: Eerdmans, 2001, 166–184.

Sasson, Jack M. *Jonah.* The Anchor Bible with Introduction and Commentary. New York: Doubleday, 1990.

Saucy, Mark. "The Kingdom of God Sayings in Matthew." *BSac* 151 (April June 1994), 175–197.

Schnabel, Eckhard, J. *Early Christian Mission.* 2 vols. Vol. 1, *Jesus and the Twelve.* Downers Grove: IVP, 2002.

Schnackenburg, Rudolf. "Matthew's Gospel as Test Case for Hermeneutical Reflections." In *Treasures New and Old: Recent Contributions to Matthean Studies*, edited by David R. Bauer and Mark Allan Powell. Translated by Ronald D. Witherup. Atlanta: Scholars Press, 1996, 251–269.

Schreiner, Thomas R. *New Testament Theology: Magnifying God in Christ.* Nottingham: Apollos, 2008.

Senior, Donald, "Between Two Worlds: Gentiles and Jewish Christians in Matthew's Gospel." *CBQ* 61 (1999), 1–23.

———. "The Death of Jesus and the Birth of a New World: Matthew's Theology of History in the Passion Narrative." *ATLAS* (n.d.), 416–423.

———. "Directions in Matthean Studies." In *The Gospel of Matthew in Current Study,* edited by David E. Aune. Grand Rapids: Eerdmans, 2001, 5–21.

Senior, Donald and Carroll Stuhlmueller. *The Biblical Foundations for Mission.* Maryknoll: Orbis Books, 1983.

Sim, David C. "Matthew, Paul and the Origin and Nature of the Gentile Mission: The Great Commission in Matthew 28:16–20 as an anti-Pauline Tradition." *HTS* 64, no. 1 (2008), 377–392.

———. "Rome in Matthew's Eschatology." In *The Gospel of Matthew in Its Roman Imperial Context,* edited by John Riches and David C. Sim. London: T & T Clark, 2005.

———. *The Gospel of Matthew and Christian Judaism: The History and Social Setting of the Matthean Community.* Edinburgh: T & T Clark, 1998.

Simonetti, Manlio, ed. *Matthew 1–13.* Ancient Christian Commentary on Scripture. Downers Grove: IVP, 2001.

Smith, Ralph L. *Micah-Malachi,* Word Biblical Commentary. Edited by John W. Watts. Nashville: Thomas Nelson, 1984.

Snodgrass, Klyne R. *Stories with Intent: A Comprehensive Guide to the Parables of Jesus.* Grand Rapids: Eerdmans, 2008.

Soulen, R. Kendall. "The Believer and the Historian: Theological Interpretation and Historical Investigation." *Interpretation: A Journal of Bible and Theology* 57 (April 2003), 174–86.

Soulen, Richard N. and R. Kendall Soulen, *Handbook of Biblical Criticism*. Louisville: Westminster John Knox, 2001.

Stanton, Graham, ed. *The Interpretation of Matthew.* 2nd ed. Edinburgh: T & T Clark, 1995.

———. *The Gospels and Jesus.* 2nd ed. New York: Oxford University Press, 2002.

Stauffer, Ethelbert. "Messias oder Menschensohn?" *NovT* 1, no. 2 (April 1956), 81–102.

Strecker, G. *Der Weg der Gerechtigkeit.* Göttingen: Vandenhoeck & Ruprecht, 1962.

Strickert, Fred. "Rachel on the Way: A Model of Faith in Times of Transition." *CurTM* 34, no. 6 (December 2007), 444–452.

Strimple, Robert B. *The Modern Search for the Real Jesus: An Introductory Survey of the Historical Roots of Gospels Criticism.* Phillipsburg: P&R Publishing, 1995.

———. "The Old Testament Prophets' Self Understanding of their Prophecy." *Themelios* 6, no. 1 (September 1980), 9–14.

Swartley, Willard M. *Israel's Scripture Traditions and the Synoptic Gospels: Story Shaping Story.* Peabody: Hendrickson Publishers, 1994.

Syreeni, Kari. "Between Heaven and Earth: On the Structure of Matthew's Symbolic Universe." *JSNT* 40 (1990), 3–13.

Turaki, Yusufu. *Tribal Gods of Africa: Ethnicity, Racism, Tribalism and the Gospel of Christ.* Nairobi: Ethics, Peace and Justice Commission of the Association of Evangelicals, 1997.

Turner, David L. *Matthew,* Baker Exegetical Commentary of the New Testament. Grand Rapids: Baker Academic, 2008.

———. "Matthew 21:43 and the Future of Israel." *BSac* 159 (January–March, 2002), 46–61.

Twelftree, Graham. *Jesus the Miracle Worker.* Downers Grove: IVP, 1999.

Ulrich, Daniel W. "The Missional Audience of the Gospel of Matthew." *CBQ* 69 (January 2007): 64–83.

van Aarde, Andries. "Jesus' Mission to all of Israel Emplotted in Matthew's Story." *Neot* 41, no. 2 (2007), 416–436.

van Buren, Paul M. *According to the Scriptures: The Origin of the Gospels and of the Church's Old Testament.* Grand Rapids/Cambridge: Eerdmans, 1998.

———. "Judaism in Christian Theology." *Journal of Ecumenical Theology* 18, no. 1 (Winter 1981), 114–163.

VanGemeren, Willem. *The Progress of Redemption: The Story of Redemption from Creation to the New Jerusalem.* Grand Rapids: Baker Academic, 1988.

van Ruler, Arnold A. *The Christian Church and the Old Testament.* Grand Rapids: Eerdmans, 1971.

Varner, William. "A Discourse Analysis of Matthew's Nativity Narrative." *TynBul* 58, no. 2 (2007), 209–228.

Verkuyl, J. *Contemporary Missiology: An Introduction.* Grand Rapids: Eerdmans, 1978.

Verseput, Donald J. "The Davidic Messiah and Matthew's Jewish Christianity." *SLBSP* 34 (1995), 102–116.

von Dobbeler, Axel. "Die Restitution Israels und die Bekehrung der Heiden: Das Verhältnis von Mt 10, 5b.6 und Mt 28, 18–20 unter dem Aspekt der Komplementarität—Erwägungen zum Standort des Matthäusevangeliums. " *ZNW* 91 (2000), 18–44.

von Rad, Gerhard. *Old Testament Theology.* Vol. 2. *The Theology of Israel's Prophetic Traditions.* Translated by D. G. M. Stalker. London: SCM Press, 1965.

———. "Typological Interpretation of the Old Testament." *Int* 15 (1961), 174–192.

Vos, Geerhardus. *Biblical Theology: Old and New Testaments.* Edinburgh: Banner of Truth Trust, 1975.

Wagner, Volker. "Mit der Herkunft Jesu aus Nazaret gegen die Geltung des Gezetzes? *ZNW* 92 (2001), 273–282.

Wainwright, Elaine M. *Shall We Look for Another? A Feminist Rereading of the Matthean Jesus.* New York: Maryknoll, 1998.

Wallace, Daniel B. *Greek Grammar Beyond the Basics: An Exegetical Syntax of the New Testament.* Grand Rapids: Zondervan, 1996.

Waltke, Bruce K. *An Old Testament Theology.* Grand Rapids: Zondervan, 2007.

Waters, Larry J. "*Missio Dei* in the Book of Job." *BSac* 66 (January–March, 2009), 19–35.

Watts, John D. W. *Isaiah 34–66,* Word Biblical Commentary. Nashville: Thomas Nelson, 2005.

Weaver, Dorothy Jean. *Matthew's Missionary Discourse: A Literary-Critical Analysis.* JSNTSS 38. Sheffield: JSOT, 1990.

———. "Rewriting the Messianic Script: Matthew's Account of the Birth of Jesus." *Int* 9 (October 2000), 376–385.

Wedderburn, Alexander J. M. "Jesus' Action in the Temple: A Key or a Puzzle?" *ZNW* 97 (2006), 1–18.

Wenham, David and Steve Walton. *Exploring the New Testament, The Gospels and Acts.* London: SPCK, 2001.
Wenham, John W. *Christ and the Bible.* Downers Grove: IVP, 1972.
Weren. J. C. "The Five Women in Jesus' Genealogy." *CBQ* 59 (April 1997), 290.
Whitelam, Keith W. *The Just King: Monarchical Judicial Authority in Ancient Israel.* Sheffield: JSOT Press, 1979.
Williams, Stephen. "The Transfiguration of Jesus." *Themelios* 28 (Autumn 2002), 22.
Wink, Walter. *The Human Being: Jesus and the Enigma of the Son of the Man.* Minneapolois: Augsburg Fortress, 2002.
Winter, Paul. "Matthew 21:27 and Luke 10:22 from the First to the Fifth Century: Reflection on the Development of the Text." *NovT* 1, no. 2 (April 1956), 112–148.
Wise, M. O. *"Temple." Dictionary of Jesus and the Gospels.* Edited by J. Green, S. McKnight and I. H. Marshall. Downers Grove: IVP, 1992, 811–817.
Wright, Christopher J. H. *Salvation Belongs to Our God: Celebrating the Bible's Central Story.* Nottingham: IVP, 2008.
———. *The Mission of God: Unlocking the Bible's Grand Narrative.* Downers Grove: IVP Academic Press, 2006.
———. *Knowing Jesus Through the Old Testament.* Downers Grove: IVP, 1992.
Wright, N. T. *The Last Word: Beyond the Wars to a New Understanding of the Authority of Scripture.* New York: HarperSanFrancisco, 2005.
———. *The New Testament and the People of God,* Christian Origins and the Question of God. Vol. 1. London: SPCK, 1992.
———. *Jesus and the Victory of God,* Christian Origins and the Question of God. Vol. 2. Minneapolis: Fortress, 1996.
Zumstein, J. *La Condition du Croyant dans l'Evangile selon Matthieu.* Fribourg: Editions Universitaires/Göttingen: Vandenhoeck & Ruprecht, 1977.

Langham Literature and its imprints are a ministry of Langham Partnership.

Langham Partnership is a global fellowship working in pursuit of the vision God entrusted to its founder John Stott –

> *to facilitate the growth of the church in maturity and Christ-likeness through raising the standards of biblical preaching and teaching.*

Our vision is to see churches in the majority world equipped for mission and growing to maturity in Christ through the ministry of pastors and leaders who believe, teach and live by the Word of God.

Our mission is to strengthen the ministry of the Word of God through:
- nurturing national movements for biblical preaching
- fostering the creation and distribution of evangelical literature
- enhancing evangelical theological education

especially in countries where churches are under-resourced.

Our ministry

Langham Preaching partners with national leaders to nurture indigenous biblical preaching movements for pastors and lay preachers all around the world. With the support of a team of trainers from many countries, a multi-level programme of seminars provides practical training, and is followed by a programme for training local facilitators. Local preachers' groups and national and regional networks ensure continuity and ongoing development, seeking to build vigorous movements committed to Bible exposition.

Langham Literature provides majority world pastors, scholars and seminary libraries with evangelical books and electronic resources through grants, discounts and distribution. The programme also fosters the creation of indigenous evangelical books for pastors in many languages, through training workshops for writers and editors, sponsored writing, translation, strengthening local evangelical publishing houses, and investment in major regional literature projects, such as one volume Bible commentaries like *The Africa Bible Commentary*.

Langham Scholars provides financial support for evangelical doctoral students from the majority world so that, when they return home, they may train pastors and other Christian leaders with sound, biblical and theological teaching. This programme equips those who equip others. Langham Scholars also works in partnership with majority world seminaries in strengthening evangelical theological education. A growing number of Langham Scholars study in high quality doctoral programmes in the majority world itself. As well as teaching the next generation of pastors, graduated Langham Scholars exercise significant influence through their writing and leadership.

To learn more about Langham Partnership and the work we do visit **langham.org**

www.ingramcontent.com/pod-product-compliance
Lightning Source LLC
Chambersburg PA
CBHW051539230426
43669CB00015B/2655

This volume is a monumental work. The topic is of immense importance, and one that has not received nearly the attention it deserves. The concept of mission is central to the theology of the Gospel of Matthew. And there is no recent, authoritative full-scale study of mission in Matthew's Gospel. The book relates mission to other key themes and motifs in Matthew, and in the process deals carefully with virtually every passage in the Gospel. Having taught and written on Matthew's Gospel for over 30 years, I myself learned a great deal from this work.

David R. Bauer, PhD
Ralph Waldo Beeson Professor of Inductive Biblical Studies
Dean of the School of Biblical Interpretation
Asbury Theological Seminary, USA

Bitrus A. Sarma's work offers a unique and persuasive missional reading of Matthew's Gospel, and particularly Matthew's use of the Old Testament from the perspective of missions. Matthew's view of missions is to be found in Israel's faith traditions, and it is developed in the Gospel under the framework of promise and fulfillment. This well-researched book has significant implications, from Matthew's perspective, for how one should read the Old Testament. Highly recommended.

David E. Garland
Dean and Holder of the Charles J. and Eleanor McLerran Delancey
Chair of the Dean
Professor of Christian Scriptures
George W. Truett Theological Seminary
Baylor University, USA

Few studies see the New Testament's use of the Old Testament beyond both the mere formal *citing of texts* and the ideology and theology motivating such exercise by New Testament authors. Fewer still go on to establish an overarching interpretive framework for understanding how NT authors use the OT—or, better still, *how* the OT *shapes* major segments and central issues within their works. Dr Bitrus Sarma's new work eloquently succeeds in these areas and more. No scholar today doubts the defining role of 'mission' for Matthew; and Sarma not only explores how Matthew weaves the OT into his *narrative* of Israel and the nations, but also shows how Matthew actually uses the OT to redefine and provide a new interpretive framework for the Triune mission in the early church. Thus, by viewing such mission "as an ongoing series of divinely orchestrated actions toward the realization of salvation in Jesus", Matthew brings under this purview "people, events, and places", among other things, as they "are divinely coordinated for the salvation of humankind through [Jesus] the Messiah". The schema of 'promise-fulfillment' serves Matthew's interpretative framework, but not woodenly, since it is the *Triune* mission that drives his theology. And it is precisely around the concrete dimensions and questions of "redemptive events and institutions, geography, prophetic ministry, and intertextual typology" that Matthew's *new people of God* emerge, with a universal mission and a new identity. This timely work greatly advances Matthean studies.

Randee I-Morphé, PhD
Chair, PhD Committee
ECWA Theological Seminary Jos, Nigeria
Director, Hokma House, Centre for Biblical Research, Nigeria